D0627182

Brett H. Mandel

Minor Players, Major Dreams

University of Nebraska Press
Lincoln and London

⊖ The paper in this book
meets the minimum requirements
of American National Standard
for Information Sciences —
Permanence of Paper
for Printed Library Materials,
ANSI Z39.48-1984.

Library of Congress
Cataloging-in-
Publication Data
Mandel, Brett H., 1969–
Minor players, major dreams /
Brett H. Mandel.
p. cm.
"A Bison original."
ISBN 0-8032-8232-X
(pbk.: alk paper)
1. Minor league baseball —
United States.   2. Baseball players —
United States.   I. Title.
GV863.AIM346   1997
796.357'64'0973 — dc20   96–32437
CIP

*To Laura for her love and support, and
to my parents for their help, love, and inspiration*

Contents

Illustrations

Preface: Play Ball

In August 1993 I was twenty-five years old and serving as the assistant to the policy director of the Philadelphia Charter Commission. We were working feverishly toward a fall deadline to present Philadelphia's electorate with a new charter that would change the rules of governance for the city. Like other staff members, I was often frustrated by the pace and results of the commission's work. The deadline for the completion of the commission's task had already been pushed back once, so it was not unexpected when the deadline for placing the new charter on the ballot was moved to May 1994. I knew it would be another exasperating nine months.

At the same time that I was growing more and more dismayed with my position, I was enjoying the simple pleasures of watching the Philadelphia Phillies drive toward the National League Eastern Division Championship. I was always a huge baseball fan and enjoyed watching and playing the game. Even though my competitive baseball career ended after high school, I was still an avid weekend baseball player, and with the Phillies making their worst-to-first run toward the pennant, I could not have been more thrilled to be a fan. As I sat up in the general admission seats of Veterans Stadium — way up in the 700 level — savoring a midweek day game and the fact that I was out of the office, I decided that when my work with the commission ended I was going to do something different with my life.

In my brief career since college I had worked in politics and government, but the work of the charter commission, with its unbearably slow pace and disheartening results, left me needing a break. Watching the Phillies defeat the Montreal Expos, I decided that what I wanted to do after the end of my work with the charter commission was play baseball—not just spend the summer playing weekend baseball as I always anticipated but play ball every day. "You know what I want to do this summer?" I asked my buddy at the game. "I want to play minor league baseball and write a book about what it's really like to be a minor leaguer and tell the world about the young men who put their lives on hold to pursue the dream of playing in the majors."

I'm sure my friend does not even remember the comment because just after my declaration the Phillies scored a few runs and we got caught up in the game. After the game I not only remembered the idea but began to follow up on how to make it happen. In between files containing information about procurement reform and the balance of power between the mayor and city council, I started logging information about how I could actually have the opportunity to play ball and write the book. After the World Series I met with representatives from the Phillies and completed my research on how I could make my goal possible: I would need to find an independent team that would make room for me on its roster, since depriving any affiliated player of practice or game time would be wasting the investment of a major league team.

I spent endless hours crafting and recrafting book proposals, making contacts in the literary world, and calling every independent team in the minor leagues. My coworkers and friends just shook their heads incredulously as the deal came together. I had been very careful not to tell too many people, as most just thought my ambitious were crazy. But I was determined to make it work and methodically pursued the idea until it finally began to take shape. By the time the charter commission presented its work to the voters I had attracted the attention of a new team in the Pioneer (rookie) League, the Ogden Raptors.

While the proposed new charter was savaged across the city by a wide-ranging coalition of unions, community groups, and activists, I was working out, playing ice hockey, and going to the batting cages. Finally, when the voters of Philadelphia overwhelmingly defeated the proposed charter and put an exclamation point on the futility of the exercise, I had a consolation — I was packing my bags and gear and getting set for the 1994 Pioneer League season.

In the months ahead I would get an inside look at life in the minor leagues. Even though I would sign a contract as a professional baseball player, I would actually be an author in a Raptors uniform. I would fund my own contract and fill a roster spot but not displace any true minor league player since the Raptors did not intend to carry the full load of players allowed under Pioneer League rules. I would experience minor league life firsthand as a player and understand the joys, pressures, and unique excitement that surround the lower ranks of professional baseball. For the summer, I would trade Sunday ball for pro ball before returning to my everyday life.

My Raptors teammates, the management, and the Raptors owners alone knew my true identity as an author. From my unique vantage point as an author in uniform I would have the chance to get to know the players through formal tape-recorded interviews and informal interaction, to present a true picture of life in the minors, and to paint a portrait of the prospects, the rejects, the managers, and the owners who chase their dreams in the small towns and quaint ballparks of the little show.

Nine months after I came up with the perfect way to forget the workaday world and the frustrations of the charter commission, I had my glove and spikes over one shoulder and a laptop computer over the other as I walked through the Philadelphia International Airport. I was leaving the City of Brotherly Love to become a minor player and enjoy major dreams.

Acknowledgments

When I first came up with the idea to write a book as an author signed to a minor-league baseball contract, even I was skeptical. I did not know if I had the discipline to write a book, and although I had played baseball all my life, I did not know if I could succeed in approximating minor-league talent. I know that I could never claim to have been successful in reaching the talent level of the men who play minor-league baseball, but I believe that this book, which resulted from my season in the minors, is a credit to those who do and is a unique insight to the fans, like me, who are thrilled to watch from the grandstand. I therefore must acknowledge all of the individuals who took this project seriously and helped make it a reality.

I thank the Ogden Raptors and team president Dave Baggott for their faith in the project and their cooperation throughout and since my season in the minors. Thanks are due to the management and the players of the Raptors, who were extremely patient with my presence in their lives and jobs. The ownership, management, and players graciously made my experience authentic in every way, from giving me ground balls in practice to fining me when I broke team rules. The Pioneer League, its teams, and its personnel are due my gratitude for affording me the opportunity to accomplish this project.

Special appreciation and fondness is reserved for Frank and Ruby Sanders, my foster family while in Utah — although they never knew that they brought more than just another minor-league player into their home. I am especially indebted to Raptors players Doug O'Neill, Tommy Johnston, Jeremy Winget, Danny Miller, and Shane Jones,

Raptors manager Willy Ambos, and Raptors coach Rich Morales for their candor in describing their experiences for me. My roommate, chauffeur, and friend Brett Smith is singled out for his finesse in coping with a minor-league roommate who carried a laptop computer among his road gear. I look forward to our Cooperstown reunion, when our mutual idol, George Brett, is inducted into the Hall of Fame.

In no particular order I must thank superlawyer Larry Ceisler for his legal aid; Marty Dershowitz for his photographic and accounting help; Randy Voorhees for his advice; Maje McDonnell and the Philadelphia Phillies for their informational input; Gaines Du Vall for providing Raptors portraits; Steve Conlin for his beautiful photographs; the staff of the Philadelphia Independent Charter Commission, who endured my seemingly endless efforts to get this project underway; and the staff of the Pennsylvania Economy League–Eastern Division, who were left to deal with me during the months I spent completing and securing the publication of this book. I am also extremely grateful for the help and support of my family and friends and the informational input of the numerous authors, publishers, and agents I consulted over the course of this project.

I must also thank the University of Nebraska Press for its faith in this book and for making it a better final product.

Finally, I thank my father for instilling in me a love of the game and for his tireless support of my efforts to make this book a reality; my mother for her enthusiasm and her willingness to help transcribe endless hours of Raptors interviews; my sister Nicole for her love and support; and Laura Weinbaum, who, more than anyone, endured the ordeal of producing this book and shared my happiness in its publication.

Take Me Out to the Ball Game

The setting sun radiated off the nearby mountains and glinted off the tinted windows of the limousines. Inside sat two dozen young men who had spent their entire lives preparing for this night. My teammates and I had carefully dressed and consciously primped ourselves in vanity mirrors. Looking good was very important. In a moment, the limousines would be transporting us not to a prom but down the right-field foul line of Simmons Field, home of the Ogden Raptors of the Pioneer (rookie) League. When the doors to the limousines opened the people of Ogden, Utah, would meet the first-ever Raptors team, and the men inside would have a chance to pursue their dreams of playing professional baseball.

Inside our limousine, and behind the tinted glass of the two limousines behind ours, were players at the absolute bottom of the baseball world. My teammates and I examined the wet bar, turned on the television, and played with every knob or switch we could find. With no sense of shame or pretense of maturity we stretched out on the plush sofa, tried to make long-distance telephone calls, and spent time looking at each other and giggling foolishly. Pausing in the face of all the possibilities and pressures that the season would bring, this ride was our last chance to allow stress and anxiety to escape in juvenile antics. Listening to the frenzied crowd cheering our arrival, each player knew that this ride could be the beginning of his trip to the major leagues. But as the ostentatiously appointed vehicles pulled up in front of the home dugout, we were well aware that our careers in professional baseball might be as brief as our limousine ride. Even though I was truly a stowaway with the Raptors, in uniform — with my spikes neatly polished and my hat newly bent — I was as excited as the rest of the team to be on my way to play ball.

When the chauffeur left his post behind the wheel and opened the door, bright sunshine flooded the vehicle and forty-three hundred fans erupted in cheers. It was opening day of the inaugural season for the Ogden Raptors and there was magic in the air — a magic that comes from the connection between the players and fans — a magic that might just be missing from the major-league baseball I grew up with. But on the fields, in the uniforms, and in the hearts of the men who play minor-league baseball, an enchantment was alive in the accessibility of the game and in the possibility of turning a lifetime of toil on the baseball diamond into a career that would skyrocket a young man all the way to the majors.

This particular magic can be found only in the minor leagues — especially at the lowest levels of professional baseball, where the game is played in its most inviting settings and fans can get as close to the game as they desire. The further the game is from the aloofness of the majors, the more pure it becomes — more and more like baseball.

Minor-league baseball is where big dreams meet slim chances and wide-eyed boys develop into big-league men — or hang up the uniform for the last time. In the minor leagues — between the chalk lines, in the uniforms, on bus trips, and behind clubhouse doors — the magic can be felt. Just as the fan can feel the excitement of being so close to the soul of the game, the player can enjoy the thrill of performing at such an intimate level. Aspiring to make it to the majors, but close enough to being out of baseball forever, he is forewarned that his involvement with the game is extraordinary.

Growing up as a fan of major-league baseball, I missed out on this magic. I could enjoy baseball and be thrilled following my favorite teams and players, but I had to do it from a distance imposed by the inaccessibility of the major leagues. As a peanut leaguer in Philadelphia, one of the twenty-four places in the world where major-league baseball was played, going to see the Phillies never brought me close to the game. My earliest memories of baseball involve walking up endless ramps to sit in the upper decks of Veterans Stadium. My father, not wanting me to miss out on a traditional baseball upbringing, always encouraged me to bring my glove to catch foul balls. That far above the field of play I had a better chance of catching a low-flying plane. Watching baseball played at such a distance, against a background of inflated player egos, million-dollar contracts, and labor strife, a fan loses sight of the souls of the players and the heart of the game.

Though I had the opportunity to see future Hall of Famers like Mike Schmidt and Steve Carlton play, I watched them perform in a monolithic concrete stadium. With players on the field so far away from my seat and so quick to avoid autograph-seeking fans, I was never able to achieve a genuine connection — baseball was a form of entertainment to be watched, not something that encouraged any personal relationships.

While today the new ballparks are designed to capture baseball nostalgia in a Disneyland fashion, there is still something less than magical about major-league baseball. Watching today's young fans, who are as likely to know a player's salary as his batting average, there seems to be even less of a personal connection. At the very least there is something not very special about wanting to know the cost of a player's rookie card rather than whether he bats from the left or right side. Could it be that my generation of fans was the last to place cards in the spokes of our bikes without worrying that they would no longer be in mint condition? Can fans today understand the intimacy of the game, the intense bond with teams and their players, or the awe of the experience of seeing a game felt by fans of my father's generation? I used to think that these fond reminiscences were the product of the haze of time.

I thought so until I went to my first minor-league game — small park, real grass, players signing autographs and talking to kids. From the moment I walked into the ballpark I could tell there was something different about this experience. Sure, the quality of Utica Blue Sox baseball was a step below the majors, but the connection with the players and the game more than made up for it. For a few dollars, fans can sit in the best seats in the house instead of the nosebleed sections;

watch ballplayers with dreams, not egos; and feel like a part of baseball, not just spectators at a baseball game.

Take the baseball I grew up watching and strip it down to its essence — remove labor strife and owners more interested in skyboxes than fans; take away artificial turf, domes, and five-dollar beers; leave just the magic of the game and the hearts and souls of its players. At its most basic and most glorious, baseball is still grown men playing a kid's game, their hopes and aspirations on display for eager fans. Baseball is at its most basic deep in the minor leagues.

The minor leagues have four classifications: rookie, single-A, double-A, and triple-A. The rookie leagues are basically a starting point for first- and second-year players where draftees hone their skills after high school or college to prepare them for their ascent up the baseball ladder. If they succeed, they will be promoted through the system through single-A, double-A, and triple-A ball. At each level the size of the towns, stadiums, crowds, and the amount of pressure all increase until a young ballplayer reaches the major leagues.

Rookie leagues — where my teammates and I would toil — are where players have the most hope for their futures, their dreams still untainted by the realization that the baseball numbers game has fated almost all of the careers to end well short of the majors. It is also the place where the most players' careers end. The lowest level of professional baseball, these leagues are generally populated with freshly graduated high-school and college players who have obvious talent but may lack the full complement of skills needed to progress into the upper ranks of the minor leagues. Perhaps a young catcher is considered too small to play the position in the big leagues, or a seventeen-year-old pitcher with a blur of a fastball needs to learn the mental aspects of pitching — and an effective off-speed pitch. These players will be assigned to a rookie league to learn their positions, gain some seasoning, and get a taste of professional competition and everyday baseball.

Because the rookie leagues are so far removed from the majors, a ballplayer there knows that he has a long way to go to reach the parent club. Every young hopeful can believe that he has the talent to make it to the top of the baseball world; but looking around the clubhouse before a game and playing with the numbers, the fact remains that there just aren't enough positions in the major leagues for many, if any, of these players to make it.

Making it to the big leagues is a notion even more remote for a player on an independent franchise. On independent, or unaffiliated teams — where players are signed as free agents by the team instead of assigned to the team by the major-league parent club — a player's only hope is that his talent will be noticed and his contract will be purchased by a major-league organization. Then, and only then, can he truly begin to think of making it to "the bigs."

A player for an independent team in a rookie league is therefore at the absolute base of the professional baseball pyramid. Each of my teammates on the Raptors, released by major-league organizations, passed over in the amateur draft, or somehow having fallen through the cracks in the talent scouting system is almost out of chances in professional baseball. But with hard work his talent could be noticed, his contract purchased by a major-league franchise, and he could progress all the way to "the show." It is a dream, perhaps, but dreaming it every night helps players endure twelve-hour bus rides, scrounging for meal money, and running out every ground ball.

Since 1939 young men from across the country and across the world have traveled to the Pioneer League to begin their baseball careers. The oldest of all the currently operating rookie leagues, the Pioneer League has a rich tradition of developing big leaguers. George Brett, Dick Allen, Julio Franco, and Cecil Fielder all started their careers in the relative obscurity of the Pioneer League to finish their careers under the bright lights of the show. Set in small towns like Lethbridge, Alberta, and Butte, Montana, this league travels by bus through frontier towns and across miles of open road. Every ballpark is intimate, every town has a story, and every player is just starting to realize his dream of playing professional baseball — or starting to fear that his dream is ending.

Each man who plays professional baseball, whether a league leader or a benchwarmer, was a star at some point in his career. But with each new team and at each new level of baseball, a player must prove himself again or fall by the wayside. The players of the Ogden Raptors would have this last chance to prove themselves or else it would be time to leave the magic of professional baseball and join the nine-to-five world. For the first-ever Raptors team, the nine-to-five world would wait for at least this opening night.

As the Ogden crowd cheered their new team, immaculate in home white uniforms with *Raptors* scrawled across the chest and a fearsome dinosaur bursting through the silver *O* on the cap, they had reason to be excited. For the thirteen years since the Ogden A's moved out of town, the city of Ogden had lived vicariously through other towns for their baseball. Now the Raptors would bring pro ball back to Ogden.

Just north of Salt Lake City at the base of the Wasatch Mountains in northern Utah and at the confluence of the Ogden and Weber Rivers, the city of Ogden lives in shadows. The noble mountains cast a regal silhouette over the city of almost seventy thousand residents surrounded by fiery canyons and ski resorts. The cosmopolitan Salt Lake City, however, threatens to obscure its growing neighbor. Once a trading post sold to become a Mormon farm town, Ogden is now a livestock and manufacturing center with a downtown returning to prominence and challenging the future. Slipping out of the shadows with their own professional baseball team, the citizens of Ogden joined the players, coaches, and management of the Raptors in dreaming major dreams.

Despite its thirteen-year absence from the baseball world, Ogden has a winning history of professional baseball. In 1901, 1905, and from 1912 through 1914, Ogden hosted teams from the Inter-Mountain League, the Pacific National League, and the Union Association, respectively. In the 1920s the Ogden Gunners played in the Utah-Idaho League, which preceded the Pioneer League. With the establishment of the Pioneer League in 1939, Ogden was represented by the Ogden Reds. The Reds won back-to-back championships in 1940 and 1941 before the league suspended play during World War II. Cincinnati Reds all-star second baseman Johnny Temple and Pittsburgh Pirates first baseman Dale Long played in Ogden, as did 1956 National League Rookie of the Year and future Hall of Famer Frank Robinson.

After the 1955 season the Ogden Reds folded and the city was without professional baseball for the next decade. In 1966, however, baseball returned to Ogden when the Dodgers joined the Pioneer League. A young Tom Lasorda managed the Ogden Dodgers in their first three years, winning Pioneer League championships in 1966, 1967, and 1968. Future big leaguers Bill Russell, Bill Buckner, Steve Yeager, and Charlie Hough played in Ogden in the late sixties. Hough, who amassed a 5-7 record with a 4.76 earned-run average for the Ogden Dodgers, was still throwing his trademark knuckleball when my Raptors team took the field.

The Ogden Dodgers (renamed the Ogden Spikers for their final year) folded following the 1974 season. Five years later, professional baseball returned. The Ogden A's of the Pacific Coast League, the triple-A affiliate of the Oakland Athletics, played in Ogden in 1979 and 1980. A young Ricky Henderson stole forty-four bases in seventy-one games in Ogden and then went on to steal more bases than any other player in the majors. The Ogden A's had a much shorter career. Poor attendance and financial problems bankrupted the team. After the 1980 season, the A's were purchased and moved to Edmonton.

Although opening night was technically the first professional game in Ogden in over a decade, a few days before the official opening-day debut the Raptors had played a scrimmage game against a local baseball team. That team, composed of ballplayers whose ambitions were snuffed out well short of professional ball, was a ragamuffin squad next to my teammates and me. Although their hodgepodge attire, sloppy work habits, and lackluster play were no match for the Raptors in pristine uniforms and solid baseball fundamentals, the opposition held their own on the baseball field.

Some of the other Raptors ridiculed our opponents and their skill level; it was evident that my teammates were less than excited about their competition. Even though the two dozen men who wore Raptors uniforms were professionals that day, they might one day be on the other side of the field playing weekend baseball. Some careers would be over even before the dog days of August.

In the dugout, however, none of the players seemed to understand their baseball mortality. Even the lucky few who go on to play in major-league organizations or in the big leagues themselves will probably be out of professional baseball within the next few years. These players are right on the cusp of professional baseball — an independent team in a rookie league. One bad outing or broken rule could land these players out of professional baseball for good.

Our coaches stressed the brevity of a professional career and the need to approach every single situation in baseball as professionals, but my teammates seemed focused on something else. Maybe it was the impending season opener or choosing a place to eat after the game, but the last thing on the minds of the Raptors was that this could be the last time they put on a uniform to play baseball. I couldn't help thinking of the cliché "youth is wasted on the young." As a weekend warrior turned professional baseball player until the end of the season when my chariot turned back into a pumpkin, I knew that any weekend ballplayer would trade almost anything to be in their shoes — young, in shape, and playing baseball for a living. My teammates, however, acted as though their careers would be endless.

Although the Raptors were enjoying heady days as the toast of the town, there would come a day when they would long to have this night back — not a night when they beat a bunch of baseball has-beens but a night when they were in uniform as professional ballplayers.

On opening night the Raptors had more than baseball and their future careers to think about. Minor-league baseball is part game and part carnival. To the player working hard to further his career, this is a mixed blessing. The hoopla and sideshow atmosphere attract excited fans who pump up the players and urge them to perform better, but the frenzied atmosphere can also be harrying. All the commotion and pressure is compounded on opening night — especially the first-ever opening night for the Ogden Raptors.

We arrived at Simmons Field early on opening night, June 17, to go through the rituals of pregame batting and fielding practice. In the trailer that served as our clubhouse, neatly aligned beneath each player's name was a new uniform. On the shelf above was a new hat, and on the chair below were stirrups, sanitary socks, and a belt. Seeing my number 5 set out against the spotless new uniform shirt underneath the nameplate with *Mandel* written on it made me break out in a wide grin. Looking around to be sure that nobody noticed how much I was enjoying looking at my locker area, I noticed my teammates savoring their own moments.

Players stood around the locker room just looking at the costume before them. Not wanting to break the spell, they considered the significance of the uniform and put off getting dressed as if the uniforms would disappear if touched. For the first-year professionals, this would be the first time they suited up in the minors, and for players with professional experience it could be the last uniform they put on as serious baseball players. No matter how well designed, beer-league shirts and factory-team outfits just do not have the same appeal as a uniform worn with the pride of a player whose career could still culminate with service in the major leagues.

The trailer quickly became crowded and we dressed, penning our names and numbers in pants and shirts, and bending the brims of hats to our liking. Like supermen who had ditched our mild-mannered cover in favor of hero costumes, we emerged from the clubhouse immaculately dressed, feeling on top of the world and maybe even a little invincible. A uniform both sets a person apart and gives him a feeling of belonging. Each player who wore the Raptors uniform was saying loud and clear that he belonged in professional baseball and that all of his hard work was worth the chance to pursue his big-league dreams.

Hours before game time in batting and fielding practice, baseball was still the game that the Raptors players had all been playing since Little League. But once the crowd began to file in and the excitement began to build, baseball became anything but familiar. After pregame drills we were gathered in the clubhouse to await final instructions — not signs and signals, but which limousines to ride in and how many speeches to listen to until the first pitch; first would come the limousines, then player introductions, then flowers for the ladies, then sky divers, then first pitches, then, finally, baseball.

Raptor manager Willy "Bull" Ambos, a mountain of a man and a former minor-league pitcher, looked more like a drill sergeant than a baseball coach in his sunglasses and double-knit pants. His chance of making it to the majors as a pitcher extinguished years ago, Ambos was attempting to rejuvenate his baseball career as a manager. For his inaugural game, the intense rookie manager not only had to deal with lineups and defensive alignments, but the production aspects of an opening game. He watched the spectacle surrounding opening night with obvious irritation — his brow wrinkling and his mouth pursing into a sneer beneath his thick mustache — as the sideshow atmosphere of opening night was interfering with his first managerial effort.

After listening to the Raptors general manager go over the timetable for the pregame madness, Ambos declared that the starting pitcher and catcher would go directly into the bullpen instead of participating in the festivities. His pitcher would miss out on the fun, but Ambos would definitely not jeopardize his starter's warmup activities just so he could join in the carnival going on around the field.

Just before we left the clubhouse to enter the fray, Ambos tried to focus us one last time. From one of his meaty hands he took off a Pioneer League championship ring he had won late in his career when he was, as he put it, "a suspect, not a prospect" for the now-defunct Salt Lake City Trappers. "This is what every one of you should be thinking about," he said as his players passed the ring around.

Like all championship rings, it was garishly large and heavy. As it made its way from hand to hand, players fondled it, reading the words *Pioneer League Champions* and admiring its gleam in the clubhouse trailer light. Watching his players recognize the significance of the gold- and red-hued ring and what it represented, Ambos spoke of players in baseball who never won a championship and the sacred opportunity that each Raptor had to join the lucky few who wore a ring. Long after leaving professional baseball, pictures and programs are nice mementos, but anyone who plays has mementos. A ring signifies that once in a player's life, he was a champion.

Some players simply glanced at the ring and handed it off. Others ran their fingers over each engraving and stared deeply into the shining metal. When it came to me I passed it from hand to hand testing its weight and deciding that nobody could possibly be comfortable with it around his finger. But reading the inscription and realizing how proud I would be to have helped earn a championship ring, I decided that I could quickly become accustomed to the heavy feeling and the weighty significance.

When the ring returned to Ambos's hands, he spoke of our privileged status as professionals, but most of all he spoke of baseball — what would happen on the field, not what would be happening for the next half hour. Ambos exited the trailer and we were left to our own thoughts.

Some players barked encouragement, others discussed the final logistics of getting in and out of limousines in number order. Players and coaches had slept restlessly the previous evening, passed the day fidgeting until arriving at the park, moved through their paces in practice anxious for the game to begin, and now had just moments to be alone with their thoughts, hopes, and aspirations. A knock came against the trailer. The waiting was over. It was showtime and soon it would finally be baseball time.

We piled into stretch limousines, offering each other incentives to make fools of ourselves in front of the opening night crowd. One player offered ten dollars to anyone who would stick out of the moon roof to strike a body builder's pose. Another declared that cracking a joke into the microphone during introductions was worth two weeks of free meals.

With the park alive with cheering fans and nervous energy abounding inside the limousines, we were ready to take part in the festivities. As the chauffeur approached the door to let us out, players angled their bodies and shifted positions to prepare to burst out onto the field. Before me in line, Chris Simmons, a fireplug of a player with a Bart Simpson haircut, angled his body out the door and into the frenzy. After being told all his life that he wasn't talented enough, Simmons had progressed from high school to junior college to college baseball and had just won the last roster spot on the Raptors. Hustling fanatically and throwing his body around the field with reckless abandon during training camp, Simmons simply would not allow himself to be cut. Having realized his ambition to play professional baseball, he smiled and stepped out of the limousine and into his dream. I followed him into the sunlight and into the spotlight.

Simmons Field, which was little more than a sandlot only months before, was now a ballpark alive with excited fans. Temporary stands ringed the field with its neatly trimmed emerald grass and manicured infield. Advertising signs — plugging everything from the Flying-J Motel to the Dry Cow Saloon — ringed the outfield wall, and trees and towering mountains surrounded the park. Given the prehistoric name of the team, fans would probably not be surprised to see a real dinosaur walk out of the wilderness that surrounded the outfield fence cutting the field off from the world. Without a cloud in the sky to spoil the evening, the sun set the neighboring mountains ablaze and leaves on the trees swayed slightly in the cooling breeze — it was a perfect night for a ball game. More than four thousand fans packed the overflowing stands and they were ready to cheer after thirteen years without baseball. In reserved seating the fans were on their feet, and along the bleachers young fans ran down to the fences to get closer to the players.

We took our places along the first-base foul line. White uniforms trimmed with teal, navy, and silver caught the sun and freshly polished spikes aligned neatly. I resisted a final temptation to cash in on the free meals and addressed the fans; "I'm Brett Mandel from Philadelphia, Pennsylvania — I'll play infield." The crowd cheered, not just for me but for every Raptors player and coach. The people of Ogden had come ready to root for their Raptors.

On opening night, catcher Brett Smith, who set a school record for home runs in his senior year of college yet was passed over in the draft, did nothing more than warm up pitchers in the bullpen but bragged, "I felt like a Roman emperor. People were watching my every move." He resisted the temptation to throw a ball or two into the crowd despite boos of disapproval when he fielded a foul ball and returned it to the field of play. Smith spent the previous season playing weekend baseball after being ignored in the draft. Having already experienced a year when he had to confront the idea that his career in baseball might have peaked, Smith was thrilled to have a professional uniform on his back and a chance at a professional career at his feet.

Center fielder Doug O'Neill, a promising player in the Expos organization until injuries derailed his career, managed to give away a few balls despite the threats of fines. Responding to the raucous crowd, he even parted with a batting glove for a young fan. "You have to do that kind of stuff on opening night," was his simple rationale. Because he had fallen so far from the heights of his career, O'Neill was happy to be in uniform but anxious to play his way back into the upper ranks of professional baseball. He could not wait for the chance to step onto the field and display his talent, to show the baseball world that he was back.

After player introductions we turned to listen to the national anthem — the defining moment of pause between all that comes before baseball and the game itself. Despite the weeks of planning, lining up everything from a new sound system to a shiny new flag, there was no one in Simmons Field to sing it. Fans stood craning their heads to search for the missing singer and players could only wonder whether the game would ever begin. Some of my teammates tried a soft *a cappella* version but it fizzled out with the first octave change. After momentary confusion the public-address announcer encouraged the fans to join him in singing "The Star-Spangled Banner," and while it was not the Mormon Tabernacle Choir, the Ogden faithful did a credible interpretation of the tune.

In the stands, fans with cowboy hats and kids with bright new Raptors caps held over their hearts sang out with loud, if not harmonious, voices. Along the foul lines players and coaches joined the impromptu choir, tapping their caps against their chests to maintain the proper meter. Even though it was a familiar song to my teammates, I had to smirk as they earnestly crooned incorrect lyrics — nobody "brought" stripes and there is nothing "for" the land of the free and the home of the brave. We would have seventy-one more games to get the words right.

With the anthem over, my teammates and I each grabbed a carnation and took it to an appreciative fan. I ran down the third-base line and found a young girl who gushed as I handed her the flower. Kids raced down from the bleachers to offer high fives and ask for any part of my uniform I might part with. Someone reached over the fence and grabbed my hand to wish me good luck. As if a spotlight was in my eyes, I couldn't focus on the crowd or on individual fans — just beaming faces and grasping hands. Remembering that we were on the field to play ball, I sprinted back to the dugout where players exchanged war stories about how they gave away their flowers and prepared for the next attraction.

Although we had arrived at the field for practice over four hours earlier, baseball was still on hold. As players and fans turned their eyes skyward, four parachutists dropped in to deliver the first balls. Four players, including myself, had a particular interest in the sky divers — they were wearing our batting practice jerseys and we were responsible for getting them back even if we had to pry them off their crumpled bodies if their parachutes failed to open. With our limited salaries we could not afford the five-dollar fine for throwing a ball into the stands, let alone the cost of replacing parts of our uniforms. The worrying was for naught. The sky divers landed, gave back our jerseys, and left the field to wild applause.

The first balls were thrown out, culminating with a fifty-five-foot change-up by Ogden mayor Glenn Mecham, and it was finally time for baseball — baseball within a circus. While the starting pitcher warmed up on the mound for the Raptors, overflowing fans were let onto the warning track to enjoy the game. For the inaugural home game, the number of fans exceeded the number of seats, leaving the Raptors ownership little choice but to seat fans wherever there was open space. Raptors fielders, warming up in the outfield, laughed as hundreds of people crossed the chalk line to take their seats — in fair territory and in play. Ogden and the Raptors were ready once again for professional baseball.

For Tommy Johnston and Jeremy Winget this was the night they had been fighting for since their major dreams were put on hold by the baseball world. Tommy, a lanky and clean-cut all-American boy, was a slick-fielding shortstop for the Pirates in single-A ball. Jeremy, a comic-book superhero of a young man with his muscular physique and jutting chin, was a hot-hitting first baseman for the Orioles assigned to play in the rookie leagues. Both had heard the speech all ball-players dread: "We don't see you making the big leagues with our organization."

But Johnston refused to pack up his glove and Winget could not put his bats away without one more try at a professional baseball career. Since Winget was a local product, his fiancée and family were part of the large crowd cheering the Raptors; Johnston, a long way from his Indianapolis home, was alone this opening night. But both were in uniform again and both had a dream in their hearts and a chance to make their way back onto the road to the majors.

Fans roared as first baseman Shane Jones knocked down a hard-hit ball and flipped it to pitcher Danny Miller covering first for the first out. Two more followed and Miller, who was neglected in the baseball draft despite his standout career at the University of the Pacific, posted his first of six shutout innings. The Raptors pitcher, whose superstitious habits and cowboy garb set him apart from the other players, was thrilled to begin his professional career so well. Without his late grandfather to watch over him, Miller's career had stalled during his first years at college. But having reconnected with his inspiration through the help of a sports psychologist, Miller was back on top of his game.

The Raptors played nearly flawless baseball, pounding the Butte Copper Kings 14–0 behind Shane Jones, who had the first hit and the first home run in Raptors history. Jones, who had been passed over in the draft despite leading all of NCAA Division I in home runs during his senior year, sparked the Raptors by going three for three with one walk and one sacrifice fly. Having been told by scouts, agents, and cross-checkers that he would never succeed in professional baseball, Jones's opening-night success could not erase the bitterness he felt toward the baseball establishment — but his smile after the game could mask it for the night.

Fans cheered the Raptors' every move and stayed in their seats despite the lopsided score. In right field the fans sitting along the warning track cheered when balls bounded their way and merely moved aside when players tried in vain to make a play. When hits found their way into the rowdy bunch, the ball became a souvenir for a lucky fan and the batter was simply awarded an unusual ground-rule double. Over the noise of the crowd, air force jets from nearby Hill Air Force Base raced across the sky bursting the sound barrier with loud crashes — "That's a dinosaur growl," a fan taunted from small bleachers set up behind the opposing bullpen.

My teammates were able to shut out the distractions of the large crowd and opening night frenzy and excel. As his players pummeled their opponents, Manager Ambos bellowed, "I fuckin' love baseball!" While everything was going right for the rookie manager, he could afford to be upbeat. With the crowd on its feet and players standing in our dugout, the final out was recorded and pandemonium broke out. We poured out of the dugout to congratulate each other and the Raptors fans joined the excitement of the first win. Initiated by those seated on the warning track, fans poured onto the field, mobbing players and asking for autographs.

We fought our way back to the dugout, protectively gathering our equipment and regrouping before facing the gauntlet of fans that gathered to greet us on our walk between the dugout and the clubhouse. Signing autographs and collecting congratulations, we found the thirty-yard walk delightfully long. Balls, gloves, programs, and bats were thrust into our hands for signatures by fans young and old. The excitement on the faces of the fans was infectious. Players and fans intermingled freely; intimate contact was an understatement. Players were not only approachable, they were downright happy that anyone wanted their autographs.

But opening night was far from over. After satisfying all autograph seekers, I returned with my teammates to the happy clubhouse to prepare for an opening-night reception. With fireworks bursting overhead and fans still packed in the now-darkened ballpark, players undressed quickly, slapping backs and exchanging handshakes. The heroes of the night gave postgame interviews to the local beat writer and the other assembled media on hand for the historic night; then it was time to enjoy the victory with the entire Raptors family.

When we finally arrived at the huge log cabin that was Ebenezer's Restaurant for the party, congratulations were exchanged all around. Players, coaches, front-office personnel, and team owners sipped beers and recounted the night's festivities. The Raptors, for the moment, had the best winning percentage of any team in the history of professional baseball. But there was plenty of baseball left to play and plenty of distractions left to fight. After opening night the chemistry on the team was almost perfect. Everybody was excited to be a part of such a

The 1994 Ogden Raptors, pictured at the beginning of the franchise's inaugural year. First row: Chris Simmons, Chris Amos, Tim Gavello, Brett Smith, Mike Carrigg, Doug O'Neill, Brett Mandel, John Homan; second row: manager Willy Ambos, trainer Dan Overman, Shane Jones, Brad Dandridge, Jeremy Winget, Jeff Garrett, Dan Zanolla, Jason Pollock, coach Rich Morales; third row: Danny Miller, Troy Doezie, Tim Salado, Paul O'Hearn, Tommy Johnston, Steve Gay, Josh Kirtlan, Jason Evenhus, Edson Hoffman. Gaines Du Vall photograph reprinted with permission.

successful group and looking forward to the year ahead. For the night we could enjoy the glory of our opening game victory, but squabbles about playing time, embarrassing losses, mindless pranks, and the dog days of baseball's endless summer awaited us in the seventy-one games and seventy-seven days ahead.

For the Raptors players who excelled in their first game, this night would be filled with cautious optimism for the future. No major-league organization passes over players forever if they consistently throw shutouts or go three for three at the plate. For the Raptors who did not get into the first game, this night would only bring more anxious waiting for a chance to prove themselves.

The season was one game old but the players, coaches, management, and ownership of the Raptors had passed their most crucial test. They had made it to opening night. One year before the first-night victory, there was no Ogden Raptors professional baseball club; but the ownership had created a professional franchise, a chance for twenty-four men to pursue baseball careers, and a new pastime for a town. The management, given nothing but a license, breathed life into a ball field and formed a team for a city without baseball. Coaches, without a team just months before, now had an opportunity to lead a ballclub to a pennant. And players, out of baseball and without a chance, now had a dream.

The Prospect

Doug O'Neill's comeback began with opening day in Ogden but was put on hold as he strode purposefully from the plate, the victim of a strikeout. The force of his mighty swing was still fresh in his arms as the ball he missed was thrown around the horn and he could only walk back to the dugout and await his next turn at bat. With his shirt unbuttoned one extra button exposing his sculpted, bare chest, and his tight uniform showing off his muscular frame, O'Neill was an imposing figure. His scowl alone was enough to make players clear a path for him to sit down on the bench. Flipping his helmet into the corner of the dugout with disdain and shoving his bat back into the rack, O'Neill finally sat down on the bench to consider this latest obstacle to his fulfilling his dream of playing major-league baseball.

The castoffs on the Raptors fell into two general categories — players who were drafted or signed by major-league organizations but then released and players who were passed over in the draft. Those who had played in organizations, like Jeremy Winget and Tommy Johnston, longed to hook on with another farm system, rejuvenate their careers, and stick it to the organization that released them. The ones ignored in the draft, like Danny Miller and Shane Jones, just wanted a chance to play the game they love, to be noticed by scouts and opposing managers, and to show the baseball world that they had the talent to move up the ladder to the majors.

For one Raptor, however, it was not a release or the opinion of a scout that landed him with the team. A serious prospect since high school, Doug O'Neill had been on his way to the majors when fate intervened and dropped him all the way out of baseball. Unlike the other Raptors, O'Neill knew he could compete and excel in professional baseball and entered the season a little cocky, anxious to tear through the league and reestablish himself as a legitimate contender for a position on a major-league team.

A seventh-round draft pick in 1991, O'Neill watched as former teammates and opponents passed him by and advanced to the majors while setback after setback left him in their wake. His latest strikeout was just one more impediment he would have to put behind him on his way back from the injuries and complications that had landed him with the Raptors instead of in the major leagues.

With the pressure to show the world that he still had the ability that was once seen in him, Doug was pushing hard to make up for lost time. His speed, power, ability to hit for average, and rally-killing glove had earned him the status of prospect. Injuries and lack of progress in his career had cast a pall over his past successes and implanted nagging doubt that he would ever be able to make it back to where he once was.

Two springs before, O'Neill played in a major-league game for the Montreal Expos during spring training; now he was playing for an independent team in the Pioneer League. Once just a few steps from the top of his profession, O'Neill was now at the bottom looking up. Standing at the plate, he gripped the bat as if trying to reduce it to sawdust and with every swing hit the ball hard enough to carry him back to the verge of the majors. But one hit alone would not do it. Having swung through one more pitch, O'Neill had no option but to wait for his next chance, trying to achieve his former stature before there were no chances left.

There was a darkness about Doug O'Neill that went beyond his jet black hair and brown eyes set deep into the tanned skin of his face, showing no sign of ease or joy. When I met Doug on my first day in Ogden he was lying on a bed watching television in a motel room with some other players. As he observed me without comment or trace of emotion, I did not dare speak or approach him. After getting to know him I got past his inaccessible demeanor, and when training camp broke I found myself enjoying his dry sense of humor and easy manner. But with his game face on, there was little clue that there was any

Doug O'Neill in action. O'Neill possessed all the tools that make scouts take notice but sometimes seemed to doubt himself. Neither Raptors coaches nor players doubted that he could someday be a star. Steven D. Conlin photograph reprinted with permission.

cheer to be found in him. Playing the game, or working at it, the darkness seemed to take over, threatening to hold back his tremendous ability.

Throughout his career, O'Neill had found himself hampered by those who were supposed to be pushing him forward and now was almost all alone. Staring at the dugout floor as if trying to pierce the cement with his gaze, the rage that he played with churned inside of him — driving him to excel on the field but also threatening to end his career. Having come so close but fallen so far, he felt a frustration that would not allow him to celebrate any success short of returning to the pinnacle of his career. Only the season ahead would determine whether the rage would destroy him or return him to the road to the majors.

O'Neill grew up in the Santa Cruz Mountains, far from the bright lights of the nearest cities and without much interest in baseball.

When his family moved to San Jose, Doug quickly adjusted and began to display his prowess at sports. Although he had always been a gifted athlete, moving to the city allowed him to compete against a larger talent pool and develop his abilities in scholastic athletics. He played soccer and tennis as a youth and was eventually ranked among twelve- to fourteen-year-old tennis players in the state of California.

When he reached high-school age he was enrolled in Bellarmine College Preparatory School, a private Jesuit institution renowned for its emphasis on academics as well as its athletic successes. Despite his own successes in athletics, O'Neill actually had to lie to make his high-school baseball team. Before high school Doug had never played organized ball. "I got dared to play by people on my dad's softball team," he recalled. To begin his baseball career, he approached the Campbell-Moreland Little League organization, a West-Coast dynasty that won two Little League World Series. He quickly found out that baseball, even at this level, was not just about merit but also about whether one was expected to succeed or fail and whether one fit a particular mold. The politics and relative impenetrability of the upper levels of the baseball world hit him in the face even as a teen. "They asked me how much experience I had, and I said, 'None,'" O'Neill said, recalling how hard it was to even get a tryout. "They stood me up like five or six times in a row."

Having learned his lesson from the reception of the Little League team, O'Neill shrewdly approached his high-school team with a different story. Even though he was still without experience, he responded that he had played at Campbell-Moreland for two years and made the all-star team. It worked for everyone. O'Neill finally was playing organized baseball and began tearing up the field, hitting nearly .400 his freshman year.

Sudden success quickly built his appreciation for the game. "It was fun because right away I started hitting home runs," he said with a gleam in his eye. "If you don't play, what do you think about when you watch baseball? Who is the best? Griffey, he hits the most home runs. You don't know anything else. So when I got into it, it wasn't like I was going three for four with three drag bunts a game, I was hitting the ball and it was easy. That was fun. There wasn't any pressure, really."

Playing high-school football was also proving successful for O'Neill. While he was fighting for a place on the football squad, the team's starting punter went down with a broken ankle. Calling on his soccer experience, O'Neill excelled as a punter, and the following season he broke the Bellarmine school punting record held by former Oakland Raider Dan Pastorini. But despite his success, O'Neill was unsure of where it would lead. "I was all excited about that," he said of breaking the record of a legend. "Just the record, not the average. I still didn't know if it was even going to pan out."

It panned out to be an eyeopener and a door opener to the best collegiate athletic programs in the country. By the end of his junior year he received 796 letters from colleges and universities interested in his punting. "At first I was kind of excited," he recalled. Displaying maturity and an ability to see opportunities, not just events, Doug thought of where the success of punting could lead. "The more it panned out, I was thinking, 'A guy my size, I should probably pursue that and use that to play baseball wherever I want.'"

When summer came Doug was ready to attend Stanford University, punt for its football team, and play for its baseball team. But for the first time in his career he learned that those who were supposed to be supporting him could let him down hard. Bellarmine Preparatory School did not make promoting their athletes a top priority, and Doug was left on his own. Stanford University had not received any films of him playing, which they took to be an indication that he was not interested in matriculating in the coming fall. Although he was crushed at first, O'Neill quickly recovered and tried to make it to college without the help of his athletics or his high school.

O'Neill applied and was accepted to Stanford on his own merits. Relieved that he could still push his career forward on his own, it appeared as if everything would work out — until Doug was informed that Stanford did not want him to play baseball. Although he had only been playing for four short years, Doug knew he had a future in baseball and a serious decision to make. He decided to forgo the advantages of a Stanford education for a chance at pursuing a baseball career. He chose a school that would allow him to continue playing ball as well as punting and enrolled at the California Polytechnic State University of San Luis Obispo.

The turmoil of the previous months left a powerful impression on O'Neill. Doug had been destined to attend a top NCAA Division I school where he could gain serious attention for his football and baseball prowess as well as get a fine education. Instead he was headed for a Division II school to try to salvage his sports prospects while sacrificing, for the moment, the considerations of academics.

"I was upset," Doug said, measuring each word for proper emphasis. "Everything had come so easy so far. They were coming at me. Now I have to fight for something. That was kind of rough but it was a good learning experience." Never again would he place himself or his career in the hands of another. He would call the shots for his future.

In his first year at Cal Poly, his team won the Division II National Baseball Championship, helping ease thoughts of transferring and keeping regrets to a minimum. O'Neill was doing well and his team was successful. His coach, a former player in the Yankees organization, attracted scouts to his games, allowing Doug to get the notice he needed to be drafted.

Punting was also going well for Doug as he was fifth in the nation as a first-year punter for the Cal Poly Mustangs, while also playing receiver; he was still considering punting as a way to continue playing football. During the summer after his first year he sat down with his family and decided to focus his football on punting alone. "What are the chances a white guy like me is going to go pro as a receiver?" he recalls wondering. The following year he took off the extra padding that he wore as a receiver and worked on letting his leg carry him where it would. That year was his best year yet. He led the nation in punting and earned the attention of National Football League scouts.

On the baseball front there were also encouraging developments. The Montreal Expos drafted Doug in the seventh round of the amateur draft and told him that the big leagues were just a few years away. As an NCAA Division II player Doug was happy to be taken so high. Had he gone to a Division I school, he certainly would have been taken higher in the draft, but scouts rarely stick their necks out for a Division II player. The commitment from the Expos encouraged Doug.

Although some might be less than enthusiastic to be drafted by a team so far from home, Doug was excited to be in control of his career. "I had a lot of friends telling me, 'Jeez, Canada, that's not really even like a major-league team' — and the Expos stunk," Doug explained. "I turned that around and tried to make a positive out of it — they're ripe, here they are with no major-league winning streak and they're taking me high. I knew they were going to bump me up fast and I was excited about that." Doug signed a contract and reported to Jamestown, New York, to play for the Expos in the short season single-A New York–Penn League. After playing in high school and college and thinking about the pros, Doug was now only a few short jumps from playing in the major leagues.

"It was great," he said. "I was excited. I was out of school. Here all I have to do is play baseball — Jesus, what a life, no studying, I don't have to worry about missing a test. This is what I waited for for three years since high school thinking that I hope I don't have any regrets." Immersing himself in baseball, Doug played with a vengeance, trying to prove to everyone that he belonged and that he would progress.

"You're out there five hours before a game and you gotta learn how to pace yourself," he explained. "Here I am, all wired up, and I want to prove with every single pitch that I can do everything. And it was after about three weeks one of the guys came up to me and said, 'I don't have any doubts about what you can do. Pace yourself, save yourself for the game.'" To Doug, this was like a sign from above. In high school and college it seemed to him that nobody was on his side — if he played well, people appreciated it, but nobody was helping him push his career forward.

With the Expos, Doug was happy to have others help him achieve his goals and dreams. But mindful of his past experiences, Doug was not going to place all of his eggs in one basket. Concerned about being the master of his own fate, Doug was still not giving up on punting and returned before the end of his first professional season to Cal Poly to spend another year on the gridiron. Already the punting option had played well for him, allowing him to negotiate a salary almost twice what his fellow seventh-round picks earned by using the prospect of a professional football career to entice the Expos into showing him how much they really wanted him.

The next year O'Neill reported to Florida for his first spring training and found the Expos intent on moving him swiftly through the organization. "Immediately when I got to spring training I started working out with the double-A club," he said. "That year we had two other single-A clubs, so I skipped over two levels." With a little luck and some success, Doug could see the majors just two or three years away.

As a first-time participant in spring training, Doug couldn't help getting caught up in the glamour and fantastic possibilities. Thinking back to his first spring in Florida, Doug reminisced, "When I went to Florida, the big-league team is working out in the same facility — I'm hitting with Larry Walker and Marquis Grissom." Having played a season in single-A, this first encounter with the stars of the organization gave Doug the chance to measure up and compare for himself.

"When they signed me, they said, 'We got a guy named Marquis Grissom and we had a cross-checker look at you and he thinks you have every bit of the tools that this guy has, if not more. With a couple years in the minor leagues, you could be right up there.'" With big-league stars, autograph-seeking fans, huge crowds, and people in the organization filling his head with such glowing comparisons, Doug could not help feeling that his dreams were about to come true.

"To the outsider," Doug explained of his excitement, "that might look like, 'Wow, you were hitting with Barry Bonds' and that's what you're thinking as a first-year guy. You're like, 'Holy crap — these guys are making millions of dollars, I'm standing right next to this guy. He's taking ground balls with me.' It's pretty phenomenal, but you just have to put that aside and realize what you're there for."

O'Neill was there to play ball and when he felt a twinge in his hand while checking his swing on the first pitch of spring training, he put it out of his mind and tried to play with the pain. Since he passed on instructional ball the previous fall to play football at Cal Poly, he was not about to mention his injury because of his drive to prove that he could make the double-A club. But after playing with pain for two more weeks and hitting about .450, Doug decided to come forward and get his hand treated before the teams headed north for the beginning of the season.

The Expos training staff diagnosed his pain as tendinitis and assigned him to their single-A club in Rockford, Illinois, to rehabilitate. But after a month in the Rockford cold he was still in constant pain and the Expos training staff decided to reexamine his wrist. This time, they found a break. Doug had a hairline fracture of the hook of the hamate bone — an increasingly common injury that had been misdiagnosed for years because of the difficulty in finding it in X-rays. Because the nerves running to the hand attach around the bone, a crack rubs against nerves and causes extreme discomfort. Now that the injury is well known and is being successfully treated, it is relatively minor, but unless a trainer knows what to look for, players often go for months in pain. Once diagnosed, however, surgery can remove the hook of the hamate bone, and a player can heal properly. Jose Canseco and Dave Hollins overcame comparable injuries and resumed their careers. Doug hoped to have a similarly bright future, but first would be out for ten weeks, then for three more for rehabilitation, before he could play again. When he finally healed, Doug was able to play only the last two weeks of the season before returning to Cal Poly for football. The next baseball season could not start soon enough for him.

Doug was still an excellent punter, leading the nation again as a junior. His punting average was higher than all but a handful of professionals and Division I players that year. The National Football League was interested and the time was right to move his football options forward. After the season, O'Neill signed documents to leave school as a hardship case and went to the invitation-only NFL scouting combines. His college athletic career was officially over. Now he would have to decide between football and baseball.

At the combines he performed well enough to draw the attention of the San Francisco Forty-Niners, but they were concerned that Doug would not be attending July minicamps or the August preseason because of baseball. They wanted Doug to make a choice between his two sports. "I had been using punting to kind of ride along this whole way," he said. "Now all of a sudden I had to say, 'What's more important to me?'" At that time the choice was easy. Baseball was still fun to Doug and he had too much unfinished business to settle with baseball to give it up.

Coming into his second spring training, O'Neill had his work cut out for him. "This is the year I gotta do it," he thought. "I went through a lot that off-season with 'Why?' Why did that have to happen? Here I was, on top of the world coming out of college, and for whatever reasons I haven't disproved myself. I just had a couple of unfortunate things happen." He worked out during the off-season and reported to Florida in amazing shape, driven, as he put it, to "get even with these external forces" that had held him back.

In his first weeks his average hovered around .500. He was called up to play in a big-league B game — a spring-training contest played primarily by non-major-league starters — against the New York Yankees. He was sitting on the bench next to the Montreal starters, Felipe Alou was managing, and Doug was getting a taste of his dream to play big-league ball — but he was not happy.

"I took it as frustration," he explained, "because I'm here — but I'm not really here. It's right in front of me — this guy is sitting here, he just signed a contract for $2.1 million — I'm like, 'Jesus, I missed all last year, I'm not on this team. He's sitting right next to me — is he that much better than me?' He's just had a different road or something so it's frustrating, not frustrating in the sense that I'm a loser, I haven't made it, but frustrating because I gotta hurry up and do this. God, right in front of me is this candy — I gotta just take it." O'Neill went one for three with a few walks in his only big-league contest and was assigned to a single-A club to begin his road back from the injuries of the previous year. With some success he could be working with the double-A club by season's end and have the chance to compete for a triple-A position or even a spot with the big-league club the following spring. Two weeks into the season he was hitting over .300 with six home runs. The turmoil of the last year had no lasting effects and he was again tearing up the diamond. But as if he were tempting the baseball gods with his talent, he was again dealt a humbling blow.

In the last few minutes of bunting practice he hopped into the batter's box for a few bunts before stretching began. He had just dug himself in when he looked up to see the ball hurtling at him from the pitching machine. "I look up and just — natural reaction — instead of jumping out of the way, I go to knock it down and it shattered my thumb," he recalled, as if he were still in disbelief that such a freak injury occurred. He was in a cast and out of the lineup for four weeks. With no baseball to release his aggressions, he got into a bar fight two weeks later and broke his other thumb.

When he finally returned to the playing field he drove himself harder than ever, trying to make up for the months he spent disabled. Two weeks after his return he pulled his hamstring rounding first after a base hit. "I was just overexerting myself," he rationalized, "trying to make up for lost time — so now I have a real injury." After aggravating the muscle pull trying to return to play too quickly, he sat out for an additional month.

"At this time I'm like, 'Hey, maybe I'm not even meant to be in the lineup. Maybe I'm not even meant to play this game,'" he explained. To top things off, at the end of the season a calcium deposit on his knee flared up and required the minor surgery that ended his third year in the minors and sent him home discouraged and frustrated.

"I didn't know what to think," he recalled. "I'm at home just more pissed off than ever and letting it get the best of me. I'm working out, I'm driving weights like you wouldn't believe, I'm boxing and doing some things I probably shouldn't be doing, but I've got so much anger to get out of me." While he was taking his mind off of baseball with intense physical activity, he also had a football career to pursue.

After his second injury-plagued year, O'Neill reported to play with the San Francisco Forty-Niners without a contract. The 'Niners were happy to have him but wanted him to give up baseball forever. Even though his two previous seasons in professional baseball were disastrous, Doug could not walk away. Not wanting to lose his talent, but unable to get him to commit to football, the Forty-Niners signed O'Neill to the practice squad where he would train until a spot on the team opened up for him.

As a practice player he could be signed by any other team, and opportunity knocked when the punter for the Kansas City Chiefs pulled a groin muscle. Suddenly, the young man who dreamed of playing major-league baseball was flying to Arrowhead Stadium for a Saturday NFL game. "I had my jersey number, the whole nine yards," he recalled. "They came up Thursday and said, 'Well, [the injured punter] looks like he'll be all right.'" Just as quickly as the opportunity presented itself, it was gone. Having come so close to the big time in another sport and seeing the chance disappear, Doug turned his attention back to baseball and back to his pursuit of success in our national pastime.

In January the Expos called and informed him that they were trading him. Despite the disappointment that he was no longer wanted by the Expos, Doug was intent on getting back on the field. But even with the early warning, Doug had a long wait to find out his fate. Two weeks into spring training, as a new crop of rookies joined the veterans in Florida and Arizona, he was still sitting at home waiting to hear news. Finally he was told to report to San Bernardino where he would be formally signed by the Texas Rangers organization.

Doug was upbeat about the new start but apprehensive about his physical condition. Lifting weights so hard in the off-season had created a pinching sensation in his arm. Given his history of injuries, Doug winced through the pain, hoping to make the most of his time with his new team. "I can't have any more frustration than I already had," he told himself. "I can't let this control me. If it got the best of me, I'd kill myself. What am I gonna do, quit baseball and punt for four plays a game and always wonder if I could have made it? I couldn't do that."

He tried to live with his injury, but the pain was too intense. There was a stress fracture in his arm that became a crack as he tried to fight the pain. In the end Doug simply asked to be allowed to go home. "Don't sign me" was all he said to the Rangers. "This might be a release to you, whatever else. I don't want this thing to go through, just release me — send me home. I said, 'Look at my two seasons. Maybe I'm just not meant to play baseball. Maybe I'm supposed to punt. Maybe it's just not meant to be.'"

But walking away from the game was not so easy. With the baseball season dominating the sports news, he began to think more and more of what might have been. "A month passes by, I can't sleep with just quitting," he said, putting his career into perspective. "I see guys like James Mouton — he's playing for the Astros — he's a right fielder. He's starting this year. I played against him three years in a row. He's my age, he's slower than me, he's got some pop like I do, he can run pretty good and he's playing right field for the Astros. This is just killing me." Seeing other players in the Expos organization who passed him by while he was recuperating from injuries make it to the majors exasperated O'Neill.

Unlike players such as Tommy Johnston or Brett Smith who traveled across the country to fight for a spot in professional baseball at training camps and workouts, O'Neill was actively avoiding the baseball world. Despite offers from major-league organizations as well as independent teams, Doug remained in self-enforced exile until he could no longer endure the separation from the game. "I came to the conclusion that it's not time yet. I have to have a legitimate reason to quit. I can't do this to myself. I can't let myself down as well as people around me." Coinciding with his decision was a call from his agent inquiring about Doug's interest in an offer from a new independent team in the Pioneer League, the Raptors. The time was right, and, just months after his retirement, Doug was going to Ogden to see if he could still be a prospect.

Through training camp Doug looked like he would quickly prove that his troubles were behind him. Pitchers marveled at how difficult it was to get him out, while fellow position players just admired how far he hit the ball. Mammoth home runs and stellar glove work had his teammates looking forward to his beating up on the rest of the Pioneer League. But as the season began, O'Neill struggled. Doug found the comeback trail to be less than accommodating to his dreams. With frustration growing, he pressed harder and harder, hoping to turn around his waning fortune. Using his glove, Doug contributed to his team's success, but striking out more than once a game and failing to produce the power expected from him, he did not satisfy his coaches — or himself.

"I've always been my own worst enemy, which probably will end up getting the best of me in the end," he noted ruefully. Looking back at his career and then looking around at his teammates and opponents, Doug could only wonder at his failure to dominate the game. He played baseball with a football mentality, using anger to drive him on the field. But pitching guile and an effective off-speed pitch could stymie the rage and leave the batter with nothing to show for his fury except a seat on the bench. As the Raptors' first season began, Doug found himself more often than not in that seat with no outlet for the rage that drove him.

If he could only stay healthy, play every game, and prove that he was not injury prone, Doug reasoned that his career could be put back on track. Considering the significance of staying injury free, he quietly rapped on a wooden nightstand to ward off the forces that had jinxed him. But it was the dream that sustained him, not petty superstition, and he spoke wistfully about his desire to make it come true.

"It's there — it's always there," he said of the dream. "It's been there since I started playing even when I didn't know what I was doing out there. I felt like I had an ability and for some reason I was supposed to be here. I didn't think I was any better than anybody. To this day I'm pretty uncomfortable about my abilities. Some days I feel like I'm on top of the world, other days I feel like I have no business in this game."

Pursuing his dreams, Doug was well aware that all that might come of them was what he had already learned. While he was playing well with the Raptors, he was not setting himself apart as someone who belonged in the big leagues. Staying injury free might remove the knock against him, but he needed more hits and less introspection if he were to ever become a big leaguer.

As he sat on the bench considering his strikeout, Doug's mind seemed to churn slowly, picking apart every facet of his swing and approach to the game for the one correction that could prove that he still had the talent that made him a seventh-round pick. Picking up his glove and trotting out to center field, Doug refocused his energies on defense and allowed his ability, not his furious attempts to exorcise his demons, to take over. If only his ability could conquer his doubts — and channel his fury into effort — he could follow his dreams out of Ogden and make one last run at success.

Doug O'Neill checks the progress of his season and courts the manager's wrath by eyeing the statistics sheet. Infielder Mike Carrigg and catcher Chris Simmons also cast a glance at their averages. Steven D. Conlin photograph reprinted with permission.

Minor Adjustments

I had been a professional baseball player for only one week, but I was rapidly adjusting to the life of a minor leaguer. Arriving in Utah a week earlier, I quickly learned that the minor leagues were definitely a step below the glamour of the majors. Carrying my own bags and hopping on a shuttle van that I had arranged myself, I looked at the sparse Utah landscape on the way from the Salt Lake City airport to Ogden. I was a long way from home and a long way from the show.

When I finally arrived at the motel recommended by the Raptors ownership, I was dismayed to find that there was no reservation under my name. Without a representative from the team on hand to orient me, I was underwhelmed by my minor-league welcome. I even had to call the Raptors main office to learn about an informal afternoon workout scheduled for later that day. Shaking my head at the lack of organization, I sought out other players in the motel and found them similarly unimpressed by their reception and introduction to minor-league life. Players who were already under contract had their hotel rooms paid for, but that was about the extent of the hospitality. For our minor-league greeting, there was no cheerful reception or welcoming committee. But we could only grumble, realize that we were thankful for the opportunity to be paid to play ball, and then head to the field.

Simmons Field, just moments from downtown Ogden, was a long way from being ready for baseball when I first saw it. Workmen scrambled to assemble grandstands along the right-field foul line as the ballplayers straggled into the dugout through the construction site. Temporary trailers, unpainted plywood, and portable toilets made up the home of the Ogden Raptors, and the sound of hammering drowned out the crack of the bat and the slap of glove leather. But once we entered the island that was a baseball diamond in the sea of construction — a well-tended field surrounded by an outfield fence that was already sporting a few of the advertising signs that would ring the park by opening night — we could envision the season ahead.

Willy Ambos made a strong first impression with his imposing presence but was lighthearted in his initial address to his players. Before he got to anything about the game of baseball, he had to make sure that his players were situated in their minor-league lives. Basically, the instructions involved simple things like making sure to complete housing arrangements and being pleasant to the families who were opening their homes to us, "Don't fuck any daughters or wives . . . unless they ask for it." The talk was elegant in its simplicity and clarity.

"Don't call me 'coach,'" Ambos said, "and I won't call you 'player.'" For the rest of the season, Ambos would be "Skip," "Bull," or "Willy." Likewise, Ambos introduced Coach Rich Morales as "Mo," "Meat," or "Rich." But just when it felt like we would go around the dugout telling our nicknames and explaining how we spent our winter vacations, it was time to get down to business.

The afternoon was spent hitting, fielding, and trying to work out some of the butterflies that were fluttering in my stomach. My talent level was a step below that of the other players, but nobody made me feel intimidated or out of place. Without the egos of first-round draft picks or the immaturity of kids fresh out of high school, these were just a bunch of guys trying to make a living out of playing baseball — not the motley crew of gym rats and muscle heads I was expecting.

I really did not get a chance to talk at length with any of the players until I was assigned my first minor-league roommate. Josh Kirtlan, fresh from his senior year at Sacramento State, had just arrived in Ogden as an uncontracted invitee to the Raptors camp. Like the other unsigned players, Josh came to Ogden hoping to win one of the final roster spots on the team. Based on the two huge bags full of clothes and equipment he carried, he was betting that he would make it. Starting early the next day, he got his chance.

After months of planning, Raptors baseball finally became official when the team hierarchy convened training camp. With eighteen players under contract, ten players fighting for five openings, and me soaking it all in — thankful that my deal with the Raptors meant that for the first time in my life I did not have to worry about being cut — Ambos drilled the significance of our situation into our heads. He told us that we had the opportunity to play professional baseball and that if we performed well enough, we could just make it big — otherwise it was back to the ranks of the workaday world. With that in mind Willy emphasized constant effort and hard work. "Baseball is your job," he warned solemnly. "Treat it like it is."

During a break between drills, Coach Morales expressed the thought in a more cheerful way. Morales was no stranger to the baseball field. His father played for the White Sox and the Padres in the late sixties and early seventies and his own career included a stint in the Seattle Mariners farm system. When he realized his career was peaking, Morales wisely hedged his big-league bets and concentrated on making a career in coaching.

While Ambos was a big man, Morales was a muscular bulldog with dark skin and dark eyes that brightened infectiously when he broke into his rare, toothy smile. "I get paid to be on grass," he said, evoking grins from his rapt audience. But his message was very serious. He spoke of friends who had quit the game and settled down to other careers but still call him, jealous of his situation — living around the game he loves, enjoying everything it has to offer, and getting paid to do it. He explained to us that what was happening in Ogden was something special: we were given the opportunity to play a kid's game for pay, and we had a chance to extend our baseball lives past the summer. But if we did not give it our best effort, we could be like the great mass of young ballplayers grown into career men — sitting around a bar, sipping beer, and always looking back on what might have been.

Since my teammates and I would be paid very little and would be at home for just half the season, the Raptors ownership had aggressively pursued foster families for us. Weeks before the season began, the Raptors advertised in the local papers asking families to house a ballplayer or two in exchange for season tickets and an official "I have a Raptor in my house" T-shirt. For ballplayers on tight salaries and families with extra room it was a perfect match.

Because of our striking similarities in interests and ambitions — or maybe because he had a car and I did not — catcher Brett Smith and I were paired together for our housing assignment. From the trailer that served as the Raptors ticket office, I called the first name on the foster family sheet and arranged to get acquainted after our afternoon practice. Despite being puzzled by the unique Utah street numbering system and taking an unscheduled detour through Hill Air Force Base, Smith and I found the Sanders residence in Layton, a suburban community just south of Ogden. With the Wasatch Mountains looming to the east and the Great Salt Lake stretching to the west, the location could not have been more spectacular.

Frank and Ruby Sanders met us at their door and welcomed us like long-lost relatives. Frank — a large, jovial man whose belly shook like Santa Claus's when he gave a hearty chuckle, and an expert square-dance caller in his spare time — tried in vain to keep the family dog from sniffing us while Ruby, a petite blonde with an angelic face that brightened radiantly with her wide smile, ushered us in, delighted to have a new crop of youngsters in the house. After apologizing unnecessarily for our directional troubles they showed us to our room: we had a water bed and an air mattress at our disposal, a bathroom, and run of the house. Anything less than the hassle of renting and paying for an apartment and dealing with phones and utilities would have been just fine, but what the Sanders offered was better than we could have hoped for.

We quickly decided that the name Sanders must be Mormon for "immaculate" because the Sanders house was kept perfectly — from the fastidious front lawn to the total state of tidiness of every room. Left on our own for the evening, Smith and I found ourselves preserving the neatness of the house by rubbing our footprints out of the freshly vacuumed carpets as we went from room to room. For the few locals who made the team, home was already in Utah, but for those of us who traveled great distances it was the one thing that couldn't be stuffed into a duffel bag and brought to Ogden with bats and gloves. It was certainly nice to return to a home instead of a bare apartment and it was definitely comforting to be greeted by a family.

While Brett and I enjoyed our first night with our Raptors foster parents, the players who were still trying out for the team spent their time back at the motel. At the park for the second day of training camp we found out that some of them were checking out early — the team had already cut a few dreamers. When Ambos sat us down in the dugout and announced that the hammer had already fallen, there was a prolonged silence.

"I've been released, Mo has been released, every one of us has been released," Ambos said, describing the careers of the coaching staff and the Ogden Raptors executives. "I don't like to do it," Ambos declared, but like it or not, some of the young men who were fighting for the last roster spots were traveling home, hoping that someone else would give them a chance to pursue their dreams. While the contracted players and I involuntarily bowed our heads in silent tribute to those who would be leaving us, the players whose careers were hanging by a thread nervously looked around for any indication that they might be next.

Although Brett Smith was already under contract, he still was without a hit in training camp scrimmage games. The night before our second day of camp, Brett and I wondered whether or not to shave and agreed that we would only remove our scruff if we got a hit the next day. Smith was good looking in a boy-next-door way, and his stubble made his smiling face look just dangerous enough to turn the heads of admiring waitresses at the Ogden restaurants. My own stubble just made me look dirty. I was sure that Smith would soon be clean shaven while I would certainly be tripping over a Rip Van Winkle beard. Not that I needed any added pressure in my next at-bat, but my roommate soon homered for his first hit of scrimmage and earned his license to shave.

Despite the increased pressure I knew that the pitcher would be grooving a first-pitch, put-this-in-your-book fastball. Suppressing my nervousness, I slapped the offering deep into the hole between short and third. The shortstop fielded the ball, but it was too late. Giddy at first base, I had my hit, permission to shave, and a measure of pride.

With my hit and my growing camaraderie with my teammates, I was beginning to enjoy my time on the field. There was nothing I could do to suddenly give myself the ability to demand that Ambos play me or trade me, but I was able to fit in and occasionally make myself forget that I was in Ogden to write a book. Although I do not think that anyone else came to that conclusion, I was able to move beyond trying not to embarrass myself as a prime motivation. As we counted down toward the first game of the season, I was concentrating on improving my baseball skills and enjoying life as a minor-league player.

With each new day of Raptors camp, Simmons Field became more and more like a ballpark. With stands, concession booths, and fresh paint being added as we practiced, the Raptors front-office hands were working as hard as the players on the field. But nobody was content to pretend that the little park was a "field of dreams." The Raptors front-office staff knew that if they built it, they must also market it to make people come.

All over Ogden, Raptors schedules were on lunch counters and in stores. Across Washington Boulevard a Raptors ticket banner greeted downtown visitors. The *Ogden Standard-Examiner* covered the team's progress in camp and published a colorful team preview in the Sunday paper that came out before the Friday season opener. To make a real connection with their hometown, the Raptors would have to become more than a story in the paper; we would have to establish a bond with the people of Ogden. After our early practice on the second day of camp it was time to be introduced to our future fans. We showered, put on batting practice jerseys, and headed to the Ogden Mall where it was Meet the Raptors Day.

Tables and banners were set up, team paraphernalia was laid out, and the coaches and players waited for the crowds to arrive. At Simmons Field we were told to expect throngs of twenty-five hundred people, but the actual crowds were significantly smaller. The lukewarm reception had players and coaches grumbling about Ogden, the public appearance, and its implications for the season ahead. Biding our time, players slumped in their seats, scanned the mall crowd for young women, and soaked in the glorious air conditioning as we waited for autograph seekers and well-wishers but received mainly curious looks. Finally it was time to do something.

"How 'bout you, Ogden," began Ambos's speech — part genuine introduction and part sarcastic greeting — to begin the appearance. As his words echoed in the cavernous mall, we just looked around hiding grins and Ambos looked back at the tables with a "What are we doing here" smile. A curious crowd began to build as we all introduced ourselves at the microphone and we returned to our places at the tables to sign our first Raptors autographs.

A shiny white ball passed down the line of players as a young fan in a brand new Raptors T-shirt watched with wide eyes as it moved from player to player. Each of my teammates added his signature, making small talk with the young autograph seeker: "What's your name? Do you play ball? Are you coming out to see our opening game?"

Slugger Shane Jones handed me the ball with his name freshly scrawled on it and I paused for a second to ponder the significance of my actions. I was about to sign my first autograph. Sure, the phone company received my autograph once a month, and my college professors saw plenty of them on midterm exams, but this was the first time I would sign my name for someone who would save it for posterity — and for its potential future value.

I tested my pen on the ball with the first big *B* and then signed the rest of my name, fully aware of the goofy grin on my face. I passed the ball to the skipper, who looked at it approvingly. He held the ball up to me. "Players sign one under another in the horseshoe," he said, pointing to the wide parts of the ball framed in a semicircle of stitches. "This," he said, pointing at the area opposite the trademark, the narrow band of space where the stitches are at their closest, "is where the manager signs." With a smooth, well-trained stroke of the pen he added his name as Morales debated fines for players who signed in the manager's space — just one more bit of pressure for professional ballplayers.

But autographs are more than pressure, they are a way of establishing an important connection between fan and player. During our abbreviated Raptors spring training, we were treated to free lunches at a local restaurant and to a lesson in fan relations. Every day, between practices, we would pile into the restaurant, devour the salad bar, and enjoy the air-conditioned comfort. The waitresses, intrigued by the team, began to ask for autographs and memorabilia, and a new Raptors hat was circulated to the team for signatures to satisfy one of the requests.

Instead of just penning their names, however, some of my teammates added some prank names for fun. It was a silly joke, but a serious offense to our host community. Here we were, their team, and screwing up the simple gesture of acknowledging their attention.

Fortunately, some of my teammates stepped up and replaced the hat, this time with true signatures. Before our stretching session the next day, Jason Pollock, a one-year minor-league veteran, called the team together. We had only met each other days earlier, but it was refreshing to see the team accepting the assertion of leadership. Pollock simply remarked about the need for us to be "professionals" and act responsibly to the people who bought the tickets that provided the money to pay our salaries. There would be plenty of opportunities in our postbaseball lives when nobody would care about our autographs, but while we were in Ogden the least we could do was show our appreciation courteously with a signature.

Getting accustomed to signing autographs is a learning process. First you have to overcome the shyness and awkwardness you feel at the fact that someone wants to save your signature as proof that they came into contact with you. Then you must get comfortable learning to distinguish when you are signing an autograph and when you are just signing your name. Paying the check at Denny's with his Visa card, my new Raptors roommate signed his receipt "Brett Smith #29." After a long day signing autographs, it only seemed natural.

Final cuts for the Raptors hopefuls came on the Sunday before the season opener. Realizing that any conciliatory remarks he could utter would seem unconvincing, Ambos went through the formality of telling us how difficult it is to make cuts. Looking at the unpersuaded players in the dugout, Ambos wryly conceded that his "this will hurt

Brett Smith, in his Lone Ranger glasses, and I sign autographs for the fans before a game in Ogden. Smith was a fan favorite with his odd but identifiable costume; I was just happy for the attention. Any fan who leaves a minor-league game without an autograph is missing a chance to form a connection with the game and its players. Nicole Mandel photograph reprinted with permission.

me more than it hurts you" platitudes were just as meaningless as "the check's in the mail, I won't come in your mouth, and all that shit."

He disappeared into his office and emerged minutes later to announce his decision. For the young men who were all trying to restart their trip to the big leagues with the Raptors, Ambos's next words would either represent another bullet successfully dodged or another stumbling block placed in their path.

In front of the new Raptors, two last ballplayers were trimmed from the roster. One of the young men, just weeks past his graduation from Yale, grumbled something to himself as he rose from his place on the bench next to me and left the dugout. If he would ever become a major leaguer, his road to the bigs would have to start with another team. The rest of the players hid relief and joyous smiles out of respect for those who were not coming along for the season.

At lunch, lucky players who came to Ogden without a contract — like Josh Kirtlan, whose gamble to bring enough clothes for the whole season paid off, and Chris Simmons, who defied the coaching staff's effort to cut him by playing exceptional ball during training camp — called home with good news and finally allowed big grins to break out on their faces. "It's been my goal my whole life to play professional baseball," Kirtlan said. "Even if it is for one year, it's wonderful, it is."

With the first-ever Raptors team established, there was business to attend to. Fines were instituted for everything from speaking with girlfriends during the game to breaking curfew, and the coaching staff laid down what it considered acceptable behavior for its club. The bottom line was a warning; "Always conduct yourself as a professional ballplayer, because professional careers are too brief. There are two kinds of baseball — professional baseball and everything else. You have plenty of time for the latter."

As the assembled players quietly considered those words, Coach Morales added one more point. "Each one of you is under a microscope," he said, enumerating a laundry list of baseball sins: not hustling, not executing fundamentals, not conducting yourself as a professional, and so on. Each time a player commits one of these sins he lets the scouts, managers, and doubters who had passed them over say, "You see, that's why we didn't draft you" or "That's why we released you." For my teammates to succeed and push their careers forward, they would have to perform well under the microscope — every game, every at-bat, and every pitch.

The seriousness of warnings and admonitions yielded to some more cheerful housekeeping details. Uniform numbers were issued — first choice to players with professional experience, then whatever was left for the rookies — and bats were distributed two to a player with replacements available for broken ones.

Players engaged in a constant debate in the dugout and the clubhouse over bats. As bats are very important tools of the trade, many players are serious about getting a good one. Each player quickly developed a favorite model that he stuck with, leaving the quality of the wood as the only variable left to fret about. The clubhouse experts declared that the best bats had the fewest grains running through them. Players therefore tormented the trainer — unlucky enough to be saddled with the chore of issuing new bats — with constant requests for something with less than ten grains. I never saw one issued to me with fewer than twenty grains. Some players were so concerned that a particular bat was of an inferior nature that they refused to use it during a game. But, according to the rules, they could only get a new one when their old one broke.

My teammates were not shy about expressing how they felt about bad bats. If a player feels that his bat is going to hold him back, he is not going to be very happy at the plate, and certainly one that is truly inferior could rob a batter of a hit or two. With nobody looking, players often splintered their bats by smashing them against hard dirt or the dugout floor. These convenient "accidents" cost minor-league clubs money and could cost players fines if they were caught, but they were one way to make sure that inferior bats were kept out of play.

With my uniform number determined — number five, my high-school number — and my bat chosen — a Rawlings thirty-three-inch model 113B — the only thing left to complete my transition from the real world to the baseball world was a piece of paper. I signed my professional baseball player's contract on Tuesday, June 14, without much ceremony, and it was official — because I was playing with a team at the lowest level of professional baseball, because this was a team of players who for some reason had been passed over by the scouts of the major-league teams, and because I was the weakest link on the lowest chain — I was the worst professional baseball player in America. My high-school coach once called me inept. I was cut twice by my college coach. But with this novel entrance into professional baseball, I was certainly surpassing their wildest expectations.

Signing my contract, filling out information for my baseball card, and agreeing not to gamble on baseball games, I couldn't help but think of all the tens of thousands of young ballplayers who would give anything to trade places with me and my teammates. Unfortunately, it is not easy to trade places. Each man who plays professional baseball, whether a league leader or a substitute sitting on the bench, was a star in his hometown. But with each new team and at each new level of baseball, a player must prove himself again, or fall by the wayside. The roads to Ogden taken by my teammates were rich and varied, but each had one thing in common: hard work and a serious commitment to the game.

Those roads to Ogden must have passed through a kindergarten class at some point, because my teammates had a tendency to speak like preschoolers. I decided this not because they were impressed that I used the word *thwart* in a sentence but because they gave everything a pet name. On the field we wore a "uni," the clubhouse attendant was "clubbie," and everybody had a nickname like Paulie or Dougie. As we prepared to go on the road, we packed our belongings in a bag that was our "roadie" and rode on a bus driven by a "bussie." As long as we were putting our lives on hold to try to make a career out of playing a kid's game it was somehow fitting that we often talked like five-year-olds.

Signs that Raptormania had swept the region appeared daily during training camp. On the front page of the *Standard-Examiner* a story touted the new navy and teal Raptor Ripple ice cream that would honor the team and be sold at home games alongside the more potent Raptor Ale.

During a break in the rigorous training schedule, my roommate and I watched a movie in our foster home as two young fans attracted our attention by creeping around the windows to see if the ballplayers were around for autographs. When we came out to the front door to sign the baseballs they produced, I noticed that one of the kids had scratched *Raptors* into his leg deep enough to make me wince. The excitement of having a team of his own to root for made this young man mutilate himself — Raptors fever was clearly catching on. After our opening night, the question became, "Can we sustain it?"

The hype of opening night — and our big victory — was soon over and it was time to begin the season as it would be played for the next thirty-five home games. Instead of a limousine ride, we played flip. Instead of sky divers, local Little Leaguers ran out to positions with Raptors players. And instead of an overflow crowd, Simmons Field had plenty of empty seats.

On the field it was business as usual. The Copper Kings came out swinging and by the end of the first half-inning we were down four to nothing. But baseball is a game of great shifts of momentum and emotions and we came back in force. As the game rolled into the ninth inning, the score was five to five when the Copper Kings put together an inning that just would not end — a balk, a bunt, an error, and then hits that found nothing but open spaces. When it was over, Butte led nine to five and the Raptors faithful were filing out of the ballpark.

More than any other sport, baseball requires an evenness of emotion and an ability to endure momentary failures and setbacks. Baseball players play every day, batting and fielding many times each game. If a player lets an error, a strikeout, or any other failure affect him for long, he will quickly fail again. The players, coaches, and managers who are best able to deal with the setbacks of the game will excel just as certainly as those who internalize their failings will continue to fail.

Unwilling to quietly accept our first loss, we yelled encouragement and stood in the dugout. After Dan Zanolla struck out to begin the inning, the ball got through the catcher and Zanolla dashed to first — safe. Slowly, a good inning began and Raptors loaded the bases.

The Raptors bench and the fans who stayed could feel some baseball magic in the air. Shane Jones, whose error in the top of the ninth helped the Copper Kings start their rally, came through with a base hit and Jeremy Winget ripped a single to right. Catcher Brad Dandridge flared a ball to right to complete the comeback. As Dandridge's hit began its descent, Simmons Field erupted. The tying and winning runs crossed the plate and we poured out of our dugout while the crowd cheered madly.

If the opening night win was for the fans, this comeback was for the team. Without the mob of fans joining us on the field, we lingered before our dugout and passed around earnest high-fives and congratulations. I grabbed my gear and joined the first group of players leaving for the clubhouse. Opening the door was like landing in Oz. We had to wade through a sea of munchkins thrusting balls, hats, and programs at us for autographs. If the fans did not take to their new team on opening night, they were sold on the Raptors now.

It was a good thing that the homestand was going so smoothly because during the games, everything except baseball was going on all around us. Between innings, promotion paraphernalia was dragged back and forth through the home dugout, frustrating the Raptors coaching staff even as it amused the players. A free haircut was a prize for one fan, another had to catch plastic baseballs, and a young fan had to race around the bases. Even though there was baseball to be played, players couldn't help but get involved in the various promotions. Batboys raced outside the outfield fence with raptor-shaped cutouts atop long sticks protruding just above the outfield fence as fans predicted the outcome of the contest. Getting caught up in the hoopla while on the bench, we rooted for our favorite raptor cutout, urged the kids around the bases, and enjoyed the breaks in the action as much as the fans.

As opening day faded into memory, we settled into the routine that would be our lives for the summer and learned to generally limit our lives to one concern: "When do we have to get to the park?" Once that was determined, everything fell into place and the routine became predictable and comfortable. When at home, we arrived at Simmons Field at about 3:00 P.M. In the clubhouse, we changed into batting practice attire and made small talk, straggling out to the field for our 3:30 stretching routine. At 4:15, home team batting practice began, giving way to visiting team batting practice at 5:05.

Batting practice was almost always a good time. The balletlike choreography and precise efficiency was soothing as players effortlessly moved through their drills. Batters, who approached the cage on cue in groups — the first three batters from the night's lineup, the next three, the next three, then the extra players — would bunt, practice the execution of a hit-and-run, slap the ball the opposite way, drive the ball to the outfield, then swing away. Those in the group who were not batting would practice running the bases, advancing a base for the hit-and-run, moving to third with the opposite-field stroke, then tagging for home. Next to the cage a coach would stroke a ground ball to a waiting fielder just after the hitter in the cage took his hack. Balls would be fielded and returned — live balls from the batter would be tossed toward a pitcher behind a screen in short-center field who was designated to gather the balls, while grounders fungoed from the coach would be returned with a majestic lob designed to reach the coach's hand on one hop. On and on the dance would continue in its mechanical fluidity until all the position players had a chance to bat and run. Pitchers tried to look busy in the outfield shagging flies, pretending to give balls an honest effort while drinking up the sun and chatting with fellow hurlers.

With the easy ritual my teammates and I could take some hacks and work on defense at a relaxed pace hours before game time. At second base I would joke around with the other infielders between ground balls as we waited for our chance at bat. After everyone had a chance to bat we would all gather around the cage for the base-hit round. Every batter had one swing to get a hit and could stay in the cage as long as the coaches judged each effort successful. When a player's turn was over we would all clamor and jostle to get in next, ignoring anyone who tried to reason that "everybody gets a turn."

Listening to the sound system blasting rock and roll and cringing when my teammates sang incorrect lyrics to the songs was always a pleasant distraction to my efforts at elbowing my way to the plate. Once in, it was not always good to be successful at the base-hit round, as the coaching staff was apt to reward continued hits with a fastball at your head or a hard-breaking curve. For the few times that I was successful enough to earn a ball at my head, I was just proud to get the chance to duck it. Soon enough, batting practice was over and it was time to be reminded that we were still in the minors — we had to walk into the outfield to retrieve our balls.

While the opposition took batting practice, we would mill around the dugout, wander into the clubhouse, or hit the concession stands for a chicken sandwich or some Raptor Ripple. Back in the clubhouse, players changed from batting-practice jerseys to game jerseys and lovingly polished spikes until they radiated a metallic black luster. The trailer quickly became littered with napkins, sunflower seeds, and discarded shirts as players lounged, attempted to rest, and focused on the game at hand. Eventually we returned to the dugout and readied ourselves for our 5:55 infield and outfield practice.

Unlike batting practice, where players seemed loose and coaches were usually in a joking mood, this encore presentation of baseball in ballet was serious business, an overture for that night's game. Out-fielders would first field four balls each, two requiring a throw to second base and two going home. With outfielders trotting off the field, the infielders would begin their routine of fielding, throwing, and covering their bags for a return throw from the catcher — get one and cover, get one and cover, get two and cover, get two and cover, a long one, bring it home. As the fielding practice crescendoed, the coach would produce a finale of pop-ups for the infielders and three final pop-ups for the catchers, hit straight into the air — "home runs in an elevator shaft" — above home plate. Coaches took pride in their ability to get their team on and off the field in mere minutes and opposing coaches would good-naturedly smile approval at each other's performance, especially if the final pop-ups were impressively grouped near the plate.

At 6:05 the visiting team took over for their fielding practice, then the ground crew prepared the field for the upcoming game, leaving plenty of time to kill. Some players played games of pepper or flip, others stretched and ran. Finally the national anthem beckoned the first pitch each night promptly at 7:00.

The schedule was not the only thing that was becoming routine as we continued our opening series. We were getting quickly accustomed to the rants and raves of our manager. After displaying his temper during the first two games, Ambos was riding the umpires hard in the third game. Misplays by his team elicited angry epithets and missed calls by the umpires drew bursts of outrage — usually mentioning the words *lube* and *bungie* in some combination. Ambos was displaying a tendency to be a little too passionate.

Although it seemed only a matter of time before his first ejection, Ambos was shown the door for the first time for something he did not do. After a close call on a play where a Copper King avoided the tag of Shane Jones at third base, the Raptors bench erupted. Though the umpire had made the right call, this did not stop me from yelling my displeasure and it certainly did not stop Coach Morales from unleashing a string of angry remarks at the base umpire. The umpire, who had had his back turned, wheeled — and threw out Ambos.

"That's it Willy, you're gone," he shouted. And with that, the rookie manager had his first ejection. He did not deserve this one, but nobody in the Raptors dugout thought that it would be his only early exit from a game. Despite the ejection, sloppy play, and an offense that did not take advantage of the opportunities presented it, we came from behind and won our third game against Butte.

Giddy with our sweep of the Copper Kings — a cooperative team composed of free agents and players from various farm systems — we prepared to play an affiliated team. The Idaho Falls Braves, whose parent club had played in the National League championship series each of the previous three years and won the pennant twice, brought their talented, if young, team to Ogden. While most of the Raptors were postcollege age, the Braves, loaded up with drafted talent including players from the Dominican Republic and even Australia, did not have a single player older than twenty-two. Eleven of their twenty-eight roster players were under twenty, including their catcher, Pascual Matos, a young Dominican with a cannon for an arm. At least according to baseball professionals, the Raptors were out-talented by the Braves.

But before confronting the Braves, we had to contend with a long day and a big public appearance. We traveled to the Eccles Dinosaur Park, a "zoo" filled with dinosaur statues from the mighty Tyrannosaurus rex to the latest star of the dinosaur world, the raptor. In addition to meeting the public and signing autographs, we were going to pose with the raptor for our official baseball-card picture.

Player appearances are a big part of minor-league life as teams try to increase interest and encourage attendance. Although the players understand the need to interact with the public, it is difficult not to let these interruptions in daily life affect their mindset or their performance on the field. Instead of arriving at the field at about 3:00 to get dressed, we had to get to Simmons Field at 10:00 A.M. to prepare for our trip to the dinosaur park. My sleepy teammates and I were frustrated to find one hundred Raptors posters to sign but among two dozen players only five pens to sign them with — autographing Raptors posters was a long, slow process.

When we finally arrived at the dinosaur park we found an enthusiastic crowd. Despite the morning's frustration, posing for baseball-card pictures and signing autographs pumped up the players and made for a fun event — for a moment. After the initial flurry of fans, autographs, and congratulations, the crowd dispersed. We were supposed to stay until three but it was not even one when we found ourselves out of fans and searching for shade to wait out the day. We were tired, hungry, and bored, but the manager of the dinosaur park was adamant about us staying around.

When we finally left for lunch, our coaches had canceled batting practice, giving us a full three hours to kill. Those who lived farther away found the clubhouse floor comfortable enough to catch some shut-eye. I joined some of my teammates there for a nap before we stretched to prepare for the game.

The long day took its toll. Balls clanked off gloves and throws sailed away during infield and outfield practice. A little more than halfway through the drill, one too many errors caused Coach Morales to call us off the field, a little chagrined and very frustrated. Ambos was not about to let our performance go without comment. We gathered in the clubhouse waiting for a storm — we got a hurricane.

We may not have been intense, but we were still undefeated. That did not matter to Ambos, who bellowed warnings that we beat a team we should have beaten but now were about to face a legitimately talented team. Each time we play, Ambos warned, the opposing manager writes a report on us that could further or doom our career. Any player labeled a dog now would find it very difficult to change that impression.

Just as the fury looked like it would subside, Ambos changed subjects and upped the intensity of his outrage. For the first time, the lineup had been altered for the game with the Braves. One player, who irked the coaches with his timid play, was benched, and the rest of the lineup was juggled with the change. Ambos said that he had heard the grumbling about the changes and he had one thing to scream at us: "Fuck you! This is *my* team!"

Stunned by our manager's extreme reaction, we left the clubhouse to play ball. Despite jumping out to score four runs in our half of the first inning, the Braves beat us by taking advantage of errors and misplays. After the game, Ambos faced the press having endured his first loss as a pro manager and commented to a reporter that his team was not intense. He lowered his voice as he suggested, "Maybe that's my fault."

For the last game of our first homestand we needed a win to send us on the road on a positive note. With the sky threatening to open up and a cool breeze sweeping across the field, we checked the weather nervously. Some players openly hoped for a day off, wishing to rest and sleep before the next day's early morning bus trip to Helena, Montana, but the clouds parted and our game was on.

Pitcher Danny Miller was on the mound for his second start in our final encounter with the Idaho Falls Braves. Working quickly and throwing strikes, Miller was again sterling. Raptors bats exploded for two home runs and the home team cruised to a six-to-three win. With no tantrums, no need for late-inning heroics, and no whining, it was a perfect way to leave town. We were four and one, in first place, and ready to take our act on the road.

The Rejected

After spring training, neither first baseman Jeremy Winget nor short-stop Tommy Johnston figured that he would ever be on a professional baseball road trip again. Released by the organizations that signed them and unable to find refuge anywhere in professional baseball, both were contemplating a life without major-league ambitions. But, having gained another chance with the independent Raptors, Winget and Johnston were ready for another season's campaign and ready to make the most of the new opportunity.

During Raptors training camp Tommy's smooth fielding and Jeremy's hard hitting made as much of an impression as their war stories from the years they had already spent in the minor leagues. Winget wore spikes issued by the Baltimore Orioles and festooned his car with an Orioles vanity plate despite having been cut by the organization just months before. In the clubhouse he was happy to tell how his Bluefield Orioles won the championship of the Appalachian League and earned him the ring he wore proudly. Johnston spoke wistfully of the success enjoyed by the Pittsburgh Pirates of the early 1990s of which he had once hoped to be a part.

As the sun poked lazily over the trees showering dawn on the bus that would take us to Helena, both players were back in baseball and gearing up for the challenges ahead. Even though the hour was early, Jeremy seemed to be relishing his second chance. "Who's this?" he challenged catcher Troy Doezie as he curled up across two bus seats, covered his face with his Orioles hat, and complained that he needed sleep in a thick Spanish accent. "Dominicans," he said as Doezie laughed, remembering his own experience in the Twins system trying in vain to get one of his Dominican teammates to share a seat.

Winget was happy, and with good reason. Just months earlier the Baltimore Orioles had informed him that he had no future in their organization. But having faced the mortality of his baseball career, he was once again playing, and playing well. He had played every game, his average was flirting with .400, and he had knocked in almost a run per game. Numbers like that over the course of the season would certainly extend his career. But his early season success did not mean that Jeremy was going to tempt fate. After every inning when he returned to the dugout he had to receive the infield ball while his spikes were still on grass; returning to the infield, he had to sweep the dirt in front of first base, and on his equipment he wrote a simple declaration, "I can, I know, I will." Superstitions could just fill in the lapses when talent waned. With a wide smile, Winget prepared for life on the road — the road that pointed toward the majors.

In the back of the bus, Tommy Johnston sat unfazed by the turmoil of players stowing gear and fluffing pillows around him. With a Walkman helping him shut out the commotion, Johnston looked as unconcerned and at ease as he did fielding a difficult short hop. Even though the season was only a few days old, Tommy was anchoring a solid defensive middle at shortstop for the Raptors, with Chris Amos at second base and Doug O'Neill in center field making opponents earn every run against the Raptors. While Tommy's glove was earning him kudos, he was still hitting on the light side. His average would have to pick up if he wanted to attract attention from any other organizations. Never one to let his face betray his emotions, Tommy just looked passively out the bus window and waited for the bus to pull out of Simmons Field.

As the game wound down the previous night, he was anything but placid. In the bottom of the eighth, Johnston was in dire need of the Raptors bathroom facilities, which were inconveniently located near the clubhouse, about thirty yards behind the home dugout and separated from the dugout by the ballpark crowd. Unfortunately for him, players had jammed the dugout door to keep it from swinging open and allowing Raptors fans at the concession stands to distract them from the game. Batting third in the inning, and unable to open the dugout door despite his frantic efforts, he was forced to keep his composure and exercise his power of mind over matter. "I'll unbuckle my belt," was his only response to how he would deal with the situation. To his credit, he took his at-bat and was able to draw a walk. But to his dismay, he was stuck on the basepaths until the end of the inning and then on the field for the Braves' ninth inning. When I ran out to deliver his glove and hat, I patted him on the behind and encouraged him, "Just don't think of raging rivers." Either his concentration or his agitation kept him from responding. Finally the game ended, and Johnston, ever polite, stopped to listen to instructions from his coach, sign autographs, and then break the land speed record to the portable toilets for a well-deserved late-inning relief appearance.

Tommy Johnston grew up on the southwest side of Indianapolis in Decatur, one of the smaller Indianapolis townships. "There are nine townships in Indianapolis and most people can't name all nine of them," Tommy explained. "We are the ninth — I can go five minutes and see the outskirts of the city or five minutes and see farms."

The baby of his family, which included two older sisters, Tommy began playing baseball in the third grade. But young Tommy Johnston actually had to be coaxed into Little League. "The very first day my dad signed me up, I didn't want to play because I was sort of shy," Tommy admitted. As a seven-year-old he was a little intimidated by the other Little Leaguers in their full uniforms and spikes, but Tommy put on a glove and went out to play. Where to play was another question.

"The coach says go to left field," he recalled, "and I'm like, 'Where's that?'" Johnston would quickly learn where left field was and eventually took to baseball. Growing up in the Hoosier state, Tommy liked playing basketball better than baseball but soon began to develop a real talent and a real passion for the game. Unlike most of his friends who were putting up basketball hoops, Tommy and a neighbor bought a batting cage. Once his interest in baseball was sparked, he began to hone his craft.

Tommy improved and played on through grade school and into

high school. When not on the diamond Johnston played football and basketball, but he was intent on continuing his baseball career. He was not drafted after high school and was set to go play ball for Purdue University after his senior year when a scout noticed his talent while he was playing in a summer league. The shy kid who didn't know how to get to left field suddenly had major dreams.

Jeremy Winget had always wanted to play baseball. During the game's golden era, his grandfather played for the St. Louis Cardinals minor-league system and his father played at Brigham Young University. A Utah native, Jeremy grew up in a small town just outside of Salt Lake City. His family moved to slightly larger Murray when he was in the seventh grade, and he attended Murray High School, where he excelled at baseball.

As a Mormon and a baseball fan, Jeremy always admired Dale Murphy, the superstar outfielder for the Atlanta Braves. Murphy, known for his tremendous ability as well as his gentlemanly demeanor, inspired Jeremy because of his actions both on and off the field. Because his grandfather was a Mormon church leader, nine-year-old Jeremy had a chance to meet fellow-Mormon Murphy when he came to Utah.

The meeting gave Jeremy someone to look up to — not just an ability but a conduct to emulate. "I like him," Jeremy said of the two-time National League Most Valuable Player, "not just because he can play baseball, but because of what he was off the field — real quiet but a great example. Not that he was better than anybody else, but he just treated people the way people wanted to be treated and respected people. When he asked you, 'How're you doing?' he'd really mean it."

Jeremy played T-ball, then moved into Little League and quickly excelled. "I never thought I was better than anybody else," he said, recalling his early baseball success. "I never looked at it that way, I would just try to go out and play hard."

Hard play soon had Jeremy thinking of where his baseball talent could lead. "I always wanted to play pro ball ever since I can remember," he said, "and in high school scouts started coming around — they wanted to know if I wanted to play pro ball or go to college. I just told them, 'I want to play pro ball.'"

Tommy Johnston was in West Virginia when a scout for the Pittsburgh Pirates approached him. "He asked me if I would like to play pro baseball," Johnston said. "I said, 'Sure.'" He did not need much time to think about the question. Even years after his entrance into professional baseball, he remembered his quick decision to sign with the Pirates. "I was thrilled," he said with a smile, and decided, "If they give me a contract, I'm signing no matter what."

The Pirates offered Johnston a free agent's contract and gave him a five thousand dollar bonus. He reported to Bradenton, Florida, to the Gulf Coast League and was playing rookie ball at the age of eighteen. With only three weeks left in the Gulf Coast (rookie) League season, Johnston was excited to be in professional baseball, but tentative in his approach. "The first day I'm sort of feeling like I don't belong," he remembered. "Everybody is wearing these Pirates uniforms." Now Tommy Johnston was wearing a uniform.

In the last weeks of the season he batted .208. "I was five for twenty-four," Johnston beamed. "It should have been six but the scorekeeper gave me an error — I beat it out." Fresh from the Gulf Coast League, he played in an instructional league in Florida then reported to school, worked out in winter, and then focused on baseball as he prepared to report to spring training.

Like many first-time professionals, Tommy was excited just to be playing pro ball in his first year in the minors, but reported to spring training prepared to work hard to push his career forward. He played hard but did not receive an assignment to a full-season team, which begins its year as the parent clubs head north for their own season. Stuck in extended spring training, Tommy bided his time until the short-season leagues began after the draft.

"Man, that's hard. Everybody breaks for spring training and you have to stay there. It's sort of disappointing," he said. After the draft, he reported back to the Gulf Coast League, where he played every day and batted .240. But with the assignment came extra pressure. With a new crop of players entering the Pirates system after the draft, Johnston could see that he had to produce to move up the organizational ladder because the hungry new kids selected in the draft would be gunning for his job.

At the end of his second year in the Gulf Coast League, Tommy was moved up to Welland, Ontario, and single-A baseball for the last week of the New York–Penn League. The crowds of single-A baseball — in contrast to the dearth of attention drawn by the games in the Gulf Coast League — were a welcome change for Tommy. "When I moved up to Welland, there's people — just tons — I was like, 'This is what it's all about,'" he said. "I hit .280 for that last week, one hit shy of .300."

After getting a taste of the crowds, attention, and intimate contact that makes the minors so unique, Tommy was ready to continue his ascent through the Pirates system. But the next year another lackluster performance kept Johnston in Florida for another year of extended spring training. He played well enough to win an assignment to Welland again, but another crop of rookies entered the Pirates system as eager as Tommy to move up to the bigs.

"I start playing once every three days," Tommy said glumly, "then once every four days, then once every five days. I was almost ready to ask for my release. I was so frustrated thinking, 'What am I gonna do?' because I didn't know how to handle life without baseball."

After Jeremy Winget's senior year in high school, the Orioles made him their twenty-first-round draft pick. Two days after graduation, he left Utah for Florida to begin his professional career. "The funny thing about it," he recalled with a grin, "was when I looked back in my books — I guess it was when the Orioles were doing good in '83 — I wrote, 'I want to play for the Orioles' when I was like eleven or twelve."

In Sarasota, Florida, Jeremy had to adjust to professional baseball in the Gulf Coast League as well as life without his family. "That was probably the toughest time in my life," he recalled. "I struggled. I went like two for thirty-four in the first month and a half. It's just tough to adjust for a high-school kid — being away from home and my girl — that was the longest three months of my life."

After struggling in his first weeks in Sarasota, Jeremy found his swing and hit near .300 for the rest of the season. He finished the 1991 campaign with a .238 average in forty-one games. Returning to the

Gulf Coast League the following season, he was hitting .331 when he was called up to the Orioles' single-A affiliate, in Bluefield, West Virginia.

"My girl was there for two-and-a-half weeks," he remembered excitedly. "I'd just taken her to the Orlando airport, I got home, and the family I was staying with said, 'Coach just called.' I called him and he said, 'We're gonna move you up.'"

He drove seventeen hours from Sarasota to Bluefield and was in the lineup the next day hitting a home run in his second at-bat. But soon he was pulled from the lineup and only playing every four or five games. "I was working real hard, but it was like they wouldn't work with me," he said. "They just kind of let me be. They gave me grounders, but they just lost hope in me."

The coaches that liked him and the scout that signed him had left the Orioles organization by the time he reached Bluefield and his new coach was not happy with him. "I had no pull," Jeremy conceded about his chances with the Orioles in his second year. For a six-foot-two-inch slugger, he simply was not displaying the power the Orioles needed. With few supporters in the organization, he knew his days were numbered.

Winget's girl — his high-school sweetheart, Jamie — stuck with him and supported him through his trying times with the Orioles. "If it wasn't for her, I probably wouldn't be where I am right now," he said with a wide smile. "She has really supported me. At times I wanted to give up and she'd say, 'You're not giving up.'" They were engaged — over the phone — while he was in Bluefield and she was in Utah.

The next year at spring training the Orioles were playing anybody and everybody at first base and instead of going north to play high-A ball, Jeremy stayed in Florida for extended spring training. When the short-season leagues began he returned to Bluefield, but when he arrived he was told that he was being assigned to a cooperative team — the Butte Copper Kings, of the Pioneer League — to get more playing time.

He drove from West Virginia across the country to Montana, where he played every other day but lacked the advantage of having the Orioles organizational people observing his performance. Although he hit .303 in forty-four games for Butte, Jeremy was unhappy. Despite his steady improvements, the Orioles were just not allowing him to progress through their system.

It was now 1993, and while Jeremy Winget toiled in Butte — over two thousand miles from where the Baltimore Orioles played in their new ballpark at Camden Yards — Tommy Johnston was facing similar frustration in Welland as the Pittsburgh Pirates attempted to defend their National League Eastern Division crown.

Even though he had seen his playing time diminish, Tommy still had a uniform on his back and a chance to push his career forward. Still proud of the budding ballplayer, his parents and girlfriend made the trip from Indianapolis across the border into Canada to see him play. While his hometown rooting section was in Welland, Tommy was told to visit manager Larry Smith's office. With his decreased playing time and .156 batting average, Tommy did not need much of a hint about the topic of the meeting. For the first time in his baseball life, he was about to be released. "The organization wants to make a change," Tommy recounted hearing that night. "We don't think you're going to make it to the big leagues with the Pirates organization."

The previous year the Pirates played in the National League Championship Series and Tommy Johnston was a nineteen-year-old shortstop moving up toward the bigs. After two-and-a-half years of watching Tommy develop, the Pirates were giving up on him and concentrating their efforts on younger prospects. Suddenly, Tommy was a twenty-year-old ex-professional walking through the clubhouse, not telling his teammates that he had been cut, wondering how to break the news to his parents and girlfriend. Tommy was headed home where he would face his first fall, winter, and spring without a baseball future.

While Tommy pondered the end of his career, Jeremy Winget worried about his prospects with the Baltimore Orioles. With spring training, Jeremy dutifully reported to Florida with the Orioles but played only a handful of games during the first two weeks while no-

Jeremy Winget, a Utah native, was a popular player and a veteran of three years in the minor leagues when he came to Ogden. Steven D. Conlin photograph reprinted with permission.

body talked with him on or off the field. Even though he had seen the writing on the wall, it was still a shock when he was called into his manager's office. "We don't think you'll make it in our organization," he recalls hearing, as his professional baseball career came to a crashing halt.

After trying unsuccessfully to catch on with other teams, Winget was almost resolved to give up baseball. The only team that was actively interested in him was the Ogden Raptors, but he was prohibited by minor-league rules from playing for a rookie league team because of his veteran status unless every team of the league consented, and the Idaho Falls Braves would not consent.

At a loss as to how to direct his life, Jeremy Winget received a call from his grandfather. Dale Murphy was in town again. Jeremy met with the ex-big-leaguer and they talked about baseball and life without baseball. Murphy then intervened on Winget's behalf and the Idaho Falls Braves removed their opposition to Winget's signing with Ogden. Once again, Jeremy had a chance to play the game he loved, and, with the increased playing time for the Raptors, the chance to put up numbers that could put him back on the road to the majors.

"I realize that if you don't know somebody or if somebody's not pulling for you, you really don't have a chance," he said, but was determined to give baseball one more time. "I thank God every day that I can play. Every day I go out there and just soak it up and I'm gonna try to play baseball as long as I can."

Like Winget, Tommy Johnston tried to move on with his life but still felt a void where baseball used to be. "Sitting in college, I was like, 'Man, I can play this game,'" he remembered. He had to give it one more shot. The scout who had signed him for the Pirates informed him about a released-player tryout camp. The Baltimore Orioles scouts invited him to spring training. "The year of college made me grow up a little bit," Tommy said. But it was back to playing a kid's game for another spring.

He was thrilled to put on a uniform again, but it was short-lived. "I had a ten-day tryout at spring training and they didn't offer me a contract," he confessed. "So I was like, 'Well, this is probably it.'" But even though the Orioles didn't want the sure-handed Johnston, his tryout performance attracted the attention of a scout who turned Tommy on to the Ogden Raptors.

"After they didn't offer me a contract with the Orioles, I just said, 'I just want to play for fun — I love the game, I love to play in front of people, I just love everything about the game,'" he decided. "I just said I want to play no matter where it's at."

"I wrote a letter to Willy saying, 'I can play but I don't really have that much money to come to the tryouts because all the tryouts were on the West Coast," Tommy said of his first contact with Ogden manager Willy Ambos. When informed that there was going to be a tryout in North Carolina, Tommy decided to drive for two days and try one more time. After seeing his slick glove work and confident fielding, the Raptors signed him on the spot and Tommy was back in professional baseball.

With the new opportunity came the pressure to move his career forward, but Tommy tried to focus on the job at hand not the career prospects he was trying to resurrect. "I don't really think about it," Tommy said. "I just go out there and try to have fun. I just have fun playing every day. I try to impress people, but I don't concentrate on impressing people. I don't think every day, 'I'm gonna make it to the big leagues.' I just want to have fun and put together a good year with respectable numbers.

"Any day you could be working in a factory. You just can't take the game for granted." He pointed to tunnel vision and a single-mindedness about baseball as the difference between the players who would move on and those who would be left behind. "They just go about their business and do what they have to do," Tommy explained. "There's no way everybody can make it to the big leagues, you just have to have the right breaks, have people pulling for you, and put up the numbers."

Unfortunately for players like Tommy Johnston and Jeremy Winget, baseball is not simply a meritocracy. Although baseball fans and baseball professionals love to hear the tales of sixty-first-round draft picks or undrafted free agents making their improbable way through the system all the way to the majors, it is often only the early-round draft picks who receive the chance. Unless there is significant money invested in a player, or significant backing by the decision makers within the organization, chances are that the average minor leaguer will end his career without ever fulfilling his dreams.

To take a real shot at baseball dreams, it does not hurt to have contacts in the world of sports, and during his tryout with the Orioles, Tommy had a closeup view of a baseball spectacle that was being watched by a curious public — a thirty-one-year-old rookie given the unusual opportunity to pursue his dubious chance at a major-league career. Michael Jordan, perhaps the greatest player in basketball history, was pursuing his own major dreams as Tommy worked at putting his career back on track.

"It was in the Orioles' spring training and I was playing shortstop," Johnston recalled. "It was Jordan's first game in the minors after being called down. In the first inning there were not that many people there because it was just on the complex and there was a big-league game going on, but by the end of the game the crowd heard that Jordan was over in the minor-league complex and there were probably five hundred people watching our game."

The Hoosier in him could not help being excited with his proximity to the basketball star, but the ballplayer in him could see that Jordan was still a long way from the majors. "I wasn't too impressed with Jordan," Tommy confessed, "but I was still in awe of him being a legend. I was playing short and he was leading off of second so I was four or five feet from him," Johnston gushed. "I said something to him but I didn't know if he would respond. He didn't really seem sure of himself. I just told him he better not get too far off the base.

"I'd like to see him back on the basketball court, personally," Johnston confessed. "I don't think he's going to play in the big leagues. He's got some ability, but he's thirty years old. His swing is just messed up. He's swinging all arms."

Because of his celebrity, Jordan had the chance that other ballplayers work for all their lives while a curious nation of sports fans followed his progress. Johnston and Winget had their chance because they refused to believe that their careers were over, and only family and friends would care about their exploits unless they could do something to once again attract the attention of the baseball establishment. As we began our first road trip there was one more reminder about the difference between the international superstar turned minor leaguer and the rejects on the Raptors. While Jordan's Birmingham Barons traveled through the Southern League in luxury aboard a customized bus, we had only a charter bus to carry us through the expansive Pioneer League.

The sun finally hailed the day with brilliant light and the bus was ready to begin our trip. Willy and Mo sat in the front of the bus with trainer Dan Overman and radio announcer Kurt Wilson behind them. I sat behind Overman with Winget and Doezie behind me. Further back, along the aisle, Brett Smith joined a card game with Doug O'Neill and Chris Simmons, and in the back of the bus Johnston was beginning to snooze.

Simmons Field faded into the rearview mirror and the Raptors bus turned onto A Avenue, then onto Twenty-fourth Street, and onto Interstate 15. For me, this was excitement. The season was stretched out like the road before us and neither lack of sleep nor the pending hours of travel ahead could dampen my enthusiasm for the days to come. For Winget and Johnston — who were once on the way to the majors in organizations intent on bringing along the most talented players to drive their major-league clubs to the World Series — the road ahead could bring either more disappointment or joyous redemption.

The Long Road Ahead

Five hours out of Ogden, the Raptors bus was quiet. Bodies lay strewn in the aisles and across seats in positions that said "neck cramp" in bold body language. In eight hours we would be on the field against the Helena Brewers, but with the bus cruising through Idaho, players and coaches were just trying to catch up on sleep.

Only truckers and tumbleweeds shared the road with my teammates and me on the way to meet the bus for our 6:00 A.M. departure. Players with professional experience who had been through this routine before arrived early, set up a pillow, and quickly fell asleep across two seats. Straggling players walked cautiously down the bus aisle looking for the friendly face of a teammate who would share a seat. They were met only with grumbles. I propped myself against the inside armrest and curled up facing the bus window so I would not even have to make eye contact.

While players were still conscious, meal money — seventy-five dollars for five days — was handed out. At five dollars per meal, none of us had any plans to save some for a rainy day. We shoved meal money into our wallets and Coach Morales picked *Fletch* from his movie stockpile and put it into the VCR as we pulled out of Ogden. By the time the bus had reached cruising speed on the interstate, most of the team was watching the film through their eyelids. When I finally found a yoga-like position that allowed me a measure of comfort, I joined them. Life on the road, Raptors style, was just beginning.

Out the window of the bus an occasional farm or weigh station broke up the view, but most of the scenery from horizon to horizon was nothing but big sky, rolling hills, and far-off mountains. As we cruised on, the only thing that seemed to vary was their proximity. We passed over the Continental Divide, but to the drowsy Raptors it was just another mile marker. After hours of bus travel, the dazzling, post-cardlike scenery was just a blur and the only thing we wanted to see through the window was a sign reading, Helena, Next Right.

I quickly learned that I did a poor job of preparing for the road trip. While some teammates brought foam pads to sleep on, rice cookers to prepare healthy food in, personal stereos to listen to, and porn magazines to read (or at least look at) I did not even bring a pillow. All I had was my laptop computer and a serious resolve to pack better for the road next time. I was also going to seriously think about bringing along a book of card game rules for my teammates.

Directly behind my seat, Jeremy Winget and Troy Doezie were busy playing cards during the trip but could not settle on a game that they both knew how to play. Through Idaho and into Montana I had to listen to an endless series of card game rules. "Just play war or go fish," I would turn around and yell every time they began to go through the intricacies of hearts or gin. At least I could console myself that by the time we were midway through the season they probably would have run out of new games to learn.

Listening to Winget and Doezie learning to play cards was not the only frustration of road travel. By the time we were a few hours from home, everyone took on a common stench and a common exasperated attitude.

To break up the trip we stopped for breakfast and then again to stretch our legs. With each stop, sleepy players — hair recently styled by the bus window and cologned by the odor of too many men stuck in a poorly ventilated bus — would blink their eyes and shuffle off, only to come back slightly refreshed and dive back into their sleeping positions.

The Pioneer League is a "carry your own bags" league, so when the Raptors bus finally arrived in Helena, each player filed into the motel parking lot with an equipment bag, a clothing bag, and a pillow. Some brought along blankets and others carried radios. For this first road trip I had drawn the dubious privilege of carrying the medical trunk and crutches. With our road-weary expressions and various baggage weighing us down, we looked like refugees fleeing some hostile ballpark. Lugging my equipment and clothes along with the cumbersome trunk and crutches, I decided that making it to the bigs would be worth dreaming about even if all it meant was that someone else carried your bags.

We had just under two hours to try out our lumpy beds, grab a bite to eat, change into our uniforms, and climb back on the bus for our game. Touring around Montana's capital would have to wait for another day.

Nestled in the foothills of the Rockies, Helena is a quaint city of about twenty-seven thousand residents. In front of our motel ran Last Chance Gulch, where men walk around in cowboy hats, sporting goods stores do brisk business selling all manner of firearms, and a taxidermist displays fearsome-looking bears and record-setting bucks. Around town, opulent Victorian mansions built for Helena's mining millionaires contrast with the Greek renaissance architecture of the state capitol and the more modern state and federal buildings. While Helena now boasts a thriving arts community, the city has preserved its pioneer heritage. Sculptures depicting miners and ranchers along the walking mall on Last Chance Gulch and the restored miners' village on Reeder's Alley give visitors a glimpse of Helena's gold-dust-sprinkled history.

Some of that gold dust should have been spared for Kindrick Field. Part of a municipal park complex that contained a large swimming pool and a small orchestra shell facing a lush green lawn, the ballpark was little more than a grandstand and bleachers surrounding a sloping American Legion field. The dimensions were small, the infield grass was overgrown, players had to run uphill from first to second, and the park was badly in need of some paint and nails. Playing for an affiliated team meant that a player was poised in a conduit to the major leagues but it did not necessarily mean that major-league luxury trickled down through the organization.

After stowing our equipment in the small and dingy locker room, we stretched and tried to get our bodies and minds ready to play ball.

We were stiff and fatigued from the long day, but the cooling breeze and the familiar sights and sounds of a ballpark helped shake off the cobwebs. Suddenly the breeze turned into a full-blown windstorm that whipped across the field and swirled dust and dirt mercilessly. With an hour to go before game time the skies looked like Armageddon was upon us, but by the time the umpire said "Play ball!" the fickle Montana weather turned a certain maelstrom into a pleasant evening. Making the most of the break in the weather, Paul O'Hearn pitched well, holding the Brewers to a single run and allowing us to cruise to a seven-to-one win.

After the game there was no celebration and the coaches laid down the law for our first night on the road. A midnight curfew was imposed, leaving us little time to do much except shower and grab a quick dinner before bed check. I joined most of the team at the Last Chance Casino for a postgame meal. Doug O'Neill introduced me to keno and then quickly moved on to higher stakes games. While Doug won dollar after dollar, I was just throwing away my meal money. As I walked away from the video poker machines, I could hear teammates cheering Doug's good fortune. By bed check I think he might have won enough to buy out my contract.

On the television, Ken Griffey Jr. was besting Babe Ruth's record for most home runs by the end of June and the Raptors players noted his talent with much awe. As we joked about the heights of Griffey's prowess, I scanned the sports ticker for a Phillies score. I was the only one of the Raptors who really followed a specific major-league team.

Unlike casual fans who talk about their favorite team's chances in the pennant race or the fantasy-league player who rattles off endless statistics, my teammates were more interested in individual players or friends and former teammates who were playing elsewhere in baseball. When talking about other players, my teammates and coaches constantly explained, "I played against him in college," "I coached him in Sacramento," or "He was on my team in the Gulf Coast League." From the outside, looking at all the names of all the players on all the teams in professional baseball, the universe surrounding our national pastime looks immense and daunting, but once immersed in it, baseball is a relatively small world.

After spending the day exploring greater Helena, lounging in motel rooms, and throwing more money at the video poker machines of the Last Chance Casino, we again traveled to Kindrick Field to take on the Helena Brewers. This night it was the Raptors who were held to a single run as the Brewers' pitching, led by twenty-year-old Tano Tijerina, an imposingly tall righthander from Waco, Texas, silenced the Raptors' bats.

This was an important night for the Raptors as we were trying to put some distance between ourselves and the Brewers in the race for the Southern Division crown, but it was more important to the Brewers. In addition to the pressure of performing for the manager's report, the Brewers had two roving instructors in town to check out the talent and lend the benefit of their professional careers to the team. These instructors could make recommendations to the parent club that could make or break the careers of the young Brewers; they could also make recommendations that could put one of the Raptors on the road to the big leagues. In warmups, batting practice, and the game, the pressure was on to make a good impression.

For my fellow bench players and me, it was just another game. Nonstarters spent the entire night staying ready just in case we were needed. For three hours we sat on the bench and tried to keep our heads in the game. During rallies we cheered. After questionable calls by the umpires, we yelled. When we felt we might be needed, we stretched. And during the rest of the game, we just passed the time.

I constantly squeezed a rubber ball and bounced it against the floor or chewed endless bags of sunflower seeds. Troy Doezie and Brett Smith spat on ants scurrying across the dirt on the edge of the dugout. Pitchers busied themselves with pitching charts. Others scanned the crowd for good-looking women. Without much to cheer or yell about, we waited in vain for our teammates to rally, or for the coach to call on us for assistance. In the seventh inning Morales called out, "Ex-players get ready." My teammates and I began to stretch lightly and get focused on the game, but it ended without incident.

For the starters it was a tough loss. For the substitutes it was also a long, uneventful evening at the ballpark. But sitting in the best seat in the house, and being at hand to go into the game at a moment's notice, was certainly not the worst way to spend the time.

For me, being a bench player was part frustration knowing that I was not going to be inserted in the game unless it became a serious mismatch, but it was also part thrill knowing that I was a professional baseball player for the summer. After sitting on the bench all night, thinking how lucky I was to be in uniform, I was always brought down to earth when Ambos declared a curfew in effect. My fellow pine riders had a much more difficult assignment trying to stay ready for action. Especially early in the season, every chance for a bench player to get into a game was a double-edged sword: a player finally had the opportunity to show the coaching staff what he could do, but if he did not make the most of it, he could be stuck on the bench for much longer. There was no denying that the pressure was on, but every man who sat on the bench believed in his heart that if he were given the chance, he could make like Lou Gehrig and win a starting position that he would never relinquish.

Again subject to a midnight curfew, we headed to the smoky Last Chance Casino for a quick dinner before bed. At the beginning of the season, Ambos had handed out a players handbook setting forth what was expected of the team and had listed a few simple rules that he would not tolerate being broken — never wear team apparel outside the ballpark, never openly question his authority on the field, never be drunk in public, and never have women in your room on the road. The rules served not only to keep the team in line but also to protect the organization from bad situations. For the publicity-conscious minor-league franchise, notoriety resulting from any unfortunate incidents would ultimately mean reduced attendance and generate an attitude that the men who wore the uniform with the town's name on it were nothing more than drunks or thugs.

Not heeding the warnings, some of the Raptors decided to take the opportunity of the first road trip to test Ambos's rules. By the time the sun rose over Helena for our final day in town, everyone was buzzing about a player who had been caught with a woman in his room and others who had been embarrassingly drunk at a nightclub, foolishly harassing the umpires who were with us for the series. It was bad enough that players broke the rules; it was just plain stupid to piss off one of the umpiring crews we would be seeing for the rest of the season. Wandering around Helena all day, I caught bits and pieces of the story as players wondered about the repercussions of these actions. Would Ambos levy fines, give a speech, scream and yell, or quietly resolve the situation?

When we assembled on the bus, the coaching staff lagged behind in their rooms. Players checked their watches: 4:30, 4:32, 4:35. The bus was to leave promptly at 4:30, but the coaches were letting the players endure a few more minutes of wondering. Finally, Ambos and Morales boarded the bus silently.

Morales stepped forward and calmly stated, "Every time I stepped onto a field, I was proud to wear a uniform on my back. You guys are lucky. As long as you have a uniform on your back, you have a chance to make it to the majors." While we listened silently, Morales continued, reserved and subdued, reminding players how foolish it was to do anything to jeopardize the chance that they have been given to be paid to play baseball, the chance to make it to the majors, and the chance to cash in on their dreams.

"This is an independent situation, gentlemen," he concluded, "so no one gives a damn about you." The words hung in the air as he turned to sit down. If any of the Raptors were released for lack of talent, or for foolishly breaking club rules, no one in baseball would shed a tear, or probably even notice. These were all men who the baseball establishment had already let slip through the cracks. Their success, not their failure, would surprise the baseball world. Doing something to hasten the end of their last chance looked like a rather immature and poorly considered action as we waited in the Helena heat for Ambos's turn to speak.

"I have the worst case of the red ass I have had in my entire life," Ambos began in measured rage. Embarrassed eyes slowly made their way to the floor as Willy talked to us like adolescents who had just been caught shoplifting. Act like a professional. Have pride in our team. Be men. "This is my last chance," Ambos concluded. "I won't let you ruin it."

After dropping a well-played game three to two we were still feeling our manager's ire. Instead of stopping on the road to Idaho Falls for dinner, we showered and ate a meal of leftover concession-stand hot dogs and hamburgers. It was all we would get, but complaining about the meal was the last thing on our minds. Having endured a loss, an icy shower, and a poor excuse for a dinner, all we wanted to do was sleep.

Our bus arrived in Idaho Falls at three in the morning, allowing us time to throw down our bags and sleep in a real bed. With no obligations until the bus was scheduled to depart for the Idaho Falls Braves field, we slept very late, and when we finally boarded the bus it was the first time we had been together as a team since the bus left Helena.

Ambos stood up and briefly informed us that justice had been served for the rule breakers. A particularly harsh suspension without pay and more than one hundred dollars in fines — almost half his bi-weekly paycheck — were levied against the young man caught with a woman in his room while public drunkenness only cost violators a few dollars apiece. Ambos had a warning for everyone else: he would personally place the next rule breaker on a bus home. With that the bus pulled out of the motel parking lot, passing the scenic waterfalls that give Idaho Falls its name, and made its way toward the field.

Along the banks of the Snake River the stands of E. F. McDermott Field rose to frame an impressive baseball facility. A solid concrete edifice on the outside, McDermott Field transformed into a bright and airy ballpark once visitors passed into the seating area. Despite its home run–denying dimensions, a large green wall with immaculately painted signs surrounded the field and gave it a cozy feel. A grand scoreboard that flashed messages and announced batters' statistics rose out of left-center field. Although large, it seemed to connect the fans to the game rather than impose itself on them. In a smaller facility, the lavish scoreboard might have seemed out of place, but the Ruthian dimensions of McDermott Field called for a scoreboard that could match its proportions.

The Braves, in their home park, took advantage of some Raptors defensive mistakes to out-slug the visitors eight to five. After failing to score with the bases loaded and one out in the late innings, the

Raptors offense wilted. Nothing cures a team's problems like winning, but the converse is also true. After this third consecutive loss, grumbling was second only to card playing as the most popular postgame activity.

At home we would disperse after games and then reunite the following day. On the road, however, we were together almost constantly with baseball — and our individual gripes — on our minds. Pitchers did not want to throw to a certain catcher, infielders wanted a different first baseman, and catchers bemoaned position players who were not tagging out runners after good throws.

The stark concern that baseball could be over forever drove players to grumbling. Especially with an independent team, one bad outing could have a player packing his bags before the seventh-inning stretch. Players simply did not want that poor effort to be caused by a catcher who could not block balls in the dirt, a first baseman who could not handle a short hop, or a player who was not hustling behind them.

For the Raptor players, the difference between joining a construction crew and signing the coveted contract with the St. Louis Cardinals could be that a scout looked at the statistics and simply determined "too many errors" or "too few wins." The Raptors knew this all too well and it added fuel to their grumblings and gave them license to complain.

Far from home — even if it was just a foster family's house — players could get awfully lonely. Getaway days, the final day in a particular town, were especially tedious. Cost-conscious minor-league clubs have players check out of their rooms and throw their baggage into a few rooms reserved to be used for storing bags until the bus leaves for the game. Where two dozen players once occupied twelve rooms, getaway procedures called for us to fit, with our baggage, into only three. When players needed to change into uniforms or use shower and bathroom facilities as game time approached, the getaway rooms became awfully cramped. With checkout time around noon and nowhere to be until late in the afternoon, we packed up our belongings and were left without a room to call home for the day. Playing poker while sitting on equipment bags, watching a motel movie with ten

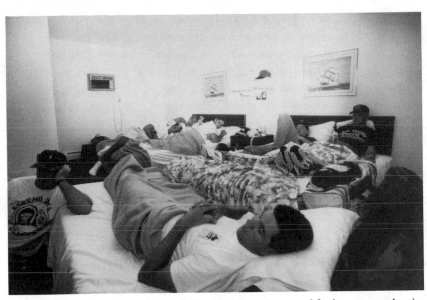

Getaway days meant packing bags, piling into rooms reserved for luggage, and waiting for the day — and the road trip — to end. Killing time are Jay Hogue, Danny Miller, Josh Kirtlan, Mike Carrigg, Edson Hoffman, Don Baker, and Doug Smyly. Steven D. Conlin photograph reprinted with permission.

teammates, or trying to nap three to a bed became the getaway day routine.

With one more game on the road trip against the Idaho Falls Braves, a win could do the Raptors a world of good. Grumbling could give way to congratulations, the torture of dealing with getaway rooms would subside, and a two-and-three road trip could yield optimism for the trip home. Without a win, it would be a long ride back to Ogden.

The American flag in right field whipped in the wind as dust swirled through the infield and into the dugouts. Hats blew off players' heads as we shielded our eyes from the blowing dirt and debris. For the final game of our first-ever road trip, we would have to battle not only the Braves but the elements as well.

As we huddled in the dugout the Raptors bats exploded for a four-run first inning. Despite the wind and dust wreaking havoc on nearly every play, Paul O'Hearn pitched us to an eight-to-two victory. Nobody was yelling at us, we were going to stop for a real meal on the way back to Ogden, and the showers at McDermott Field were even warm.

After two wins in five days on the road, we were all anxious to return to Ogden, not just to gain home-field advantage against the Helena Brewers, who would be in town for three games, but to return to our comfortable routines. For at least the next few days there would be no more "When does the bus leave?" or "Are we showering here or at the hotel?" At home we could enjoy baseball and the ease of following a routine. More than getting last at-bat, home-field advantage meant home-field peace of mind: knowing when to get to the park, what restaurants serve satisfying food, and what to expect from an average day. When the bus rides, the uncertainty, and the constantly changing schedules yielded to the normalcy of home, even the longest or losingest road trip ended with the happy news that home was just one more ride away.

Back in the friendly confines of Simmons Field, we battled the Brewers back and forth until the game was tied in the bottom of the ninth. The Raptors responded by loading the bases and bringing an unlikely candidate as a hero to the plate.

Starting shortstop Tommy Johnston had been hit in the hand by a pitch in Helena. Back in Ogden, team doctors discovered a break, sidelining Johnston just as he had pushed his batting average to .300. With the lineup juggled, utility infielder Mike Carrigg got a rare start and stood at the plate with a chance to make an impact. Rising to the challenge, he lashed a single up the middle to bring in the winning run. For Carrigg, relegated to bench duty for much of the early season, it was a chance to shine.

Each time a player steps on the field there is a chance that someone will notice his talent. Given his chance, Carrigg shook off the pressure and succeeded. Perhaps the Brewers manager's report for the evening might include a note that an infielder named Carrigg could play a little baseball. When the Brewers consider their needs for next year's draft, perhaps they will say, "Why draft an infielder and shell out bonus money when we can just buy Carrigg's contract?" In the clubhouse after the game, wearing a big smile and debating how many newspapers he should buy the next day, Carrigg was an unlikely but happy hero enjoying his chance to dream.

We were now only a game behind the first-place Brewers, but despite our seven-and-four record and the late-inning heroics of the night before, the Raptors management was not satisfied. Deeply concerned about attendance and reports that some scouts felt we were talented but playing without heart, the front office wanted a change.

Raptors vice president and general manager John Stein gathered us in our clubhouse after batting practice. With two dozen ballplayers nervously averting their eyes, Stein made it clear that management was not content with their effort, and with good reason. If the talent on the team was not performing well enough to attract positive attention from scouts, the franchise would not be able to earn significant revenues by selling players to major-league organizations at the end of the season.

Stein, who played four years of professional baseball — bouncing from the Chicago White Sox organization to the Dodgers and Pirates organizations until a shoulder injury ended his career — understood what makes baseball players into big leaguers, what makes teams win, and what makes franchises succeed. Questioning the players' heart and commitment after a rash of errors and lazy play, Stein was not reluctant to consider roster moves.

Unlike clubs that serve as farm teams for major-league organizations, where winning can take a back seat to talent development, an independent team must succeed on the field. The Helena Brewers might keep a seventeen-year-old shortstop in the lineup despite some shortcomings because he is being groomed to be an impact player in the majors five years down the road. If the same shortstop is having trouble with the Raptors, there is no reason to keep him around when another player could be brought in to do the job. With a talent pool consisting of every single player who is not currently playing professional baseball, an independent team has plenty of young men to consider adding to the roster if its players do not succeed.

With their desire and heart questioned, my teammates glumly took in all Stein had to say about playing with a chip on their shoulder, going all out, and showing the baseball world that they had what it takes to move on into one of the major-league organizations. Heads bowed beneath navy and teal hats, and eyes darted around the clubhouse trying to measure up likely victims of management's wrath. We would travel to Butte to take on the Copper Kings after the series with the Brewers. After that, Stein declared, "changes would be made."

After Stein walked out of the clubhouse there was an involuntary moment of silence. Players scanned the room sizing up who was safe and who was on the bubble. The ones who knew that their careers and dreams were in jeopardy hung their heads with angry yet anxious expressions on their faces. We were only one-sixth through the season and many of the players who were in danger of being cut had received a dearth of chances to display their talents. The first sound in the clubhouse came abruptly, spat out of a player who stalked into the training room: "What an uplifting speech."

John Homan made the remark. Homan, a left-handed starter who came to the Raptors from the University of Wyoming, did not need any additional pressure on him. He was credited with half of the Raptors losses with his 0-2 record and 5.00 ERA. Against the Brewers that night he was due to make another start. After hearing Stein's words, Homan knew that his third start could very well be his last if he did not produce.

Before the clubhouse could again come alive, Ambos and Morales walked back in to survey the damage. Homan had retreated to the training room to begin preparing for the game. I followed him to grab a bag of sunflower seeds — my own preparation for the evening — and stepped back into the clubhouse to hear Ambos utter the fateful words, "Baseball is a business."

Any speech that begins with "baseball is a business" is not one that a player wants to hear. For the Raptors getting their first taste of professional baseball, the words *baseball* and *business* simply did not fit together in their dreams. For the players who had already experienced the cruelty and quickness of a cut from a professional team, the words were just a bitter reminder of how unkind the game could be.

After the speeches, some players griped about their chances, or the lack thereof. Most, however, came out with something to prove, and the Raptors jumped out to a four-to-one lead after one inning. As had been our custom, however, we could not deliver the knockout punch and let the Brewers back into the game. Sloppy fielding that always seemed to precede timely hitting by the opposition allowed the Brewers to catch up, sending Homan to the bench with another early exit and leaving the Raptors questioning whether they would ever coast to a victory again.

In the dugout I could hear the boos echoing from the stands as fans made plain their feelings about the performance. I could only imagine how loud the sound must have been to John Stein, sitting behind the plate. Willy Ambos furrowed his brow, pursed his mustached lips, and looked hopefully for relief from his bullpen.

In the end, players exchanged congratulations after a sloppy come-from-behind win. Homan, who spent the remainder of the game sitting quietly, shifting his eyes from the field to the dugout floor, just sat in the dugout and looked out at the empty field. He had raised his ERA to a disturbing 9.00 while allowing the opposition to hit .451 against him. He would have to hope for one more chance or else face the dire fact that his major dreams were ending.

For the final game of the short homestand, Danny Miller again led the Raptors to victory and earned his league-leading third win. After the game we celebrated the win that put us back into sole possession of first place as we packed our gear for the next day's road trip to Butte, Montana. We joked, passed around congratulations, and left the clubhouse as a team, but players who considered themselves on the bubble gave the trailer a second look knowing that it might be the last time they left it as a Raptor.

On the bus to Butte, a report came over the radio that basketball superstar turned baseball wannabe Michael Jordan was considering leaving minor-league life after his brief stint in double-A ball with the Birmingham Barons of the Chicago White Sox organization. While some of my teammates admired Jordan for pursuing his own dream, many real minor leaguers were quick to focus their ire on Jordan for his dalliance with the game. "He's a cunt," yelled out one angry voice. "What a joke," called another. Putting it into perspective, Ambos stated simply, "If you have enough money, you can do anything. Meanwhile, he is taking the spot of someone who has worked all his life to get there."

Morales agreed in a more colorful manner: "If I were catching, and Jordan came up, I would say, 'Mr. Jordan, it's a pleasure to play on same field as you.' Then I would give the sign," he said as he pantomimed, indicating the sign for his pitcher to throw a beanball. We shared a laugh and spent the rest of the trip to Butte debating Jordan's chances.

Once a grand mining center dubbed "The Richest Hill on Earth" because of the valuable ores lying beneath its surface, Butte is now a transportation and tourism mecca attracting fishermen, outdoor enthusiasts, skiers, and even speed-skating Olympic athletes who train in Butte's High-Altitude Sports Center.

To the west of historic uptown Butte, on the campus of Montana Tech, Alumni Coliseum, home of the Copper Kings, offers a panoramic view of the Rocky Mountains surrounding Butte. The ballpark, actually a converted football stadium, is a modest facility, worn by the years and in need of refurbishing. A covered grandstand with a small press box rises behind home plate and folding chairs along the first- and third-base foul lines form box seating. Sitting in the tiny dugout looking at the chicken-wire fencing and dented corrugated metal surrounding the field, the nicest thing to be said about the park was that it had a great view — nothing but mountains and the setting sun beyond the outfield walls.

As lightning bolts crisscrossed the sky, we picked up our fifth straight win while storms threatened to shorten the game. After a brief shower, rainbows of perfect clarity arched against the sky between the outfield wall and the Rocky Mountains. At least one dream, not a pot of gold, lay at the end of this rainbow.

Brett Smith came into the game hitless in six at-bats and worried that pending cuts would include him. He had a big night, getting two hits and catching a winning effort behind the plate. I could not have been happier that he had come up big. Smith — my roommate and my most valuable player because he drove me back and forth to the park — was barely able to check his exhilaration over his outing. When we returned to our motel room he excitedly called family and friends to tell them of his success. With the quality game he could put aside worries about cuts and once again dream his major dreams.

After putting ten runs on the board the next night, we lost in most dramatic fashion as backup catcher Greg Rosar hit a bottom-of-the-ninth, two-out, three-run home run to win the game for the Copper Kings. Sullen players walked off the field toward the bus. The suddenness of the loss, taking certain victory from the Raptors, left us quiet. When a pitcher throws the last out, there is a certain logical conclusion to a game. But when a batter ends a baseball game, it is a glorious victory for the winners and a shocking defeat for the losers.

On the bus, waiting as always for play-by-play man Kurt Wilson to finish his postgame show so we could head back to the motel, the team was as silent as the Montana night. For one Raptor, however, maintaining the silence and demeanor of a player on a losing team was a torturous end to his evening. Struggling to maintain his own place on the team in the face of the pending roster moves, Chris Simmons had suddenly gone four for four. Prior to the game in Butte he had not recorded a hit and was one of the players clearly on the bubble. Unable to celebrate or express joy on the trip back to the hotel after his performance, Simmons was awkwardly quiet in the loss-induced, shellshocked silence of the bus. He would have to wait to get back to his motel room to let out a few loud whoops to celebrate his personal victory.

Although we were loose prior to our last game with the Copper Kings, the night proved to be a difficult one as a cold front blew into Butte, dropping temperatures dramatically and putting a chill on the Raptors bats. The Copper Kings exploded for a big lead before we could answer.

With pitcher after pitcher unable to muzzle the Copper Kings bats, Ambos called on John Homan with the Raptors down seven to nothing. Not only was he being asked to hold the Copper Kings, he was being given a chance to save his spot on the team. Homan strode to the mound with a runner on and his career at stake. He promptly gave up back-to-back home runs, a single, and a double. After the fourth straight hit, Ambos had seen enough and made the walk to the mound to remove his pitcher. Homan just waited until the skipper arrived, handed him the ball, and walked off the field. For the rest of the game he sat quietly, either numb to the cold or too focused on his fate to shiver like the rest of the team. Perhaps he would have been more excited if he realized he was about to witness a small bit of baseball history.

"Now batting for the Raptors, Brett Mandel," came the words from the public address announcer at the end of the losing effort made more insufferable by the frigid weather. As soon as I was told to grab a bat, neither the score nor the weather mattered. Picking up a batting helmet and pulling my bat out of the rack, where it had languished unused in each previous game, all I could think about was the significance of the moment.

Unlike every high-school standout, sandlot legend, Little League all-star, and college player who did not make it to professional baseball, I was coming to the plate. Considering the vast universe of people who have played the game but never made it to the pros, I would be joining a remarkably small fraternity by appearing in a game. I was nervous for myself attempting to do my appearance credit, but I was also excited — excited about taking my first professional at-bat and excited about what might occur.

We were losing fourteen to seven in the ninth inning, Brett Smith stood on third, there was one out, and my head was spinning. Sensing my anxiety, third-base coach Morales called me over to talk. "You don't want me to squeeze?" I asked, suddenly horrified about the prospect of having the pressure of a do-or-die bunt in my first-ever at-bat. I recall him saying something about looking for a fastball in this situation, but I was too conscious of my beating heart and wavering legs to hear and comprehend his exact words.

Digging in and listening to the public address announcer intone my name, I tried in vain to hold back a smile. Thoughts rushed to the forefront of my consciousness: keep your hands back, open your hips, watch the ball hit the bat, hit a first-ball fastball, I hope someone gets a picture.

The always sparse Butte crowd had all but dispersed into the chilly night, but I was very conscious of the fact that I was entering a game where a crowd of people paid to attend. Driving it home on all the Butte Copper Kings uniforms, the "125th anniversary of professional baseball" patch made it clear that I was suddenly playing professional baseball. Practicing, riding the bus, and signing autographs was one thing, but I was intimidated by my pro debut. If there had been a sudden noise, I was so wound up and tight I would have jumped clear out of the stadium. But I was not there to savor the moment and I was not there to watch pitches go by. I was going to swing as hard as I could at anything close.

Shane Hill, a tall righthander from Oklahoma, reared back and threw a low, inside fastball. I swung, hitting the ball solidly on the ground toward center field. I sprinted down the line as fast as my legs could carry me, my body instinctively reacting to the situation as I was still far too nervous to make a conscious decision to run. Watching the bag getting closer, my mind raced my churning legs, urging them forward as all I could think was "hit."

The shortstop reached the ball and threw me out by half a step. Smith, rooting for my ball to reach the outfield, almost neglected to run home, but my ground ball was enough to earn me an RBI. I did not get a hit, but I did do the job.

Off the bat, I thought the ball would go through the infield as it would have back in my Philadelphia recreational league, but against a professional shortstop it was just another long-ranging play to the left. After hearing the slap of the ball in the first baseman's glove just before I hit the bag, I slowed to a stop along the right-field foul line. Suddenly, the thrill of being an author in the game gave way to a more natural reaction as a player. I was out and wanted another chance to prove I could hit. As I wheeled around to return to the dugout, I was disappointed.

My teammates, however, had flooded out of the dugout as if we had just won the World Series. Everyone congratulated me, Morales handed me the ball, and I suddenly realized that not only was I officially a professional, I had produced in my first-ever professional at-bat. I tried to be cool about it, but I was far too excited to pull it off. I accidentally left my bats and my hat in the dugout when I went to shower, and only because Brett Smith was picking up for me did I avoid some heavy fines.

I could not even try to hide my wide smile, and neither the Raptors loss nor the Butte cold could quell my euphoria over my first official game appearance. I probably wasted more energy trying to act subdued than I ever could have in shouting out my excitement over my pro debut.

Back in Philadelphia, my friends and family would finally see my statistics in the Area Players in the Minors column in the sports section of the newspaper, and for the rest of my life I could recount the story of my first at-bat. Leaving Butte, I could not have been more pleased. I slept well on the way to Ogden, finally getting a taste of my own major dreams but mindful that across the aisle John Homan silently contemplated the end of his.

Back home in Ogden, cuts awaited, but so did our big reward for our efforts on the field — our first paycheck. Above every name in the Raptors clubhouse was the wonderful slip of paper that makes professional baseball separate and distinct from all other forms of baseball. We were paid $325, before taxes, on the first and fifteenth of each month. On the road, meals were subsidized with our meal money and lodging was on the Raptors. Foster homes in Ogden were offered at no charge and many local bars offered free beer to players. But no matter how the expenses were cut down, the paycheck did not go far. Considering that we put in seven or eight hours each day at the park, not counting endless hours on the bus during road trips or time spent making personal appearances, our pay worked out to only a few dollars per hour. That deep in the minors, it was the chance to play and the chance to pursue the dream, not a lavish salary, that made it worth the struggle. But out of meal money and strapped for cash, players welcomed the checks like long-lost friends before slipping on their uniforms.

Like the rest of the team, John Homan pulled on his stirrups and home whites and joined his teammates filing out into right field for stretching. Before he could get across the foul line, the words he had been dreading echoed across the ballpark: "Homan, John Stein wants to see you." Players who were just beginning their pregame jog paused momentarily to consider the words and then made their way across the outfield grass. As Homan disappeared into the clubhouse, we could only continue on our run to the First Security Bank sign in left field as if nothing was happening.

From the clubhouse, Ambos emerged and walked over to his players. Interrupting our stretching, he gathered us around him and spoke somberly, if not eloquently. "I lost my cherry as a first-year manager," he said, explaining that he had just cut Homan. Each Raptors player and coach had been through the pain of a cut or release, and Ambos was quick to point out that he, too, had been on the receiving end of the speech that he had just made to Homan. Only a few years before, Ambos himself had been released just weeks before he thought he was headed to spring training with the Seattle Mariners. "When you see him," Ambos said, feeling for his former player, "give him a pat on the ass."

Moments later Homan emerged from the clubhouse. Without his uniform, he looked like just another fan as he walked through the bleachers to say good-bye to his old teammates. Beginning with the pitchers, players began to break out of their stretching ranks to say their farewells. When I shook his hand, Homan did not seem bitter or sad. He had taken his best shot at playing baseball and was just informed that his best was not good enough. With nothing to be ashamed about and having gotten his chance, he was headed back to Wyoming to finish his schooling.

The next day, outfielder Jason Pollock, who had learned the hard way that he had to work to fulfill his dream to play professional baseball and was reduced to lying about his age to get his chance, was cut as well. But baseball continued for us without a pause for our parted teammates. The game waits for no one, and there is no time to worry about those who fall by the wayside while pursuing a dream.

The Neglected

Independence Day was an appropriate respite to take stock of the significance of the Raptors franchise and its first few weeks of baseball. Decked out in our special holiday hats for the Fourth of July (everything from our dinosaur logo to our three official hat styles helped pump up the bottom line with merchandise sales), we were happy to be off the road and thrilled to be in first place in the Pioneer League Southern Division. Although that may have been reason enough to celebrate, with a round of roster cuts behind us many of the Raptors had more than America's birthday to be happy about.

Doug O'Neill, Jeremy Winget, Tommy Johnston, and a half-dozen other Raptors players had spent the previous year with another minor-league team after being acquired through the draft or signed as free agents. Now they were trying to rejuvenate their careers after being cut by other organizations. Fourteen other players, however, were passed over in the baseball draft and were only able to enjoy major dreams because the owners of the Raptors created an independent franchise which gave them a chance to keep playing. Having survived another threat in the roster cuts, these players could again concentrate on their baseball futures.

Each year, thousands of college players end their baseball careers without being drafted by a major-league franchise. They have little choice but to put their trophies on their shelves, put their gear in their closets, and give up hope of pursuing their baseball ambitions. But for the lucky ballplayers seeking a second chance, the unaffiliated Ogden

Raptors were a salvation. For them, every day was "independents day."

The win that brought us back into first place was thrown by our most reliable pitcher, Danny Miller, giving him a perfect record at four wins and no losses. For the slim, tanned six-footer who liked to wind down after a game by donning boots and a cowboy hat and two-stepping the night away, it was, quite literally, a feather in his cap. Miller made a habit of placing a plume inside his hat before games, just for luck. Without a loss in his professional career, Miller was not about to change any of his superstitious habits, from hopping over chalk lines to pacing around the mound to pick up the ball to begin an inning. Even with his impressive record, like the other Raptors passed over in the draft, every day he wore a professional uniform was a victory. After years of labor on the baseball diamond, Miller had a right to savor each new success.

Little Danny Miller grew up in a small town called Poway, just northeast of San Diego at the foothills of the San Diego Mountains. "As far as I can remember, I grew up with a baseball in my hand, always playing the game," he said, recalling his formative baseball experience. "Probably the person who was the most influential on my baseball was my grandpa. The year that he retired, I started Little League. Ever since then he never missed a game, so I always grew up loving the game. That's what you live for, just going to bed on Friday with your bat and glove underneath your pillow — maybe you can sleep in a uniform when you're real little — then grandpa coming over maybe six o'clock in the morning to take you out to breakfast."

While he was still very young, he began to think that baseball might be something he could see himself doing all his life. "My mom pulled out a story I wrote when I was in first or second grade — 'What I want to be when I get older' — and I said, 'Play professional baseball for the San Diego Padres and play in front of a lot of people.'"

By high school it looked as if his dreams might come true, until a broken thumb on his glove hand took him out of the infield and placed him on the pitcher's mound — and onto center stage. With a soccer sock over his cast and a big softball glove ready for defense, he

Danny Miller surveys the field and waits for his next start — and his next chance to show that he can make it in professional baseball. Steven D. Conlin photograph reprinted with permission.

toed the hill for the junior varsity team. "The first game I pitched, I threw a no-hitter," he said matter-of-factly. "The next week I pitched again. I had maybe thirteen or fourteen strikeouts." The following day the varsity coach told him that when the cast came off, he was going to move up to varsity.

He raced home and sawed off the cast. The next day he was on the varsity bench when, with his team ahead by two runs, the coach put him into the game with one out and a runner on second in the final inning. "I got out of the inning," he said, "ended up picking up a save, and ever since then I was up on varsity. The bad thing about that is my thumb never got a chance to heal, so I couldn't grip the bat the rest of the year or do anything. My thumb was pretty much a mess. It still is to this day."

Through his freshman and sophomore years he compiled an almost perfect record as a varsity pitcher, but as he began to contemplate playing college ball, he had a decision to make. A high-school quarterback, Miller had to consider whether to pursue football or baseball. In the end, the extra work and dedication to football would have interfered with summer baseball leagues and his pursuit of his dream.

Football was fun and he had a talent for the game, but baseball was too deeply ingrained in his life to do anything that would diminish his passion for — or chance to have a career with — his favorite sport. "When I was five and six years old I would go to Padres games every day that my grandpa [a commercial fisherman] wasn't at sea, and I knew the starting lineups. I loved the game — looked up to Dave Winfield, who was probably my favorite player growing up, saw all the great guys playing then, saw the Chicken hatch down in San Diego. I just loved it."

He decided to put his efforts into baseball, but had a setback after he came into the year a bit too confident. "I probably didn't work as hard after my sophomore year, thinking I was six and one as a sophomore, thinking that I'm just going to come back and dominate the next year," he conceded. But by redoubling his efforts he rebounded for a strong senior year, which began to draw the attention of professional scouts. Especially with his grades lagging behind his ERA, scouts were eager to have the hard-throwing righthander eschew college for the minor leagues. Miller definitely felt the added pressure.

"Going into the fall of my senior year when everything started to roll around and I had a lot of the pro guys coming up to the house and going through all the tests and stuff, it was tough. But I sat down with my grandfather and he said, 'Don't worry about it — it's the same thing you've been doing ever since you were little. Just go out and have fun,'" Miller said. "Senior year came around and I started off 6-0 leading San Diego in everything — strikeouts, earned run average, pretty much everything. At that time, I had a lot of decisions to make.

"I told scouts that there'd be no way I'd sign. Nobody in my family ever graduated college, a lot went but never graduated, and that was a big thing. My grandpa really wanted me to go, and my parents wanted me to go to school, and I figured after three years of school there might be something better for me."

He finished his senior year with a record of thirteen and one, received All-American honors out of high school, was named All-

League, All-San Diego Co-Player of the Year, and first team All-State. That summer he went to Japan and played baseball with the All-American team, which was composed of some of the brightest talent in the baseball world. "Everybody on that team is playing professional baseball," Danny said. "I think after this year's draft there might have been six first-round draft choices I played with on that team. Kenny Henderson was a first-round draft choice, Jacob Cruz was a first-round draft choice — his teammate Antone Williamson — there's a bunch of guys that I played with that were incredible."

For a month the team traveled through Japan like royalty, barnstorming the countryside. "I'll never forget it — the best experience I ever had in my life," he said of the trip. "High-school baseball there is a lot different than it is here. It's everything there. High-school baseball is like the pinnacle there. They're treated like gods, the high-school players there. Every night we went out there were buffets and banquets for us every town we went to — Osaka, Nagoya, Tokyo, Kyoto."

Fresh from his trip overseas, even though he was drafted by the Philadelphia Phillies, Miller began school at the University of the Pacific in Stockton, California, where he received a full scholarship. "My grandpa wanted me to go to school so I went to school," he said simply. "That was pretty much it."

But being away from his grandfather was difficult for Miller as a freshman and he felt the separation immediately. "My grandpa and I had a relationship that was even tough to talk about because he was the most important thing to me in my life. More so than my parents, more so than my brother, more so than anybody in the world. He was the important thing to me. He wanted to come up on his birthday, but nobody in my family would let him. They didn't want to let him drive up by himself and nobody could take the time off to come up and watch one of my ballgames up there.

"I was walking to class and coach pulled me in and said, 'We got to talk.'" Miller's inspiration, his grandfather, had died.

"It took the life out of me," he remembered. "I hated U of P, I hated school because I was up there and I felt that if I was down there my grandpa wouldn't have died. I blamed myself a lot. He was in perfect health. He just had a freak heart attack."

The shock to Miller's system was evident in his pitching and he went through his freshman year as a poor player for a dismal team. "We were horrible," he confessed. "We couldn't do anything right. I got beat up really good — one and seven, my ERA was seven-point-something, but my heart wasn't in it. I really felt that I made the wrong decision and really thought about dropping out of school."

But by the end of his junior year his baseball success and his future prospects were picking up and he was attracting the attention of major-league scouts, figuring he would once again be drafted. "After my junior year, 'Oh,' I thought, 'for sure,'" he said, recalling his confidence. "I had workouts with the Dodgers. I had workouts with the Orioles. I felt I was physically and mentally ready to go after my junior year. It turns out I didn't get picked up. That was a shock. That hurt a lot.

"So I came back down again that summer, went to a tryout camp and pitched rather well and got a lot of opportunities to sign as a free agent after my junior year. I told the scout with the Orioles, 'Thanks for the opportunity, but I think that I should go back to school and finish out because if I can sign as a free agent this year I should be able to sign as a free agent next year, and if I have a good year next year I could probably be drafted.' He said, 'Yeah, that's probably the case. You go up and have a good year next year, everybody's got a card on you, you should get drafted.' So I turned it down mainly because it cost twenty-two thousand dollars a year to go to school, and they wanted to offer me between two thousand and five thousand dollars. There'd be no way I'd ever go back and finish school, not at U of P, which at that time, after three years, I only had a year to finish. I was that close, I really felt I should go back. I worked really hard in the off-season, got to where baseball was the most important thing again."

But there was one element of his success that was still missing. His senior year he put the final piece back into the puzzle. "I really felt in touch with my grandpa again," he said. "I was working with a sports psychologist, one of my professors. I took a sports psychology class and we got to the point where what was missing my first three years up at school was the fact that I wasn't pitching with my grandpa around, I wasn't feeling he was there, I was feeling he was lost and somewhere else and all kind of metaphysical out there. But we got back to the point where he was in my heart again and I was so comfortable on the hill going out my senior year."

With Miller at his best and reconnected with his inspiration, his University of the Pacific baseball team enjoyed the nation's longest winning streak, winning twenty-one games in a row. He finished the year at eight and four with a 2.60 ERA and 121 innings pitched. He felt that he had done everything possible to get picked up in the draft and was ready to take the next logical step in his career, into professional baseball. But again, he was not drafted.

"I was pretty much angry," he recalled. "I felt I did all that I could to get picked up to at least have a chance. My junior year a girl got drafted in the fortieth round — I mean, a girl gets drafted and has no intention of playing minor-league ball, but they waste a draft choice on her. Now how does that look when you have a kid whose only dream is to play baseball and you don't get picked up? I was pissed, absolutely enraged, that I didn't get picked up. I felt that I should have had the opportunity to play."

Through the baseball grapevine Miller heard that he did not get drafted because scouts felt that he was playing hardball with them, waiting to sign on his terms. Once he was ready to sign, the scouts apparently played a little hardball with him to show the young prospect that he should sign on their timetable, not his own. But Danny was not willing to give up even if it meant entering professional baseball with a team that was not affiliated with a major-league franchise. When he learned about an opportunity with the Ogden Raptors, he took some money out of the bank, flew to the tryouts, and was signed as a free agent. Not only did he impress the Raptors coaching staff enough to be signed, he earned the right to pitch the first-ever Raptors game.

"The rush that first night was something really comparable to what I felt in Japan when I was playing for my country," he said with a smile. "I can't even explain it. It was the biggest rush in the world playing in front of all those people — first professional game, it was great."

Even though the thrill of opening night gave way to more success as he seemed unbeatable in the early season, Miller was unsatisfied.

"Every time I go out, I look at the other pitcher and think, 'This guy was drafted in the fourth round, it's almost a joke, what are scouts looking for?' So every time I go out, I go out with a strong intensity that I'm going to show these people, that I'm going to prove them wrong. It's to the point where everybody keeps saying that there's a lot of scouts looking at me and they're going to find me a place to play with an affiliated team. There's a lot of scouts watching me pitch, and I see them back there in the backstop and I think to myself, 'You guys are full of shit.' I can't say that they're full of shit. I should say that baseball's so funny that you can't take anything for granted just because people are looking at you and I'm putting up good numbers now. What's the difference between putting up good numbers now and the numbers I put up in college? I already put up the good numbers. How much more do I have to do? Until it happens, until I get picked up, I'm not going to count my chickens or anything like that. I'm just going to go out and play.

"I'm playing professional baseball. That's what I said when I was in first or second grade when I wrote that story, that I wanted to play professional baseball, so I guess I've done that. I'd really like to be playing baseball three years down the line. Honestly, I would like to be playing for an affiliated team. If it's independent, that's fine because I'm having a great time here, but I'd still like to be playing baseball."

Miller knew that establishing a career in professional baseball is not just about playing baseball and performing well on the field. Every time he took the mound he was pursuing his dream. Having been neglected thus far in his career by the affiliated establishment, he knew that everything he did on the field might still not be enough to penetrate the upper ranks of the minor leagues. Keeping an undefeated record would certainly be a feat, but being signed by the Padres would be true victory.

"I would say, if you truly believe you can play, then you set your goals one day at a time going from there. Then you can do it," Miller said, offering advice as well as looking toward his future. "Just don't take anything for granted. Never burn any bridges — never take anything for granted." Having pitched the Raptors back into first place, Miller could just bide his time relacing gloves, looking for a new feather for his hat, and waiting for his next start — his next opportunity to take one day at a time.

Much of Ogden came out to Simmons Field to celebrate Independence Day with the Raptors, and even though the odometer counting bodies that walked through the gates of Simmons Field was climbing steadily — and the Raptors were hovering near the league lead in attendance — the team needed to draw better to satisfy its owners. For the big Fourth of July game with its accompanying fireworks, a big crowd was expected and, given the ownership's lust for increased attendance, desperately needed.

As we went through our pregame workouts, the skies clouded over and intense weather blew through Ogden. Winds and rain quickly turned a beautiful day into a serious storm. Gusts of wind blew dust from beyond the field, causing players and fans alike to huddle together for cover. Thoughts of a sellout were quickly replaced with thoughts of a rainout when a sudden calm swept over the park. A tree had blown over, taking the power with it. As the storm subsided, the park was silent with nervous anticipation over whether the game could be played without power to fuel the lights and the public address system.

An Ogden city police cruiser made its way across the field, informing the large crowd about the mishap as workers moved quickly to salvage the game. The concession stand did a brisk business and my teammates and I circulated among the crowd to sign autographs to keep the fans happy. Parents beamed with pride as their young ones mustered up the courage to approach the ballplayers and little eyes lit up as players made small talk while signing gloves and balls. In rescuing what might have been a dismal evening waiting for the power to come back to the park, players and fans were able to further develop their blossoming affection.

With an apprehensive "test, test," the public address system stuttered to life, signifying that power was back and baseball was soon to follow. Fans cheered and players made their way back to their dugouts for the game. Less than an hour after the game and its big crowd were feared lost, the perfect combination — baseball and the Fourth of July — was on again.

All the way down the left-field foul line a group of fans took their place in the Tar Pit, a small set of bleachers adjacent to the left-field foul pole. The 400 Foot Club had made the short trip to Ogden to follow their favorite Raptor, Shane Jones. Jones was a lively addition to the Raptors and a team prankster who gave as good as he got. That came in handy because his baby face atop a muscular body, made to appear even more bulky by additional girth around his midsection, made him an easy target for his teammates' ribbing — especially for the way he plodded around the bases when his mighty "yaks" failed to clear the fence. The 1993 NCAA Division I home-run king had had the 400 Foot Club cheering for him at the University of Utah and was pleased to have them cheering on his successes in Ogden. But like Danny Miller, Shane Jones was passed over in the draft despite his collegiate success. At third base, pulling on his cap moments before the end of the national anthem and turning away from his rooting section back toward home plate, Jones could only go to work knowing his fans were behind him, hoping that his efforts with the Raptors would be enough to earn a signing by an affiliated team at the end of the season.

Shane Jones grew up in the little town of West Jordan, just sixty-five miles south of Ogden. His father played fast-pitch softball and his two older brothers played high-school baseball, encouraging young Shane to develop an interest in the game. "I wanted to be the one that went on in baseball," he said. "I had one cousin that played college baseball, which was good because I was just getting into high school while he was in college and I thought, 'Wow, this looks pretty fun, I want to do what he's doing.' So that motivated me. But a lot of time hanging around my dad when he was playing softball got me interested in the game."

The youngest child in the family, Shane grew up as a very competitive young man. "I still am today," he confessed. "It's a competitive nature in our family. Whether it's golfing, hunting, we always want to outdo the other, and I think that's good because that's where I get my

Always an intense competitor, Shane Jones puts on his game face. Applying the eye-black is Raptors trainer Dan Overman. Steven D. Conlin photograph reprinted with permission.

competitive drive. I get it from my brothers, from my father, and I think if it wasn't for them I wouldn't have that edge."

That edge allowed Shane to excel in his youth baseball games. By the time he entered high school, the young man from a town of forty thousand people, hundreds of miles from any major-league city, knew he wanted to play professional baseball. "I don't know why," he said of the dream. "It was just something within, that I thought, 'This would be a cool job, this would be something that looked fun.' When I was a sophomore, I devoted my life to baseball. I wanted to play baseball and get paid for it. That was my goal. So I devoted my time to baseball. I quit every other sport in high school but baseball. I played basketball and golf. I quit them. I did something to do with baseball every day in high school."

But just because a young man devotes his time to baseball does not automatically get him a contract with the New York Yankees. Jones had to work hard to move on from high-school baseball up the ever-narrowing baseball pyramid. "My senior year, when I got an opportunity to go to University of Utah, I thought, 'Maybe this is a step,'" he recalled. "Everyone plays Little League baseball. Only a few go on to play high-school baseball, and then only a few go on to play college baseball. So I thought my goal out of high school — I want to play college baseball."

Jones accepted a full scholarship to the University of Utah and suddenly attracted the attention of the Cincinnati Reds. But with the scholarship and the chance to play baseball at a Division I school, Jones declined an offer to go to a Reds camp. "I had the scholarship to the University of Utah and I thought, 'Well, this is good enough. If they want to draft me then they can,'" he said. "The draft came along out of high school, nine people got drafted out of Utah. Out of the nine people that got drafted, no one's still playing pro ball. So I was happy that I went on to college and that I got the opportunity now because the guys that got drafted out of high school aren't playing. I've always said that my goal in life out of high school was to play baseball as many years as I could out of high school. Right now I'm on number six and those guys are done." The big disappointment came when he was not drafted after college.

"That was a hard two days for me. The talk was that I was a post-fifteen guy, which means that I'm not going to go in the top fifteen rounds but between fifteen and thirty, and I said, 'All right, I can handle that.' So the first day wasn't bad; the second day I spent worrying, biting my nails. I went fishing the whole day. I come back — nothing. I talked to my mom and that's when I found out that my buddy got drafted in the forty-first round, and then I'm thinking, 'If they're in the forty-first round, I didn't get drafted.' I was pissed off for two days. I didn't want to talk to anyone. I thought about all the hard work, all the dedication — I don't have anything to show for it. It pissed me off because people didn't have the faith in me. The scouts don't know what they're doing. I've said that from day one. They'd rather take a guy that runs track — a 3.6 to first base and hits a buck ten — than take a guy that can hit .360 and not run a lick.

"To teach someone how to hit a baseball is really hard. You've got to have talent. Hitting a baseball thrown ninety miles an hour at you is pretty hard. To teach someone to hit a baseball in a year — I think it's ridiculous. That's what they gamble on. I mean, if that's what they're going to do, then I have no control over that. I always say I don't worry about shit I don't have control over. Yeah, it bothers the shit out of me to go to a baseball game, watch a guy go 0-4 with three strike-outs, a shortstop who's not that good, and after the game have seven or eight scouts line up and time him. They're after speed. They're not after the real talent of the game.

"You can't steal first, that's what I say. If you could steal first there'd be other people that should be in the game. But, I don't know. To hit a baseball, I feel, is the hardest thing. For me to work at it for fifteen years, hard for the last eight years, devoting all my time, and them bringing in someone who can't hit, it's tough."

Having spoken with people from the Ogden Raptors before the draft, Jones did have an option after his disappointment. With his parents lending him support, he made his decision to take one more shot at baseball as a career. "My mom and dad were really supportive, they've been supportive throughout my whole life. They were disappointed," he said of their reaction to his being passed over in the draft. "They couldn't understand why. I couldn't understand why. My parents said that there had to be a reason why." Two days after draft day he signed a contract with the Raptors.

"Guys that get drafted — you've got to fight for a position then, and I thought, 'Wow, that would be tough to fight for a position my first year in pro baseball,' and I haven't had to deal with that, ever," he said, putting a positive light on the chance to play on an independent team. "So when I came to Ogden they said, 'Hey, you'll be playing every day.' So I looked at that in a positive way and kept saying, 'I'm going to get four to five at-bats a night. I'm going to get three hundred ABS this summer and my buddy that got drafted by the Cardinals is going to go to an organization that might not play him every day.' So that was good, and my mom and dad helped me to really understand that." The perspective helped get Jones through the difficult weeks after the draft, but it did not remove all of his bitterness.

"I hit .340 in four years. I started every game but two in four years at Utah. My last year I had twenty-five home runs. I tied for the most home runs in the 1994 season in college baseball, which to me meant a lot, but I really don't have anything to show for it. Usually a guy that leads football in yards rushing has something to show for it — he has a big check to show for it. Usually the guy in college basketball that scores the most points has something to show for it. I led the nation in home runs and I really have nothing to show for it but the twenty-five home runs, which I'll always look back on. I can always say, 'Yeah, I led the nation in home runs that year,' but I don't have anything to show for it."

Scouts told Jones that he was too old, that he was not good enough at third base to play professional baseball, that his home-run prowess only proved that he was one-dimensional. Scouts drafted speedy players, convinced that coaches could teach them to hit, and tall players, convinced that coaches could teach them to field, but would not draft a power hitter who had proven himself at the Division I level. The incongruity and unfairness of this method of talent evaluation — of who is allowed the chance to compete — was not lost on Jones.

"It's hard to swallow," he said, "It's like a letdown on everything that you worked on. All the blood, sweat, and tears that go on in baseball — and all the hard work — and for someone to come up and say, 'You're not good enough,' it sort of pissed me off. I want to go out and prove that I am good enough, but it always seems that they'll find something wrong with me. That's how it's going right now, even in the Pioneer League, right now they're saying there's always going to be something wrong with me, whether they tell me I'm throwing sidearm from third, I'll start over the top they'll find something wrong. I have a mark on myself and it's hard to get rid of and I don't know how I got that mark. If I didn't have the mark, I would have been drafted. I'm not taking away anything from one of my best friends at the University of Utah who got drafted by the Cardinals organization, but he got drafted in the forty-first round and I had fifteen more home runs and forty more RBIs than him and he gets drafted and we're the same age. So right there I knew there was a mark against me somehow. I'm just trying to prove to the scouts that they're wrong."

Having graduated as a sociology major, Jones did not need to be reminded that many factors besides talent and potential enter into the baseball decision-making process. "That's something that upsets me — that kids don't see what stars in the major leagues have to go through," he explained. "Politics is a big part of baseball, and that's what I'm seeing right now. You take a guy who gets drafted in the first round compared to a guy that gets drafted in the fiftieth round. The guy in the first round is going to get more chances than the guy in the fiftieth round because he got drafted in the first round. See, one thing about scouts is, they're afraid to admit they're wrong. Because most of the time they are wrong."

Recounting a conversation he once had with a scout who offered the encouragement that his franchise had three guys in the majors who were never drafted, Jones noted the irony. "I said, 'Doesn't that show you that you scouts don't know what you're doing, because you've got three guys that are in the big league on your team and they didn't get drafted? That shows that you guys aren't doing your job because you see one guy and you think he's okay and you don't look at anybody else. You guys are afraid to admit that you are wrong,'" he said. "When they've got their mind set on someone they're going to give him all the chances in the world.

"When I go to a park, I always look at a guy across the park playing my position. I feel I could play just as well as those other people, but I just don't feel I'm getting the breaks right now. So if I've got to keep on doing what I have to do, I'm going to go to the yard every day playing hard — give 110 percent. Maybe one day I'll get a break. Maybe one day someone will see me and give me a chance. That's the only thing I can hope for."

For a game that almost every American knows the rules to — one, two, three strikes you're out — baseball can be very complicated. Even in the minor leagues, players are still learning the subtleties — positioning, offensive and defensive theories, specialty plays, and the tricks of the trade that make good players great. Talent is never enough to make a major-league ballplayer. When the young men arrive in the minor leagues, it is clear that they have a talent to play the game. Once they polish up on the subtleties and the craft of their position, they can combine their talent with an understanding of the game that will enable them to further their careers.

Fielders who understand how to position themselves can compensate for weak arms or lack of speed. Hitters who only swing at strikes can increase their batting average despite other weaknesses at the plate. Professional baseball players are all very gifted athletes, but only the ones with heart and an intelligence for the game are likely to make it to the big leagues. For the Raptors who had already been passed over by the baseball world, mastering the fundamentals and perfecting their craft was essential to disproving the people who passed them over and restarting their trip to the major leagues.

Some days I would come to the yard before practice to see Shane Jones standing alone at home plate hitting balls off of a tee by himself, swinging mercilessly and grunting with each contact. "Drive the ball to the opposite field every time," he would remind himself. Then he would walk into the outfield, gather all the balls, and walk back to home plate to do it again. Jones understood that he not only had to prove to the scouts that they were wrong, he had to prove to them that they could not pass him up again. To make the scouts eat their words, he was going to make that kind of single-minded effort every game. But when saddled with a hitless performance or credited with a multiple-error game, it was difficult not to feel the immense pressure that weighed on his shoulders.

"Right now, I'm a little disappointed in the way I performed," he said as he struggled through a slump. "I'm sure I let a lot of people down — you know, they've had a lot of expectations of me that I feel I haven't lived up to. I really wanted to have more RBIS. I want to hit over .300 and I'm only hitting .270. In college when somebody hit .270, that's not good, but in pro ball it is, and I've got to learn how to deal with that."

Hurling his helmet into the dugout or fiercely barking at himself as he took a seat on the bench, Jones often let his emotions get the best of him. But having played the game for so long, he understood the ramifications of every strikeout and every failure at the plate — it made it that much more difficult to bring his average up, that much more difficult to earn himself a signing at the end of the season. For almost a decade Jones had focused on extending his baseball career for as long as possible, but seeing its possible end often made him press too hard and let his temper interfere with his performance.

"I press every day and I wish I could stop it," he said of his passionate outbursts, "and I'm going to try from here on out. My goal is not to show any emotions after an at-bat. After I ground out — oh, well. If I strike out — oh, well. Because maybe if a scout sees me not showing emotions, maybe he can see that I can play at the professional level." This was easier said than done, and just one more goal to strive for in his difficult journey through the baseball world. But a little help from his mother and a little PMA went a long way, which is why he wore it on his wrist.

"I put 'Mom' on my wristband for me to look at that and control my emotions," he said. "My mom doesn't like when my emotions show on the field, so when I get out I look at 'Mom' and it keeps me from getting too emotional. The PMA stands for positive mental attitude. It's something just to keep my attitude positive, my mental attitude, because I feel right now that baseball's probably 80 percent mental at this level. Everyone can swing, everyone can field, and everyone can throw it, but the mental game is what's going to help me succeed. So I look at the PMA just to help me keep that positive mental attitude."

It helps to have a mentor, and Jones was lucky enough to find another young man whose experience with the baseball world was similar to his own. "When I was growing up I didn't have anyone, but now there's sort of someone that keeps me going, and that's Denny Hocking, from the Twins," Jones said. "He got drafted in the fifty-second round. They didn't believe in him and he's in the big leagues. When I go to the park, I think of him knowing no one had faith in him, just like no one has faith in me now. He's proved all his critics wrong. So there's someone out there who's proven the system wrong.

"He's in triple-A now, but he's been up and down for the past two years. They sent him to triple-A in Salt Lake; that's where I got to know him, and he's just an inspiration — no one had faith in him but he's in triple-A. I said, 'Denny, my name is Shane Jones, I play baseball at the University of Utah. I'm talking to scouts right now and I don't quite know how to handle them. Is there a way we can get together?' I called him and ever since then our friendship's grown. He wants to see me prove them wrong just as he did."

With the right numbers, the right performance over the season, and a little bit of good fortune, Jones could do just that. So every day Shane Jones taped up his wrists, wrote "PMA" and "Mom" on his wrist wraps, and took the field to pursue his dream. Danny Miller looked for a new feather for each start and prepared to prove that the scouts that passed him up were wrong. Celebrating "independents day" meant celebrating that they still had a chance. Tim Gavello, who used a spread-hands grip reminiscent of Ty Cobb to hit .370 with thirty-nine RBIs at San Jose State, was told that he was too small to play first base in professional baseball but still had a chance. Chris Amos, who led all of NCAA Division I in stolen-base percentage but was not drafted, still had a chance. Brett Smith, Jeff Garrett, Tim Salado, and Chris Simmons were each passed up in the draft but still had a chance. Every day the Ogden Raptors took the field, independents day meant that someone passed over by the baseball world could end up proving everyone wrong, making it to an organization and all the way to the show.

"That's my biggest goal," Shane Jones declared, having focused on it throughout his playing career. "That's what I want to happen. I don't know if it'll happen because last year in the draft no organization took me. So I've got a big question mark in my mind. I want to be picked up by an organization. I go to the yard every day hoping I get picked up, but if I don't get picked up, I can look in the mirror and say, 'Hey, I gave it everything I could.'"

Minor Troubles

At high noon, with his players gathered around home plate, Willy Ambos grimly surveyed the scene and began to lecture. The one-hundred-degree-plus temperature and the oppressive sun beat down on my teammates and me, and we wanted no part of this early workout. Although we usually arrived at the park in the cooler hours of the afternoon, our presence at this scalding early practice was well deserved. The previous evening, five errors gave our opponents five unearned runs. Booted balls, missed signs, and too many strikeouts contributed to a sloppy outing, which warranted the practice in the blazing Utah sun. Independence Day may have been a reason for the Raptors to celebrate their place in pro ball, but after the Fourth of July the team fizzled like a wet bottle rocket.

Ambos was still fuming about misplays and what he perceived as the complacent attitude of his players. Having seen his career peak well short of the majors, Ambos knew how it felt to play the game, and with his debut as a manager, he also knew how it felt to watch others squander their chances by not putting their heart into every game.

"Baseball is the greatest game in the world," he said, as his players squinted against the glare. "If you're not going to give it the effort it deserves, then you're an asshole." Again and again, in motivational speeches and furious fits, he lectured us on the meaning of being blessed with the talent and opportunity to play professionally. Looking back on his career, it was easier for him to appreciate the solemn commitment and tunnel vision necessary to make dreams come true than it was for his players, who were at the height of their ability and feeling invincible. Most players learn too late that only those who appreciate the mortality of their careers, respect their opportunity, and work earnestly at the craft of baseball can succeed in extending the pursuit of their dreams.

Later that night, the hard workout and harsh words appeared to have affected my teammates as we ran out to a big lead against the Helena Brewers, but the performance soon fell apart. Fielders kicked balls around the infield and pitchers walked the Brewers around the bases. My teammates turned an easy win into a frustrating loss as Helena overcame a seven-run deficit in the sixth inning to steal a sure Raptors win. After our day of working on fundamentals, the Brewers' comeback was something we just could not explain. Stunned, we lost our third game in a row, extending our post–Independence Day slide and dropping to a game and a half behind the Brewers in the hunt for the Pioneer League Southern Division crown. More important, our coaching staff was at a loss as to how to motivate or direct the team. We left the field silently, avoiding Ambos's angry gaze, but had no time to worry about our poor effort. It was ten-thirty and the bus to Great Falls was leaving at two in the morning. We had to get a quick dinner, pack our bags, and get back to the park.

It was always good to be home, but the comfort and routine of returning to the roost also meant distractions. After the disastrous series with Helena, we were grateful to leave the scene of the crime. On the road there was almost nothing to consider except baseball. All we had to do was eat, kill time, and play ball. At home there were girlfriends and wives, free beer at local bars, mail to read, bills to pay, and everyday life to prey on the mind of a ballplayer.

Beginning the first extended road trip of the season, the last thing we needed were additional distractions. But the Raptors owners continued to promote their team in any way possible. A camera crew from a local television station was coming along for the trip. The extra attention was not necessarily a problem, but the fact that the news crew was taking up two seats for the eleven-hour ride was a major concern. We certainly would have let an entire truckload of media travel behind our bus without comment, but the loss of seats meant that the Raptors bus was even more like a sardine can than usual. Noticing the extra passengers, players scrambled to establish elbow room. Steve Gay and Dan Zanolla crawled up into the luggage racks, and Jeremy Winget stretched out on the floor. These less claustrophobic Raptors curled up to sleep while I leaned against a window and consoled myself that in another twelve hours the trip would be a bad dream.

With twenty-six games in twenty-six days behind us, we left town for the nine-day road trip — seven games in Great Falls and Billings sandwiched between two travel days — that would roughly complete the first half of the season. As we struggled to sleep, we could comfort ourselves that the next day, for the first time all season, was a day off.

Most American workers have weekends off. According to the Bible, even God took one day off. Professional baseball players, however, rarely get a break. The teams of the Pioneer League, like those in the majors and throughout the minors, play weekdays, weekends, and holidays for the pleasure of the fan. For players, days quickly merged together and soon after the start of the season, questions like "What time does the bus leave?" or "Who do we play tonight?" meant more than "What date is it?" or "What day is today?" For the Raptors, the only way to tell the days apart was that we wore teal holiday hats and our batting practice jerseys on Sundays. Otherwise a Thursday was just like a Saturday, which was just like a Monday.

After a brutal bus trip where poker, neck cramps, and bad jokes were more plentiful than sleep, we arrived in Great Falls just after noon and enjoyed our holiday from baseball by stocking up on food and catching up on sleep. Watching a sunset out of uniform and eating dinner before ten o'clock was simply foreign after more than three straight weeks with a game every day.

Although we had become accustomed to playing ball, eating a quick dinner, and then having a few beers before bed, on this off day, dinner and beers left plenty of time for more and more beers. My teammates and I watched the major-league All-Star Game in awe of the talent being displayed and longing for the days when the hard work and hard life of the minors could be replaced by the glamour, attention, and lucrative paycheck enjoyed by the All-Stars. By the time Tony Gwynn won the game for the National League by sliding under

Ivan Rodriguez's tag in the tenth inning, we had had more than our share of beer and more than our share of jealous longings, but the night was still young. After more beer, our day off ended with us stumbling home, faithfully obeying our midnight curfew as the routine of our lives once again took over. After our short vacation, it was back to the daily grind of minor-league baseball.

Great Falls, the second largest city in Montana, with a population of about eighty thousand, is one of the bigger cities in the Pioneer League. Casinos, theaters, malls, and clubs offered us many diversions to take our minds off life on the road. While I spent some of my down time wandering Main Street and Doug O'Neill again tried his luck at the video keno and poker machines, Chris Simmons and Shane Jones purchased Montana fishing licenses for a more bucolic pursuit. With the news cameras in tow, the two former University of Utah teammates traded bats for poles and tried their luck at Montana fishing. Simmons, who had made the most of his playing time despite his utility-player status by batting .364, was still chomping at the bit to get into games but waiting patiently to have the chance. Jones, who was still leading the league in extra-base hits and doubles despite struggling since his torrid start, was in definite need of the calm of fishing to take his mind off his slump. He could not have picked many sites with more stunning scenery to refocus his intensity and drive back into the calm rhythm needed to draw him out of his funk.

Just an infield fly from the new Raptors fishing hole, along the crystal-clear Missouri River, the majestic waterfalls that give the city its name cascade just down river from Legion Park, home of the Great Falls Dodgers. The park was vintage minor leagues with the Marlboro Man rising above the left-center field wall, flag poles — in play — in center, and cozy, blue grandstands lining the field. Pillars supporting the overhang, chicken-wire fencing protecting fans from foul balls, and painted signs around the outfield walls made Legion Park look like it was built in baseball's golden era and preserved for today's ballplayers.

Were it not for the fact that it was a Dodgers facility, the park would be an ideal place to play, but the home-team attitude served to make visitors feel only one way: unworthy. While the Idaho Falls Braves exuded the Johnny-come-lately cockiness of their parent club with its recent success, the Great Falls Dodgers seemed to reek of the holier-than-thou pureness of the Dodgers organization with their speeches about what it means to be a Dodger and their proud tradition. The Great Falls Dodgers had pristine white uniforms with their names on the back and used only pearly white balls for batting practice. The organization was trying too hard to ooze class, from the batboy who greeted our bus upon arrival to the necrology page in their program detailing all the members of the Dodgers family who had passed on to the great Ebbets Field in the sky.

To me, my teammates, and especially our coaches, this all contributed to an impression that we were supposed to feel as if we did not belong on the same field as the Dodgers. But the upstart Raptors promptly pounded the home team into submission fifteen to six behind Jeremy Winget, whose two-for-four performance added four RBIS and a majestic, mammoth home run to his gaudy statistics that were among the league leaders in almost every category. The offensive explosion snapped our losing streak, won the first game of the long road trip, and earned a little bit of respect from the haughty Dodgers.

Even in the midst of the Dodgers' arrogance, my teammates and I could appreciate certain details of the class and funds that a major-league organization provides to its affiliates. Throughout the ranks of the minor leagues are instructors, coaches, and managers with big-league experience. In the Pioneer League, these former major leaguers were usually players that only serious fans or card collectors would know, like Idaho Falls Braves manager Max Venable, who traveled through the majors with the Giants, Reds, and Angels. Occasionally, however, a bright star from the majors would cross our path.

When Dodgers pitching coach Luis Tiant — who as "El Tiante" won 229 major-league games, leaving his mark on the baseball world by almost single-handedly defeating the Big Red Machine for the Boston Red Sox in the 1975 World Series — walked on the field, we could not help noticing. It was one thing to be told that the opposing manager was in the bigs, but it was another to recognize immediately that we were in the presence of someone familiar. Watching Tiant walk to the mound was a reminder of why minor leaguers try so hard and work so diligently. Being on the same field as a legend makes the whole experience of the minors seem temptingly close to the show. It was easy to focus on the game at hand or the day-to-day misery of bus rides and fast food meals and forget that the majors are not all that far away. But watching a former major-league star, it was hard to do anything but dream.

To reinforce our dreams, a representative of the Topps baseball card company visited our hotel in Great Falls to officially sign us to contracts. We filed into a conference room, more giddy over getting free cards than over the prospect of making it to the majors. Two contracts with five-dollar checks attached were handed to each of us for signatures. The contracts gave Topps the right to use our pictures and guaranteed us income based on card sales — once we reached the majors.

When I was a card-trading kid being ripped off in trades for my favorite players — "my Ron Cey and Steve Garvey for your extra Larry Bowa, sure" — I never imagined that one day I would be putting my name on a baseball-card contract. Topps was getting our signatures on contracts because we were some of the very few people in the world who had a chance of making it to the majors. We walked out of the room with two checks that we all planned to save forever, two packs of cards, and "borrowed" Topps pens that nobody planned to give back.

In our rooms we opened the card packs and looked at the faces of players who had fulfilled their major dreams. More than ever it seemed that a few years and a few breaks could have Raptors faces on the cards while a new crop of rookies signed their own Topps contracts. Between the cards of Ken Griffey Jr. and Andres Galarraga were players who were in our shoes just years ago. Flipping the cards over to get a glimpse of the players' careers, my teammates could barely hide smiles to find some who had passed through the Pioneer League. In my pack of cards was Mike Ignasiak, who played for Helena in 1988 and was in Milwaukee in 1991, and Angel Miranda, who was on the mound in Butte in 1987 and was in the majors six years later.

Someday a Tommy Johnston or a Doug O'Neill card could show a similar route and future Ogden Raptors could look over their statistics with a sparkle in their eyes and a dream in their hearts. Staring up at the baseball pyramid, the journey through the rookie leagues to single-A, to double-A, to triple-A, all the way to the majors sometimes looked like a long trip, but seeing it neatly mapped out on the backs of the cards of those who have made the journey, it didn't seem distant at all.

Later that evening, with new baseball cards tucked in hats for luck and two wins against the Dodgers already under our belts, we looked forward to extending our winning streak. But as the third game wore on in a two-two tie, neither the visiting Raptors nor the home team could break the deadlock.

Buoyed by utility fielder turned starting pitcher Dan Zanolla's escape artistry that extricated his team from trouble, the Raptors scored a go-ahead run in the top of the tenth, but the Dodgers struck back, tying the game in the bottom of the frame. With the Dodgers still batting — two outs and a runner on second — a ball rocketed into left-center field that appeared destined to end the game and ruin the Raptors effort. I joined the other players who were holding their breath as Doug O'Neill sprinted after the ball. Diving fully extended toward the wall, he snagged the ball, brandishing it proudly for the umpires after he slid to a stop, and extinguished the Dodgers threat.

The catch could not have been more spectacular. Not only had O'Neill caught the ball, but he saved the game and kept us alive. Struggling at the plate — batting .250 with only two home runs and almost forty strikeouts — O'Neill somehow managed to clear his head and focus on defense when he took the field. Despite his frustration at not being able to recapture the form at the plate that once made him a seventh-round draft pick, stellar play in center — consistently hitting the cutoff man, notching assist after assist with strong throws, and making highlight-film catches like the one that prolonged this game — continued to make O'Neill an invaluable part of the lineup.

In the dugout the game was growing painfully long, and I joined the other bench sitters as we killed time with dugout baseball (land a ball on the first step for a single, the next step for a double, the top step for a home run), scanned the crowd to ogle young women, and tried varieties of rally caps and good luck charms to ignite our teammates. Mike Carrigg's hollowed-out cups on the ears could not help, nor could any of Chris Simmons's cheering or my rubbing lucky stones. We switched seats, held our breath, and yelled encouragement to no avail.

As the fourteenth inning began, Carrigg turned his sunglasses upside down as baseball black magic to get the run we needed, and the voodoo did the trick. Josh Kirtlan singled Jeremy Winget home to break the tie, and with runners on first and third Tommy Johnston drove a ball off the mound that popped high enough in the air to score Kirtlan and allow Johnston to reach base safely. The hit was especially satisfying for Tommy — back in action after nursing his hand back to health — who had been hitless until the fourteenth inning and was struggling to get his average above .200.

With the giddy bench yipping and cheering, the rally ended, leaving the Dodgers down three runs in the bottom of the fourteenth. But nobody told the Dodgers that they were supposed to go quietly into the night, and they promptly loaded the bases and brought the winning run to the plate. We held our breath until the Dodgers rally died with a final line-out to Shane Jones, allowing us to finally erupt in a celebration that carried from the field through the locker room to the bus.

"That was the greatest game in the history of the franchise," gushed Willy Ambos to loud cheers that echoed in the bus. Bubbling over with rare praise about his team's heart and perseverance, Ambos, who had often shown frustration with his team, seemed genuinely pleased to be associated with his players.

In the middle of the celebration, however, one Raptor was silent. Starting pitcher Dan Zanolla was sullen despite his remarkable effort that night and all season on the mound for Ogden. Zanolla, who held the Dodgers to three runs over ten innings, strode to the front of the bus to deliver some news. Just after the final out was recorded, Zanolla was informed that he had to leave the team.

In an effort to cut costs, the Raptors ownership had entered into an agreement with a team in the independent Northern League that allowed Zanolla to be loaned to the Raptors, where he could compete in the Pioneer League. Now that he was playing so well, his Northern League team wanted to recall him, effective the following morning.

As the bus quieted, Zanolla, with tears in his eyes and a shaky voice, informed his teammates that his team was recalling him. "I will do everything I can to stay here," Zanolla said, but the deal had already been done. The raucous bus went quiet as players looked about, unsure of what to say or feel. A respected member of the team and a good friend was being taken away. Had he been picked up by a major-league franchise, the mood would have been jubilant, and if he had been released, the mood would have been tinged with the knowledge that there was reason to let him go. But leaving for a team where he had a questionable future while he was playing so well left his teammates dismayed and subdued.

Mellowed by the bad news, we returned to the hotel. With the announcement that, after the big win, there was no curfew, we dispersed to celebrate the victory as Zanolla patiently phoned everyone he could think of to enable himself to stay with the Raptors. By morning he was gone, along with his strong arm and easygoing manner. Two days later a new player was with the team wearing Zanolla's number three.

While Zanolla's private drama unfolded, the Raptors celebration raged into the night. My teammates and I, quite comfortable with the town after three days in Great Falls, made our way to familiar watering holes and hot spots. By morning we were nursing hangovers, recounting war stories, and sluggishly moving baggage into getaway rooms. Everyone spent the long day sleeping, watching a player's homemade adult video of his exploits the previous evening, and trying to avoid loud noises until game time.

A step slow after the long celebration, without many starters, who were getting a well-deserved rest, and facing the Dodgers ace, we lost the final game of the series despite a gutsy late-inning comeback. Dodgers starter Dennis Reyes, a seventeen-year-old lefthander from Higuera de Zargoza, Mexico, inspired nothing but respect from the Raptors bench. Reminiscent of former Dodgers great Fernando Valenzuela, not only because of how he mowed down batters but also how his ample frame filled out the Dodgers whites, Reyes was in Great

Falls but seemed destined to take his 1.85 ERA to Chavez Ravine in years to come.

Looking at mediocre players in uniform for the affiliated teams in the Pioneer League, my teammates were left thinking, "You were chosen but I wasn't, you have my job, I should be playing for your organization before you, I should have the chance that you have." But there was an excitement and an admiration for players like Reyes who had a chance to make it.

In our first test against foes from the Northern Division of the Pioneer League, we won three out of four away from home against the Dodgers. A single win in the next three games against Billings would ensure our first winning road trip, which would, according to an early-season promise, win beer for the trip home courtesy of the coaching staff.

But our coaching staff was not satisfied. After watching Jason Evenhus — starting pitcher for the final game against the Dodgers — slink back to the hotel well after breakfast, the coaches renewed their disgust at what they saw as their players' lackadaisical attitude toward the game. Barking at us to keep our heads out of the stands and keep our minds on the game, our coaches had once again turned surly toward us, and antics such as Evenhus's staying out late before his turn in the rotation seemed to be tempting fate.

Our bus was loading and we were scheduled to arrive in Billings at four in the morning, where our next day's game against the Mustangs was scheduled for that afternoon at one. We needed dinner and sleep; there was no time to worry about whether the coaches cared for us or even if we lost ground in the pennant race. As we desperately tried to rest on the trip, even the route itself conspired against us, and the road to the major leagues got a little bit rougher on the trip between Great Falls and Billings. While I gazed mindlessly at the movie in the VCR, hoping it would lull me to sleep, the bus suddenly lurched over a bump. After another series of bumps, I began to take notice of the surroundings. The main road was being repaired and the directional signs had led our bus on a barely paved detour.

Riding on what was little more than a dirt road, the bus headlights were the only light source for as far as the eye could see. If any Raptors were ever to progress along the road to the majors, we would first have to get back along the road to Billings. We had often joked about making sure that the bus driver was awake, cringing any time anyone saw what may have been the driver's head bobbing drowsily, and suddenly confronted our deepest fears. "Did we veer off the road?" Anxious eyes and calculating minds were finally put to rest when the bus re-entered civilization and the interstate system. By the time we reached our motel in Billings it was just before dawn and all we cared about was getting sleep after our bumpy ride. Nobody said that the road to the majors would be easy, but I expected it would at least be paved.

Waking up in Montana's largest city was a pleasant surprise. Earning the name Magic City, Billings sprung up in a span of five months around the Northern Pacific Railroad in 1882. Today the city remains an oasis of urban activity in the vastness of central Montana. As a transportation and commercial hub with a bustling downtown framed by distant mountains, Billings attracts visitors bound for all parts of the Northwest, including Yellowstone Park, the Little Bighorn Battlefield, and the scenic Beartooth Highway. A population of ninety thousand, a downtown with tall buildings, and a legitimate nightlife made even a city boy like me feel almost at home.

Just outside of town the Rimrocks form a cliff wall surrounding the city and provide a dramatic backdrop for Cobb Field and its Billings Mustangs. With neatly trimmed grass and dragged infield, the park was a beautiful facility befitting a major-league farm team. The field, within walking distance of downtown Billings, was coated with stucco and rather impersonal on the outside, but inside the stadium was cozy. Dark tunnels where fans stocked up on hot dogs and cotton candy opened to the brightness, grass, and dirt of the field. A covered grandstand kept box seats in the shade while bleachers along the first- and third-base lines allowed fans to soak in the Montana sun while they took in the game.

Overstuffed recliners above the visiting dugout provided perfect viewing for winners of the "best seats in the house" promotion, which gave the park a minor-league feel, but the Harry Caray sound-alike on the public address system gave the park a major-league sound, and there was nothing minor about the home team's success. As evidenced by the gaudy flags in left-center field, the Mustangs were the two-time defending Pioneer League champions and their supporters — who led the league in attendance with over one hundred thousand fans over thirty-six dates — were leading lusty cheers for a third championship.

In the tunnels beneath the stadium, a proud but subdued sign touted the members of the Mustangs Hall of Fame. In the very center of the top row, a glossy eight-by-ten picture of George Brett stared out at fans between Larry Shepard and Gorman Thomas. I could not resist taking a picture of the man for whom I wore my number five. Somewhere back in Philly, packed up among my belongings, was an autograph that read, "To the other Brett — best wishes — George Brett," signed while he was in Philadelphia playing against the Phils in the 1980 World Series. Striding through the stadium that gave Brett his start, I could not help wondering if someone with the Raptors or with the Mustangs would one day similarly inspire one of today's youngsters.

The Mustangs played hard but joined the growing list of teams that found out the hard way that the Raptors were intent on winning a championship ring. Behind undefeated ace Danny Miller, who pushed his record to six wins and no losses and a league-leading fifty-three-and-a-third innings pitched, the Raptors held off the home team to record a five-to-four victory despite only a few hours of sleep on the bumpy ride to Billings. It was just one more feather in the quirky pitcher's cap as his quest to hook on with a major-league organization continued.

The win, however, was not very pretty. Plagued by poor mental play, we again spent the day at the ballpark missing signs and infuriating the coaching staff. Bristling from the coaches' perpetual anger toward us, we were growing tired of put-downs and insults as motivation. As we warmed up at second base, Chris Amos and I tried to laugh about the growing tension, but when he told me that he was thinking of quitting, it was suddenly no joke. After a strong start to the season, injuries had slowed him down and his batting average began to plummet. As his production decreased, the coaches were riding him hard, and the constant lack of privacy that came with being on the road was grating on him. I could not help thinking to myself that thousands of kids would kill to trade places with Chris, yet he was actually talking about leaving the Raptors. It looked as if the team might just fall apart on its own if the brewing confrontation between players and coaches did not tear it apart first.

Each day that we were on the road, the official Pioneer League statistics were made available to our coaching staff. Since statistics represented the currency of the baseball world — how players would be judged when general managers decided whether to inscribe them in the book of baseball for another year or to end their careers through their indifference — most players had a more than casual interest in getting a peek at them. Although no player wanted to be termed a "stat-rat," everybody wanted to cast a glance at the numbers much as growing children like to look at notches on the wall that assure them that they are indeed growing every year.

As I found myself sitting next to the statistics sheets on the bench in the Billings visitors dugout, I caught a teammate's eyes straying from the game to the sheet and back again. Our mutual view was interrupted by a meaty hand's swipe at the statistics as Willy Ambos ripped the sheets from the bench, tore them to pieces and threw the scraps of paper to the dugout floor.

In the attempt to climb the ladder to the majors, the statistics that mark individual progress were the only measure that truly mattered to each player in the long run. In stark contrast, a manager's achievement is measured primarily by the performance of his team. By shredding the statistics sheets in Billings, Willy let us know his feelings on the odd dichotomy. Since relations between manager and team were strained, any indication that a player was not giving his all for the team was cause for Ambos's anger. We would have to come together as a team to please the manager — or find more appropriate times to catch a look at the statistics.

Amid the conflict that was growing in our dugout, we had a closeup view of a piece of baseball history to keep our minds off our internal troubles and our hands off each other's throats. Aaron Boone, son of Bob Boone and grandson of Ray Boone, was trying to join his brother Bret in the big leagues and become part of the only three-generation major-league family in baseball history. The Mustangs' third baseman was hitting well but struggling a bit in the field when the Raptors entered Billings. Despite Boone's success or failure, it was a treat to encounter anything that made the majors seem not so far away. Like signing our baseball-card contracts, watching Boone, with his major-league connection, was just one more reminder that the cold war simmering between the Raptors players and their coaching staff was worth putting up with because the majors were still waiting for those with the talent and toughness to endure.

Like the month of March, the Raptors were making a habit of coming in like a lion and leaving like a lamb. With home just a bus ride away, bags packed and stowed, and the wear of the road weighing on players' shoulders, it was difficult to be excited about the getaway game. Fresh off the bus, we had an impressive five-and-one record in the first game of road trips. Unfortunately, a one-and-five record on getaway days tempered that success. In Billings, the road again took its toll and we dropped our final two games to end our trip. Looking back, however, we had reason to be proud. We had beaten the then-first-place Dodgers three out of four times in their home park and then beat the Mustangs, who had taken over first place in the Northern Division after we conquered the Dodgers, at their field before running into some trouble to end the trip with four wins and three losses.

Leaving Billings, we should have been happy with our effort. But after eight days on the road, eight days of close proximity, and eight days of battling for a share of first place, the road had taken its toll. Not only did we receive no beer for our winning road trip, there was barely any conversation between coaches and players as our bus pulled away from Cobb Field.

Ambos and Coach Morales constantly stressed taking pressure off their players. They only wanted us to simply follow their instructions on when to run, when to bunt, and when to change defensive alignment — and to play fundamentally sound ball. But too many times for our coaches' liking, players stood dumbfounded at first base as Morales signed for a hit-and-run, tried stealing third base with two outs instead of allowing the batter to do his job, or just plain gave less than a 100 percent effort.

Because of their proximity in age to the players and because their playing careers were not so impressive as to command awe, Ambos and Morales, both in their late twenties, had resorted to establishing themselves as leaders of the pack by belittling and insulting their players whenever possible. In the clubhouse, on the road, and during practices, we quickly found abuse par for the course.

"Is it that fucking hard to read the signs?" or "If you don't fucking hustle, I'll put a pitcher in at your position" was often the most significant communication between the coaching staff and players during the game. Ambos sarcastically barked at his charges and Morales — who had shaved his head before the trip, making him look downright nasty in a "Fuck-the-world-I-don't-care-how-I-look" way — eyed us with looks that could kill. Opposing players would quietly ask, "What's the deal with your coaches?" and we could only shrug.

Ambos and Morales had an almost religious zeal for the game and took it as an insult to them and to all of baseball if players committed sins on the field, especially the sin of not giving the game the respect it deserved. As the long road trip dragged to its conclusion, a chasm was widening between coaches who resented their players' approach to the game and players who were getting fed up with their coaches belittling them and showing them up on the field.

By the last game of the trip, players were actively avoiding coaches and coaches were throwing at players' heads during batting practice; players were talking openly about quitting, and coaches were questioning whether players would be around for the next road trip; and despite the overall winning record of the trip, players and coaches boarded the bus as if they hadn't won a game.

Walking onto the bus as it prepared for departure in Billings, Ambos turned toward his players as if to start the trip home with some words for us. He spun his head, slowly puffed out his cheeks, exhaled with a frown, and then turned to face the road — he had nothing to say. When the bus stopped for dinner, Ambos used the opportunity to address us. "Bus leaves at eleven-thirty," he said, then turned to leave the bus and mumbled, "Hopefully, some of you won't be on it."

As we spent dinner shoveling fast food into greedy mouths, players complained that the coaches backed out of their promise of beer and discussed the dissension brewing on the team. Coaches spoke ominously of the future and what players were in for upon our return to Ogden.

Ambos and Morales had a right to be concerned, not only for how their team performed but for how individual players responded to their tutelage. It was not just their jobs with the Raptors but their own major dreams that were at stake. If the baseball world saw that they were an effective staff, future managerial and coaching opportunities would open up for them. If not, Ambos and Morales could find themselves out of professional baseball altogether.

Back on the bus after dinner, the Raptors were quiet as card games and movies faded into the night. Players and coaches slept an uneasy sleep, concerned about the future. The next day was another travel day — our second day off of the season — so we would have a cooling-off period before we again took the field. But the damage was done. Only the fact that we were not losing kept the situation from getting ugly. With players threatening to quit, management threatening releases, and thirty-three ball games' worth of confrontations before us, the bus drove back to Ogden along well-traveled Interstate 15 and into the darkness ahead.

The Management

Willy Ambos and Rich Morales had a difficult balance to maintain. Both sincerely wanted to create an atmosphere that would give their players the best chance to further their careers. They also wanted the team to reflect positively on them so that their own careers could move on from Ogden. Although these two notions did not necessarily have to conflict, the dissension between team and coaches increasingly meant the ambitions were at odds. Players did not feel that they were being treated properly, and the team was not playing up to the standards set by the coaching staff. Ambos and Morales could push neither their careers nor their players' careers forward if the team was not responding to them. But Willy and Mo knew what their players were up against, how hard it is to build a career in baseball, and all they wanted was for the Raptors to make the solemn commitment necessary to earnestly pursue their dreams. As former players, when they did not see the proper respect and commitment to the game, their reactions were sometimes extreme.

"Excuse me. Get out of the way!" That was enough warning for me to duck as Ambos hurled a plastic chair against the dugout wall, shattering it into pieces that fell with a clatter to the cement floor. After watching his Raptors fall short of another ninth-inning comeback with rally-killing gaffes, Ambos could do nothing but grind his teeth and offer me the warning as he vented his frustration. I suppose it was a sign of respect or concern that he did not throw the chair right through me, although maybe he was intent on demolishing the chair and realized that the only reaction he would get from hitting me with it would have been a yelp.

As a manager for an independent team, Ambos's job was to win, not to develop talent. Losing was simply failure — acceptable failure if the Raptors were out-talented but impermissible if the Raptors were out-worked. In the game that provoked Ambos's unique redecorating style, the Raptors were out-worked, and Ambos was incensed. As a rookie manager, he was well aware that his job was never secure as long as his players were not putting their hearts into the game. He understood his situation, but the manifestation of this understanding — often in mercurial bursts of fury in the dugout and clubhouse — showed how much he had to progress to continue his career in managing. To make it as a big-league manager, or at least prolong his career in baseball, he would have to learn to control his temper and work more positively with his players. Until then, the Raptors ownership would have to endure its rookie manager and increase its budget for plastic chairs.

Much of the frustration felt by Ambos came from his intimate knowledge of his players' situation. Just years before this first managerial experience, he too was an independent player trying to make his career last. He knew what it was like to be a baseball reject. He knew what it took to pursue a dream from that vantage point. Now he had to find a way to translate his experience into a motivation for his players. If he could not, he would lose his job — and his chance to once again make a career in professional baseball — trying.

Willy Ambos grew up on Long Island, New York, the youngest of six children in a middle-class suburban family. Ambos played baseball as young man, following in the footsteps of his brothers, but never really thought about pursuing a career in the game. "It actually was a mistake that I got to play professionally," he confessed with a smile. "Even out of high school, I wasn't a prospect. I just played because I was pretty good at it. I didn't even know if I wanted to go to college, but I got a scholarship offer. After a while, after I started to grow and mature, I figured out that I was pretty good at this. I was what's commonly referred to as a late bloomer, and I started to figure things out, ended up transferring schools, and ended up in the New York Institute of Technology."

He was a quality pitcher in a college program, but his sudden bloom of promise was dealt a serious blow when he hurt his shoulder after his junior year. Before the injury, he had attracted some interest from major-league scouts, but once he became "damaged goods" his career was in serious jeopardy. While his coach gave him the time to recuperate, Ambos underwent six months of physical therapy, five days a week, and by the end of his senior year he came back to pitch three starts in a row, going the distance and beating some good teams. In the final game of his college career he pitched a complete-game victory to end a satisfying rehabilitation tinged with the thought that it could be his last game of competitive baseball.

But an important figure for his baseball future was in the stands looking to make sure that Willy played again. After the game, Van Schley, of the independent Salt Lake City Trappers of the Pioneer League, approached him and asked if he wanted to play professional baseball. "Me, being the eternal smart-ass, asked, 'Is this a trick question?'" he remembered. "Two weeks later I was on a charter plane to Salt Lake City not knowing what I got myself into." Just weeks before, he was contemplating the end of his career and suddenly he was playing professional baseball.

"You have all these things going on in the back of your mind, and it's always a confidence check when you get to this level," he said, recalling his first days in the minor leagues. "I just went out there, I guess it was — I don't want to say a nonchalant attitude — more like, 'Fuck you. I'm just as good as you guys are,' and I was leading the league in wins that year and they were able to sell my contract to the Seattle Mariners, which brought me to the next level."

Willy led the Pioneer League that year with nine wins and was impressive enough on the mound to warrant the attention of visiting scouts. Not only had Ambos beaten the odds to get a chance to actually play professional baseball, but he had managed to move from his last chance with an independent team to an opportunity with a major-league franchise. The unexpected change in his fortune made him confront the notion that, with a few breaks, he could be in the majors in a few years. As he prepared for his first spring training, his career was no longer simply serendipitous, his fate was now resting on his throwing arm — and his heart.

"Getting ready for spring training is scary the first time," he said, "especially as a free agent guy, with no guarantees. It's a harrowing experience, just lockers and lockers and lockers of guys, and as spring training progresses guys go — rows of people, 'Thanks for coming.' You walk in there in the morning, there was a guy that waited at the gate and if he said they needed to see you, that was it, you were done. Pack your stuff, just throw it in a Hefty bag."

Ambos performed well enough to avoid the man who passed out the Hefty bags and to earn an assignment to high-A ball in the California League. His excitement in his first spring training — making the organization's top single-A club and realizing that he actually had a chance to progress up the organizational ladder — was tempered by his first experience with the business of baseball. "I was in a bus one day riding with a third-round pick who just signed — high-school kid, had money invested in him. He was saying how he misses his girlfriend and thinks he's going to go home for a few days to see the girlfriend," Ambos said incredulously. "I'm sitting there going, 'What kind of shit is that?' Two days after that he was allowed to go and then two days after that my grandmother died. I asked one of my coaches if he thought it was okay if I could go home for the funeral, and the answer I got from them was, 'Yes, you can go, but you're borderline.' I called my grandfather and my grandfather told me I didn't need to come home, that my grandmother would have understood, and I stayed there and I pitched that day and I was so angry about the whole thing. All that kept clicking in my mind was they let a kid go home who they had money invested in to see his girlfriend and was homesick and I had my grandmother pass away and I was told I was borderline. I knew right there that me and the Mariners would not get along at all.

"All I recall from that season is going six months straight with about ten days off during that time — probably 150 ball games. It's taxing physically. It's taxing mentally, especially when you're a middle reliever and you don't see the ball for ten, twelve days straight. Fortunately, the easy way out for me was that I hit the booze quite a bit, which was, I guess, a normal reaction. I'm stuck in San Bernardino, California, which is not exactly a hotbed of entertainment, and just being bitter all the time because you look at guys that were draft picks that have price tags hanging on them and there's nothing you can do because the managers and the organization get a list of who plays and your name's not on it — you're an RF, a roster filler, and I was an 'organizational player,' as they put it, and it was a very difficult season."

After the season, Ambos was released, and as his earlier time with the Mariners organization foreshadowed, he was not happy with the way he was let go. "Actually, if I would have been released with the numbers I had put up in my two years in pro ball — I was fifteen and two — if they would have released me at winter meetings, I probably could have gotten a contract with somebody else. So what transpired was that, lo and behold, about February first I get the call that I got released. When I talked to the minor-league director I said, 'You're a fuckin' asshole. Why couldn't you just release me back in winter meetings to give me a chance?' It's always when you get the speech over the phone they talk to you like they're reading from a piece of paper. Like, 'At this point — comma — we've decided to give you an unconditional release — comma — so that you may pursue . . . We're releasing you now so maybe you can hook up with somebody else.' You know fucking goddamn well that at this point there ain't a contract out there. It just left a real bad taste in my mouth the way they did it."

Willy Ambos was twenty-four and just married. Now he was out of baseball. After the wedding he returned to New York with his bride for a reception with family and friends, where he had to confront the end of his baseball career head-on. "There were my friends and relatives I hadn't seen in god knows how long and of course the first thing that everybody asks is, 'Hey, how's baseball?'" he remembered with a grimace. "So early on in the evening I say, 'Not so good, I got released,' and then about fifteen or twenty beers later, somebody new shows up at the party and says, 'Hey, how's baseball?' and all of a sudden I say, 'I got fuckin' released, fuckin' leave me alone, baseball sucks!' I probably could have been able to deal with it better, but you're also talking about a brash, cocky New Yorker who doesn't want to hear from anybody about rules or anything like that. And sometimes you need to be a company man, and I could never do that."

Even though he had been released by the Mariners, Van Schley called again, the Salt Lake City Trappers took him back, and Willy was able to extend his career as a member of an independent team. After a sub-.500 year, the Trappers needed a quality season to appease their rabid fans, and a veteran pitcher like Ambos was a big help. Just as quickly as he was released, he was back in baseball — and more important, he was wanted.

"It felt good to be wanted in that situation, because somebody went out of their way to say, 'We liked what you did for us two years ago. We'd like to have you back so you can do it again and maybe help some of the younger kids along,'" he said of his unlikely homecoming. "That's a good feeling because, if nothing else, I knew baseball. I knew the game and I was a fierce competitor, and that's what they liked about me. Statistically, maybe my best season was in 1990 — I led the league in ERA, had a great strikeout-to-walk ratio, and we won the Southern Division — lost in the playoffs to the Dodgers, but shit happens."

Another season had come and gone, and Willy was getting older and again had to contemplate what would be next. His career professional record was twenty-two wins and six losses, and even though he was still young enough to forge a career with another organization, nobody called. The Trappers asked him back for the 1991 campaign as a player-coach just as his body began to betray him. "Once you have shoulder problems, then you get elbow problems, and it was tough to make every start, but I did," he said, recalling a pain-filled year. "I had cortisone injections, stuff like that. If I told you some of the things I went through to be able to make a start, it would shock you — between local anesthetics, steroid injections, cortisone injections — just to be in a position, so I could be in a position, to go out and compete."

He finished his career gaining exposure to the coaching side of baseball, winning a championship ring for the 1991 season, retiring, and then having his number retired the following year. "This was 1992, and it was at the end of the season and the Trapper front office — I guess as a tribute to me — decided to retire number thirteen," he said modestly. "I didn't know about it so it was a surprise, and to stand out there in front of ten thousand people and they give you a standing ovation for just some poor slob that hung around long enough to win a few ball games, I almost started crying on the field. They gave me my jersey and people started standing up and clapping. This was just bizarre, this just doesn't happen, and it was very nice to be recognized like that." The ceremony ended his playing career, and Ambos was out of baseball again.

"I left quietly," he said. "What do you do? I was a career A-ball pitcher and my arm had just totally given out on me. I would have liked things to work out differently. All I really wanted was a chance. After that '89 season with the Mariners, I wanted a chance to go back to spring training, compete at the double-A level, and I would have just loved to have gotten my brains beaten in and then been released because then I could have said that I reached my ceiling, had maxed out, and that was as good as I was going to get, because then there's closure. I was never given that opportunity, so that left a bitter taste in my mouth. Once the hurt goes away you figure out that it's a fuckin' business and that's it."

Attempting to put his days behind him, he began to raise a family and tried to fill the void in his life by coaching high-school baseball and trying to teach his young son, Kyle, how to throw a slider. A few professional coaching opportunities came and went, and each time Willy would become excited about the chance to coach or manage, only to be let down. But he focused on learning more about the game, being patient, and waiting for his turn. "There's probably 160 minor-league teams in the United States of America, so it's not easy to land a managerial job," he said, putting his waiting game into perspective. "I always thought pitching coach, something like that, and then when this job became available — I know [Raptors vice president] John Stein and [Raptors president] Dave Baggott, I've known them for five or six years — I figured I might as well throw my hat in the ring and see what comes out. I was going to send my resumé, but the letter I wrote said, 'What could I tell you that you don't already know? All I can tell you is, I'm interested running your ballclub.'"

Like the players who traveled to Ogden to play independent baseball, all Willy wanted was a chance. When the Raptors ownership put their faith in him, he had one. The question was, could he do the job and could he do it well? Years spent sitting in the bullpen or on the bus second-guessing managers and grumbling softly finally yielded to the opportunity to actually make the decisions himself. As a former player, Ambos naturally figured that his experience could translate into a vision for his players, that they would respond to without hesitation. But when the season began, that optimism had to be balanced against the reality of managing a professional baseball club.

"It'll be great to run a ball club," he recalled thinking before he got the opportunity. "These guys will do whatever I want them to do. You just have those rose-colored glasses on and everything's going to work out great because I'm a great communicator and they'll want to play for me and this and that and you can't ever expect all the hurdles that you have to jump — you can't. Because if you did, you would never take the fucking job."

From the first meeting with the press to the first experience "babysitting" his players to the pressures placed on him by the ownership, Ambos found that managing professionally was not just about filling out the lineup card and determining who would warm up in the bullpen. "Dealing with the front office, making appearances, making speeches to rookies, dealing with fans — if your team wins, you're a great fucking guy; if they lose, you're a bum" — is how Ambos described the actual day-to-day life of a professional manager. "The players think that when we lost a game that they feel bad about it. I feel bad about it, but there's always reverberations and shit rolls downhill, and I'm usually the middleman so I have to eat shit and give shit at the same time. A lot of the times I don't even relay some of the crap that comes from the hierarchy solely because I'm trying to protect them, but they don't understand that, so when I do give shit they go, 'Oh, Skip's just given us a fuckin' hard time,' when in fact after every loss I have to swallow shit."

Certainly nobody told him that it would be easy, and given Ambos's competitive nature, managing would not be as rewarding if it were not challenging and draining. Many of the disappointments of the job disappeared once the game began and the thrill of his continuing involvement with baseball encompassed most of his thoughts. Winning eliminated almost all the rest. But one of the biggest frustrations of the job simply could not go away, and Ambos dealt with it daily — he was no longer a player, and as much as he would have loved to turn back the clock and give himself a second chance, or at least be able to live vicariously through some of his players, he was stuck in time and in the manager's chair.

"There's no compensation for not playing, never will be," he said of the desire to replicate the rush of competing. "I'd give my eyeteeth to be where some of these guys are if I could. One of the frustrating things about it is there are certain guys you take as they are, yet there's other guys you see something in and you try to give them — I can't give these guys any physical tools — the only thing I can give them is maybe a shortcut or something that might register and put them over the top. That's all you can do, and when you get a guy and you try to work with him and he's not receptive — they just don't get it — that becomes so frustrating because you just want to grab the ball and throw it and say, 'This is how you fuckin' do it, asshole.'"

For the rookie manager, every game brought a new learning experience and every off-the-field incident taught a new lesson. Experimenting with motivational styles and disciplinary techniques, Ambos muddled through the difficulties presented by the two-dozen personalities and ambitions on the team. Bristling, but coping, he managed to stave off the intrusions of the ownership, including threats that his job would not last the season. Dealing with fans, the media, and the demands of his family was often stressful and disheartening. Through it all it was Ambos's love for the game that not only allowed him to cope with the difficulties of the job but made him grudgingly enjoy the ride.

"No matter what I do with my life, I'll always be involved with baseball in some capacity, whether it's with my high-school team or professionally or college," he said. "You just can't turn it off because if you adapt to baseball, your life's attitude is based on baseball. Baseball is based on life, also based on failure. You hit three out of ten, you're doing good. In life you have to learn how to deal with struggles and failures. I've seen guys that just walk away from it. I could never figure that out because they never had that love for the game."

That does not mean that Ambos necessarily aspires to go all the way with his new managerial career. After dealing with professional players from the manager's seat for only one year, he knows that major-league managers must face even more stress. "I don't know how big-league managers manage," he confessed. "I don't know how you can do that. How do you motivate a guy that's making seven million dollars a year. He walks off the field and says, 'Fuck you, Skip.' What are you going to do, fine him? You fine him five grand he'll pull his wallet out right there, because you know when push comes to shove, and there's a problem between manager and ballplayer, who goes — manager. It's amazing. I can't even fathom managing at the big-league level. I deal with one or two reporters, maybe the occasional TV interview. These guys have cameras and sixteen beat writers and everything else going on. I can't imagine what they go through. It's scary.

"Being a rookie skipper you kind of have to keep everything in check. It's so hard and frustrating sometimes because you know that your guys are capable of doing better and they're just not, and you don't know how to drill it out of them, and sooner or later you just resign yourself to the fact that they're either going to do the job or they're not going to do the job. That's a tough thing to do because you can't play, you're not an active participant. You're an innocent bystander most times."

Sometimes Ambos was even moved to seek divine assistance. One Sunday during the season, he rallied his team and told us that there was going to be a "baseball chapel" in the bullpen before the game. Not surprisingly, the entire team flocked to the "voluntary" revival. Father Jonathan Vorhees, an old friend of Ambos's, strode into the bullpen area wearing a priestly black shirt that looked like it was far too dark for the more than one-hundred-degree heat. Bowing my head in the only sign of reverence I could think of, I saw rather unpriestly Birkenstock sandals on his feet as he delivered his message. With a lesson that never once mentioned that the Bible actually begins with a baseball verse — "In the big inning" — Father Vorhees talked about the need to take advantage of the time allotted to us in this life. Overhead, the public address system blared that "time keeps on slipping, slipping, slipping into the future," Steve Miller making the case almost as eloquently. I don't know if the heavenly guidance helped us, but it was a nice thought on Ambos's part and it was certainly easier on the plastic chairs.

"Trust your instincts," he advised first-time managers. "Don't second-guess yourself. Let what baseball has taught you dictate what you do. There's nothing you can do that hasn't been done already. You can't relearn the game. The game is here. It's been here for a long, long time and there's nothing you can do as a manager — whether it's a hit-and-run or a pitchout or anything — everything's been done. All you can do is try and communicate what you want done to your players, put them in a position to perform, and then hope that they are able to do so. The toughest thing, especially for me being as volatile as I am, is to keep my emotions in check. I've always been self-aware and if there's one thing I wish I could control more it is my emotions, and I haven't been able to do that."

That was a point that did not need to be emphasized to the Raptors players, and as the conflict between coaches and players deepened, whether Ambos could curtail his anger was a major question. But by his side, Ambos had a coach who tempered his fury with a level-headed, cerebral approach to the game. While Rich Morales often softened Ambos's intensity, he was just as unforgiving when it came to dealing with players who did not give baseball the effort he felt it deserved.

When Ambos took the job managing the Raptors, he did not hesitate to call his friend and former teammate to be by his side as his coach and confidant. They shared a love and respect for the game and a disdain for anyone who did not. Over and over throughout the season, Morales and Ambos would commiserate over the injustice of high bonuses paid to average players, the poor talent level of the minors after baseball expansion, and how they would give anything to have another shot to play the game, give it the effort it deserves, and see their careers culminate in a promotion to the show.

When one of their players dogged it, they were angry, but they were downright enraged when a player for an affiliated team denied the game an honest effort. While Josh Kirtlan laughed on the bench

Raptors manager Willy Ambos makes his point to a Pioneer League umpire. Always intense and passionate about the game, Ambos was often less than subtle in expressing his feelings to the men in blue, or to his players. Steven D. Conlin photograph reprinted with permission.

about the poor performance of a Dodgers outfielder, Morales was quick to point out that the outfielder was taking Kirtlan's job. Josh smiled, but Morales was dead serious. Nothing hurts more than seeing someone make a mockery of what you hold dear. Morales and Ambos loved the game of baseball enough that even after being released they returned to remain close to it. Watching players treat the game with a nonchalance and approach their playing careers as if their days in uniform were endless, they could just shake their heads and wish that they had one more chance to combine their ability with their knowledge of the requisite effort to succeed. Short of that, they could just scowl at lazy ballplayers and immature young men giving the game they loved a second-class effort.

Growing up, Rich Morales could not help but love baseball. The game was not only all around him, it actually put bread on his family's table. "When I was born, my father was a minor-league shortstop for the Chicago White Sox," he said. "He didn't see me for three weeks. He was on the road when I was born, but he did hit a home run the night I was born. That was a rare feat in itself because he wasn't a power-hitting shortstop."

Rich was born in a little suburb called Pacifica, just outside San Francisco, but home was wherever his father was playing baseball. "We followed him all the way up to the big leagues," Morales said of his nomadic childhood, "so I had my friends during the school year as a kid growing up, but I was everywhere, and I didn't know any different. It wasn't like baseball was forced upon me, it was just one of those things — 'What does your dad do?' 'Oh he's a baseball player.' 'What do you want to do?' 'I want to be a baseball player.'"

If it was not going to be baseball, some sport seemed destined to attract Rich's attention. His father's father was a professional boxer and his mother's father was a professional soccer player in Glasgow, Scotland. But in the end it was baseball and following his father that turned out to be the focus of his young life. "I was born in 1964, and he first got called up in 1967, at the beginning of the year, so I can't really fathom that," he said of his earliest memories. "But I can remember 1969 when he was up there for a little bit of time. I can remember living in the Delprado Hotel, which at the time was one of the swankiest hotels in Chicago, and then until the beginning of 1973, when he was traded to the Padres, I can very much remember exactly where I was.

"I always thought everyone's dad played big-league baseball. I didn't really think that my dad was anybody different except that I noticed that kids would always want to be friends with me just for the fact that my dad played in the big leagues. I never thought it was that special until I started noticing that people paid more attention to me because of who my father was, even though he wasn't a Pete Rose–caliber or Willie Stargell–caliber player. He was a big-league player and you get a lot of attention that way. One kid came up to me in the third grade and said, 'Are you Rich Morales?' I said, 'Yeah.' He goes, 'Your dad's Rich Morales?' And I said, 'Yeah, he is.' And he goes, 'Can I be your best friend?' Just out of the blue in the playground one day growing up in Pacifica he said that to me, and it was kind of funny because if my dad was Joe the groundskeeper, he wouldn't even have spoken to me."

Rich got to use Comiskey Park as a playground, meet some of baseball's brightest players, and learn the craft of the game from its stars. While Rich developed from a toddler to a Little League catcher, his father's career rose from the minor leagues to the Chicago White Sox to the San Diego Padres but eventually came to an end. "It was a shock for me because all of a sudden my father wasn't a baseball player anymore," he said of his father's retirement. "But for me it was great because my dad was always around and I didn't look at it, 'Oh God, my dad's not a professional player anymore, what am I going to do?' It wasn't like that. My dad was with me all the time, so I loved it."

With his father's playing career at an end, it was time for Rich to concentrate on his own baseball ambitions. "I love baseball," he declared simply, "not because my father instilled the love of the game in me. When you grow up around it, if your father's a great musician, chances are that you are going to either love music or hate it. I happen to love baseball. I grew up around it and I loved it on my own. When my father got out, he knew I wanted to be a baseball player. My father didn't tie me to a post and hit ground balls to me like some people are led to believe. He used to say to me, 'Don't expect me to come in your room on Saturday morning at nine and take you up to the field and throw batting practice to you, because I'm not going to do that. But if you come into my room at nine in the morning and ask me to throw batting practice for you, I'll do it.'"

Morales's career took him to the University of San Francisco for his college ball, where he started as a freshman and made the all-freshman team as a catcher. As a senior he hit .355 and threw out 50 percent of base stealers. But then a broken foot derailed his hopes of being drafted, and while teams expressed interest, nobody chose the five-feet-nine-inch singles-hitting catcher. He went through the tryout circuit and played summer ball back in California, but nobody picked him up. At the state championship it seemed as if Rich Morales might have reached the end of his career.

"It was the saddest point in my life," he said of that final game, "because I figured that was it, it's gone, and I cried my eyes out for four hours — just bawled continuously. It was tough. I think it was more a part of my life than the average kid because of the fact that baseball put clothes on my back and food on the table for my entire life. It got me my education — I had a baseball scholarship. So everything I had up to that point was all because of baseball, and all of a sudden it's gone. It's taken away from me. So I went out in the working world and was working for an advertising agency in Brisbane, California."

But the lure of the baseball diamond was too strong and Morales began to coach on the side while he became accustomed to working nine to five. That eased him back into playing Sunday baseball, which quickly rekindled his passion for the game. He was still in shape and playing well and could not resist the urge to give his career playing baseball one more chance. "I wrote the four clubs that were interested in me as a senior — the Cubs, Padres, Mariners, and the Tigers," he said, as if he were sending a resumé to any prospective employer. "I just said, 'Hey, I'm still in shape, give me chance. I'll sign for a hot dog and a Coke, be a bullpen catcher. I just want a chance to play.'"

In what Morales called a miraculous turn of events, a catcher in the California League suddenly pulled an arm muscle and the Mariners followed up on Rich's letter. "I get a phone call at work saying, 'Do you want to play professional baseball?' and it was just a no-brainer."

Having been away from the game for two years, Morales cherished the opportunity to play and approached his new minor-league career with a zealous diligence. Playing for the San Bernardino Spirit, he met Willy Ambos. Like Ambos, Morales did not always get the chance to play, but kept himself in a constant state of readiness. Every appearance in a game was a blessing and every time he put on the uniform was one more game that he was never supposed to play.

"There wasn't always a game tomorrow for me," he explained as he talked of his approach to his career. "That was instilled in me by my father at a young age. He always said, 'Always play hard, because your next at-bat might be your last.' He used to say that when I was in Little League. And it's more appropriate when you're a professional because in Little League you know you're invincible, but his thinking was, you might get run over by a car, you might blow out your knee, you might break your arm and never be able to play this game, and you don't want to look back at your last game and your last at-bat saying, 'I could have run a little harder,' or 'I could have played that game a little harder.' I've always felt that if you play hard, regardless of what your talent is, especially when you don't have much talent, nobody notices that you don't have talent. It's when you have talent and don't play hard that people notice. Play hard, play like it's going to be your last game, because it might be. That's one of the things I always adhered to."

When Rich Morales Sr. visited the Raptors, it was easy to see not only where his son developed his love for the game but also his fatherly manner in instruction. Watching the ex–major leaguer slip roles from father to instructor was charming. One moment he was expressing concern for his son's lingering stomach illness and the next he was at second base talking to infielders about positioning. In both roles, however, his passion came through. "This game is better than all of us," he said to players as an instructor while he offered fielding tips, but as a father he quickly reminded us that best thing to do with your baseball experience was to "pass it on."

Before he began to worry about passing the Morales message on, Rich Jr. was still concentrating on his own playing career, and after playing the 1989 season in San Bernardino, Morales went to spring training with the Mariners looking to make the double-A club and place his unlikely comeback firmly on track to put him in the majors.

After playing an inspired spring training, Rich received the heart-breaking news that he was being reassigned to single-A ball. He took the news well, but was crushed inside and only slightly buoyed by the promise that he would serve as the Mariners' organizational catcher whenever there was a vacancy in their minor-league system. He reported back to San Bernardino but held out little hope for his future. After fifteen games he had not caught an inning, had not had a pinch-hit appearance, and only stepped inside the chalk lines during practice. When his manager finally called him into his office, Rich thought his career was over. He received what might have been worse news.

Because of injuries to catchers playing in the extended spring training league, the Mariners were sending him back to training camp to help out the organization. "It's baseball's version of purgatory," Morales recalled with a shudder, "because you're with a bunch of kids who can't speak English — seventeen, eighteen years old. They all throw ninety-five miles an hour. They don't know where the ball's going, so you're going to get killed behind the plate or at it."

When his assignment for five days dragged on into its twelfth day, he received even more unlikely news. "We were playing against the Brewers in Chandler, Arizona, and one of our players came running around the dugout," he remembered with a smile, "and said, 'Rich, you got to get on an airplane, you're catching in Colorado Springs tonight. You're going up to triple-A.'" He went from the bottom of the barrel to the verge of the majors in one day. After spending a three-week stint in triple-A, Rich traveled throughout the Mariners system and ended the year as the everyday catcher for the single-A club. But when the year came to its end, Morales figured his life in the minors had come to its conclusion.

"I figured my career was over," he said. "I just turned twenty-six years old and I wasn't a prospect, but I do know that the coaches in the organization liked me because I kept my mouth shut, I played hard, and I played smart. Some of them recommended to our minor-league director that I become a player-coach or a coach. That's exactly what I wanted. Then it was one of those things where during the off-season I was rehabbing my knee. The day the doctors released me so I could play, the very next day I got a certified letter in the mail, I thought it was my contract. It was my release papers, and that's a very sad, empty feeling when you see the thing that says you've been unconditionally released because you're like a leaf floating in the wind — what do I do now?"

While Morales tried to find himself a coaching job, major-league organizations seemed only to be interested in bringing him aboard as a backup catcher. Having already played the role of an organizational catcher, he was reluctant to go backward in his career when fortune again smiled on him. A representative of the Office of the Commissioner of Baseball called inquiring as to whether Morales would be interested in coaching with one of their cooperative teams, semi-independent teams maintained to develop talent that for some reason did not fit into other teams in the minors. With an offer finally seeking him out, he took a chance and asked for more. "I don't want to coach, I want to manage," he said, boldly approaching the job. But the commissioner's office was concerned about allowing a twenty-six-year-old to manage.

Morales convinced them that it did not matter if he were twenty-six or thirty-two — a first-year manager was a first-year manager. All he wanted was the opportunity. Finally, the commissioner's office called. "He said, 'Well, the good news is you're going to manage one of our clubs, the bad news is, you're going to be in Pocatello, Idaho,' and I couldn't have cared less." He spent the 1991 season managing in the Pioneer League and, given the opportunity, the challenge became whether coaching could fulfill him as playing did and whether he could handle the life of a manager.

"I was trying to decide whether I wanted to be like my father," he said of his foray into managing. "I saw my father managing in the minor leagues for a number of years and wanted to see if I wanted to live out of a suitcase. I wanted to see if that was part of my life and I found out that yes, I did love it, but at the same time, it gets lonely. As much as you might be friendly with the players, you can't hang out with them, and if you don't have a girlfriend with you, you spend a lot of lonely hours, and so what I always used to do to fill my time was spend more hours with the players on the field.

"It was one of those things that as much as baseball has given me, baseball has taken away from me. I mean, I didn't have a stable home life, my parents were always fighting because when you're on the road all the time it's rough on a family. It was one of those things where I wanted to see if I wanted to be an adult the same way I was a kid, growing up around that environment. But I don't have any regrets because I absolutely love what I do. I mean, I wouldn't be here right now if I didn't love what I do. A lot of people look at it as a great summer job. Yes, it is a great summer job, but I want to see the game of baseball played the right way. I want to see kids receive coaching that I never really received."

Having seen the benefits of good coaching and knowing what the right instruction could mean in a career, Morales wanted to be everything in a coach that he would have wanted for himself. He was philosophical about what it means to be entrusted with the power and responsibility of a manager. "When you have a kid out there, you have a piece of clay," he said, "and you can mold that kid into something productive, not just on the field but off the field, by how you interact with that kid. I always thought that it was a privilege to have the capacity to do that, and I felt I did and I owed it to the game of baseball to do that. I love baseball so much that I just want to see it played the right way, I want to see kids given the opportunity to be coached, to have played for somebody, and to say, 'Man, he made a difference in my life.' Whether it has to do with anything that he does on the field. I mean, 99 percent of these kids are never going to make it to the big leagues, but six or seven years down the road if that kid still remembers me in some way when he's out in the working world, then that makes it worth it."

After the year in Pocatello, Morales coached for the Salinas Spurs and then traveled to Czechoslovakia to spread the gospel of our national pastime with Baseball International. But when Ambos called with another opportunity to coach young players, Morales quickly agreed. Observing him from a player's vantage point, his love and passion for the game was easy to see. Whether instructing us in fundamentals or warning us, "Keep your head out of the stands, you'll be there soon enough," Morales was always attempting to help us further our dreams. Looking to the future, he had dreams of his own to pursue.

"My ultimate goal when I was a kid," he said, "if I can't make it as a player in the big leagues, I want to coach in the big leagues, and I still have that goal. Is that going to happen? Probably not. It's very hard to move up as a coach in the big leagues considering that you never made it to the big leagues. But it has happened. That's my ultimate goal. Realistic goal? I'd like to manage rookie ball until I die because this is the level where you can still teach kids, and this is where they need to learn it, because kids aren't learning in the triple-A level, they're not learning in the double-A level, this is where they learn. I'd love to do that the rest of my life because I think you have a direct influence not only on kids and their lives but on the game itself, and I just don't think enough teaching is going on at the lower levels as much as it should. So I would love to be a minor-league manager forever."

To players who are looking to make the jump to coaching, Morales offered simple advice: "I would say, don't expect the players to play like you did because they can't and they won't. You've just got to take them for what they are as players and try to mold them in the right way. That was the thing my father told me a long time ago because I was almost a deranged player out there. I played hard, I played to win — that's all I wanted to do is win. And he said, 'You're going to be a coach someday. You're going to have to tone that intensity down. You can't expect players to play as hard as you did because nobody's going to.' So that's what I tell a young coach, what I told kids that I coached who are now coaches. I tell them, 'Patience, you have to have patience. There's going to be times when you lose your patience, but most of all you've got to keep it positive and don't expect them to play like you did.'"

Both Morales and Ambos were passionate about the game they loved and the almost sanctified opportunity to make a career in baseball. Seeing their players waste a chance to establish a career in professional baseball was often more than they could take. What was worse than players wasting their gift was that they were wasting their gift on a

Coach Rich Morales (left) with his father Rich Morales Sr., who was visiting Ogden to see his son's team. The elder Morales played for the Chicago White Sox and San Diego Padres. Both have baseball in their blood and look as if they could still take the field today. Brett Mandel photograph reprinted with permission.

team run by two men who wanted so badly to continue their own involvement in the game.

For Willy and Mo the challenge was not just to instill in their players a love of the game and a respect for the opportunity to play professionally. It was not just to teach. Having seen their playing careers fall short of their ambitions, coaching was all that was left of their major dreams. The challenge was to take this bunch of players — rejects and discarded talent — and make them a success. Willy Ambos and Rich Morales needed to make a serious run at the pennant and show the baseball world not only that their players had talent but that they themselves had the talent necessary to move their own careers forward.

Pennant Racing

Back at Simmons Field, after our successful but divisive road trip through Great Falls and Billings, players and coaches unpacked the bus and dispersed quickly, eager to get away to nurse bruised egos and crumpled spirits. Brett Smith and I threw our bags in the car and anxiously sped out of the parking lot without a word to our teammates or coaches. We were not going to waste another moment of our second day off of the season dealing with Raptors acrimony.

To welcome us back from the road, our hosts, Frank and Ruby Sanders, had planned the perfect homecoming — a family barbecue. Home cooking and the comfort of our foster family was just what we needed to take our minds off baseball and Frank and Ruby's children and grandchildren were eager to interact with their new ballplayer foster relations. The adults were fascinated about life in the minors and the youngest grandchildren bombarded us with questions and regaled us with tales of their own baseball experience. The adolescents played it cool and pretty much ignored us after a perfunctory introduction. Forgetting all about playing baseball for the evening, we played catch, ate real food, and told stories through the long dinner and into the night.

Frank and Ruby Sanders had more than opened their house to us, they made us a part of their family. Before games they would come over to the fence and chat encouragement and during games they cheered madly when we came to the plate. When we returned from the road, we found our dirty clothes washed and folded, our beds made, and our room tidied. If I needed to borrow the family truck, all I had to do was ask. When Smith's car needed some work, Frank had a family member take care of it while we were away.

On the road, Smith and I bought souvenir spoons for Ruby's collection and at home we had their granddaughter take part in the race around the bases. Although our time together was brief, and made briefer still by our conflicting work schedules, it was reassuring to know that there was someone at home who cared if we were eating well, if we were getting playing time, and if we were happy.

After a day spent puttering around the golf course and happily devouring corn on the cob and barbecued chicken, we were back at Simmons Field, rested from our day off, and suddenly all smiles. Gone were the snide remarks traded back and forth as well as the tantrums and temper flare-ups that had been common when our road trip stretched past a week. Having taken a day off to recuperate aching muscles and stung pride, we were loose and ready to once again enjoy playing baseball.

Since we had been away for a long road trip, we were not surprised to find that some changes had been made at Simmons Field. A new batboy suited up for the Raptors but had no idea about the torment that he would endure. After he approached me asking for the bag of hashish, "you know, for the bats," I knew that he was in trouble. The other players had sent him on a wild goose chase and it was not going to end with me. Pointing to pitcher Doug Smyly, I said, "number thirty-two usually carries the hashish." The batboy was off and running.

For the youngsters, it must be a strange mix of emotions, being so near the ballplayers and the game, yet paying for the privilege by enduring the taunting and teasing of a team of overgrown adolescents. But even though they were known to us as Booger or Snacks, we were always ready to play pepper with them or pat them on the helmet after they chased down a foul ball. I saw our new batboy, breathless as game time approached walking toward the umpires gathered around home plate to review ground rules and preside over the exchange of lineup cards. Oblivious to the trick being pulled on him, he asked the head umpire for the hashish before Ambos could shoo him away. If he lasted long enough he would certainly be asked to find the "key to the batter's box," "a bag of left-handed curveballs," or "a right-handed broom." Eventually, the period of his rite of passage would expire, but for now he was wise to ask someone he trusted before following any instruction from any of the Raptors.

We started our homestand on a high note as Danny Miller notched his seventh win and a tremendous home run by Shane Jones led us to a five-to-one victory over the visiting Great Falls Dodgers. But two Raptors infielders had their minds on matters other than baseball. Upset with life in the minors and questioning whether he was playing baseball for himself or for his parents, Chris Amos had made up his mind to quit the team, work for a living, and finish his schooling as soon as possible. Mike Carrigg, however, was considering a more permanent life change. After the game, he was going to ask his longtime girlfriend to marry him. As we dressed in our clubhouse, we wondered if Amos would leave and if Lisa would say yes.

The next day Carrigg's girlfriend wore an engagement ring and Chris Amos wore a smile, but his happiness was more relief than joy. Frustrated about not being able to perform well after an early-season groin injury, tired of a life in the minors that he saw going no further than the Raptors, and irritated by the friction between himself and the coaching staff, Amos decided that he no longer belonged on the field.

"I never really wanted to play pro," he said bluntly, as if pro ball wasn't the dream of tens of thousands of youngsters. "My dad talked me into it." He figured a summer as a ballplayer was as good a job as any other. But as soon as he arrived in Utah, his doubts began to materialize. "Ever since I got to Ogden, I was like, 'What am I doing here?'" he recalled. By establishing early friendships and enjoying success on the field, Amos was able to become excited about playing baseball, but as the season wore on he said that "there wasn't a day that I didn't think about going home."

Playing through hitless games and becoming worn down living on buses and eating fast food, Amos began to think about finishing school and beginning his life. The sedentary nature of life off the field began to grate on him. "I feel like I'm a loser because I don't do anything during the day," he said.

Walking away from the game, Amos was philosophical. "I tried," he said. "I saw what it was like and I didn't like it and I know it's not for me. Baseball is just a game — too much money involved, too much politics, just too long of a road — if you're not a first-round draft pick, you're nothing. If it's your dream, then go for it. I don't think it was ever my dream. I think it was more my parents'."

A subdued announcement from Ambos during stretching was all the notice the team received of Amos's defection to the real world. Weeks later during a Raptors youth camp a young fan asked me what happened to Chris Amos. When I told him that Amos quit, he looked at me quizzically. "How could anybody quit baseball?" he asked, incredulous. "I don't know," was the only answer that I could honestly give.

In Ogden for an extended homestand, the demand on players for public appearances increased dramatically. Raptors youth baseball clinics, appearances in Utah's Pioneer Day parades, and autograph signings at a movie opening kept players as busy off the field as we were on the diamond. With oppressive heat topping one hundred degrees each day, I was thrilled to draw movie-theater duty and had to sign only a few autographs before enjoying a movie in air-conditioned comfort.

Enjoying the time at home, Smith and I joined some teammates on a trip from Ogden to Salt Lake City for a night out. At one night club we ran into a fellow professional athlete who was getting considerably more attention than we were. Basketball star Bobby Hurley, in town for the Rocky Mountain Revue summer league, was drawing quite a crowd of well-wishers. Even though we were in a pennant race while Hurley was only playing exhibition basketball, we Raptors couldn't buy attention. It was a good thing, because the money saved went to bail out a pitcher who struck out with the Salt Lake City police. After being ignored in favor of another professional athlete and almost losing a player to the Utah penal league, returning to the adulation and friendly confines of Simmons Field never felt so good.

Sporting a new close-cropped hairdo and a cocky, "hit-me-if-you-can" attitude, Paul O'Hearn next took the mound. The Raptors' number two pitcher was often overshadowed by Danny Miller, but throwing ground balls and befuddling the Dodgers, O'Hearn picked up his own seventh win. It was gratifying but frustrating to be doing so well. After being drafted by the Chicago Cubs, O'Hearn passed up the opportunity to play professional ball and went to college. But when he went undrafted after his college career despite posting a twenty-four-and-three record for Arizona State University and Northern Alabama University, he came to Ogden looking for a second chance. Taking another shot at baseball with the Raptors, O'Hearn was having great success, but it was tinged with the possibility that it could be coming too late in his career. Even with his outstanding performance, would a major-league organization sign a crafty twenty-four-year-old? "I doubt it," he answered during the waning weeks of the season. "My age — and I don't throw super-hard — the way they're talking, they're trying to package me with one of the other guys that are marketable and hopefully I get a shot at spring training. Usually when that happens they use the guy for batting practice and send him home. If someone called and said they want me, not just for spring training and they'll put me somewhere next year like a high-A or double-A, I'll think about it, but this probably is my last year of playing organized baseball."

But those thoughts could do nothing but break his concentration and O'Hearn couldn't worry about anything past his next start. Given his success, he could be nothing but upbeat. With his eight-to-nothing shutout giving us back-to-back wins, O'Hearn had cemented a new positive outlook into place. Even Willy Ambos was able to enjoy the mood as he took some time out from steering his team through a pennant race to be a family man. Ambos's son Kyle was at the park showing that, given some seasoning and assuming that he had not topped out at two-and-a-half feet tall, he could follow in his father's footsteps as a baseball star. After working on Kyle's fastball in the bullpen, it was back to pennant racing for our skipper. "Daddy's got to go to work," he said, turning his attention back to trying to extend our winning streak.

Just when everything looks optimistic, the game has a way of humbling even the most proud players. With the score tied at five in the sixth inning of our final game with the Dodgers, the still struggling

Doug O'Neill stood in at the plate looking to change the score. A fastball bore inside on him and bounced back toward the mound with a loud crack. The Dodgers pitcher quickly fielded the ball and threw to first, and even though Raptor players and coaches argued that the ball hit O'Neill, the umpire recorded the out. Doug just trudged back to the bench silently.

Watching him nurse his hand, I knew he was hurt. Tentatively testing his thumb and looking around to make sure that nobody noticed his pain, he winced and grimaced. When the Raptors finished batting, he picked up his glove and returned to the field.

The mind can only conquer the body for so long, and returning to the bench after the inning Doug could pretend no longer. As he sat down on the bench next to me I saw the thumb was already swelling. "You don't think it's broken, do you?" I asked, as if phrasing it that way would help me get a no for an answer. He simply nodded. Unable to grip a ball properly for a throw, he tapped Ambos on the shoulder and asked to be taken out of the game.

Raptors trainer Dan Overman was quick to examine the stricken center fielder and began the painful process of poking and prodding to help make a diagnosis. O'Neill just winced and reacted with obvious discomfort. He had made his own diagnosis and was clearly despondent. After two years of hand injuries, broken thumbs, hamstring pulls, and an arm fracture that had taken him from the threshold of major possibilities to a last chance with the Raptors, O'Neill's mind was preparing him for the worst.

Tommy Johnston, who had endured his own broken hand earlier in the season, observed O'Neill's examination. "Get hit in the hand?" Johnston asked helpfully. "It's the worst."

"Tell me about it," O'Neill responded, not needing to be reminded of how hand injuries had already affected his career.

While icing his hand to hold down the swelling, O'Neill stared at the field shaking his head and pursing his lips as he considered the potential significance of his injury. As the Dodgers rallied on the field, taking an eleven-to-five lead, the only change in O'Neill was his posture. Slumping on the bench he declared, "I'm outta here. I'm not going to play through this thing."

The Dodgers won, but the last thing on O'Neill's mind was the individual game. His whole career hung in the balance of a diagnosis on the following day. Having already overcome so many setbacks in his career, Doug felt the familiar dread at the prospect of enduring another injury. Bones heal and bruises go away, but self-doubt lingers.

In the end, O'Neill's worrying was for naught. The thumb was seriously bruised, not broken. After a few days of nursing it, he was back in the starting lineup. If he continued to heal his head as he had healed his body, Doug could have a bright future; if not, the mental anguishes, not the physical ones, could doom his career.

With the Billings Mustangs bringing their Northern Division–leading record to town for four games, we needed quality efforts from all our players but only managed a disappointing split in the series. A tremendous baserunning mistake, missed signs, and poor relief pitching threatened to sweep us out of our own park, but a tremendous play at the plate and some team character brought us to the starting line of the pennant race on a winning note.

Late in our second game against the Mustangs, with shortstop Tommy Johnston on second base and Tim Gavello on first, Johnston missed a hit-and-run sign, causing Gavello to be hung up in a rundown when the batter failed to make contact. Just as Gavello was tagged out near second, Johnston inexplicably bolted for third only to be tagged out to end the inning, the Raptors threat, and the last real chance to salvage a win.

After the game, Johnston was almost inconsolable. Feeling the pressure to perform, he was letting anxiety interfere with his play. The normally stoic shortstop, who stood unfazed before the most difficult groundball, was fiddling with his batting stance, working on throws before practice, and spending a good deal of time worrying about his future in baseball. His boneheaded play would certainly not put his mind at rest. Where an affiliated team stresses talent development and teaching, independent teams must win. Johnston received glares, not instruction, from coaches and the cold shoulder, not support, from teammates.

Having fallen two-and-a-half games out of first place before our last game against Billings, we were in need of a gut check. With our most crucial stretch ahead of us, Ambos and Morales addressed their troops to give them something to think about. First, Morales spoke about our inability to execute fundamental baseball, which was not only hurting the ballclub's chances of winning but endangering the longevity of players' careers. Morales threw out the names and statistics of some players who had furthered their careers after playing for other independent teams. "He's still playing," was all Morales had to remark after reading statistics. The point was simple: if we, as players, produced and executed, our careers could continue. If not, our careers would end shortly.

"Pressure is not having a uniform on right now and trying to make a fucking living without a college degree," Morales said. "Pressure is what your parents do on a mortgage payment. Pressure is not being successful on a hit-and-run. Pressure is not fielding a ground ball in a crucial situation.

"What we have here is a fire sale. You are trying to sell yourselves to an organization by playing hard, by running hard, by getting the job done." Challenging us to give our best effort as the most crucial part of the season approached, Morales asked us to consider whether we were each giving baseball the effort it deserved. "If you can't say yes," he concluded, "then you're cheating yourself, you're cheating anybody that ever believed in you, and you're cheating the game."

Ambos was more philosophical and uncharacteristically subdued. "If you feel like we're putting pressure on you," he said softly, "well, we are. That's baseball. This is an independent structure. We have to win — we have to produce. Rich and I as a staff have to produce.

"This is a tough game. It's based on failure, and how you deal with it that shows whether you are going to go on or not. The bottom line is that it is still a fuckin' game, and the only way I know how to have fun playing this game is by winning. I can jump up and down, I can scream, I can yell, Rich can scream, Rich can yell, but it's only because our expectations of your talent warrant that at some times. Sometimes I'm not so sure you think you're as good as we think you are."

After one final exhortation to victory, Ambos turned his charges loose. With outstanding defense including a play at home plate where Brett Smith saved a run by tagging out a runner in a phenomenal collision, we escaped a late-inning rally to win our final game against the Mustangs. On the bench, Smith was dazed from a concussion and barely coherent enough to enjoy teasing about how far his prescription sunglasses flew after the impact at the plate. The rest of the team was thrilled to have beaten tough righthander Jason Robbins, who came into the game with a 1.38 ERA and would go on to record a perfect game before the end of the season, and was looking forward to another day off before heading to Helena to challenge the first-place Brewers.

Our win, combined with the Brewers' getaway game loss in Lethbridge, left us just a game and a half out of first place on our way to Montana for a showdown with our Southern Division rivals. Eight of our next twelve games would be against Helena, and because these games with the Brewers would be our final head-to-head confrontations, their importance could not be overstated. The pennant race was truly beginning, but looking at the schedule we knew that it could be over too soon if we failed to perform well in the crucial stretch against Helena.

On the road to Helena, the mood on the bus was light. In the back of the bus I sat in on the Raptors floating poker game while other players tried to catch up on sleep. Under the makeshift card table, Mike Carrigg curled up in a blanket unaware that my meal money was being taken from me just above him. The bus was the quickest place to lose money playing cards, as the smallest denomination of a bet was the smallest bill in your wallet. The only time poker was more difficult was when we used an X-rated deck, which made it all too easy to tell who held the ten of diamonds or the three of spades based on the eye-popping response the cards always drew. Based on my losings on the bus, I would have to skip two meals a day for the trip to break even — or take some tips from my experienced teammates to save some money.

Away from the card table, the Raptors players had a knack for trying to work anything for free. For players on a limited budget, freebies became another source of income. Finding a bar to give out free

Long bus rides on lonely highways meant pleanty of time to dream about the major leagues — and plenty of time to lose a trip's worth of meal money playing poker. Brett Smith, Shane Jones, and Don Baker look to add a few dollars to their meager salaries as the bus rolls on. Steven D. Conlin photograph reprinted with permission.

pitchers was the equivalent of a twenty-five dollar bonus every week. Golfing for free each homestand was worth at least ten. Sometimes these minor-league discounts were borderline thievery. If a player's picture was in the paper, he would pay fifty cents in an honor box and take ten copies. Practice baseballs disappeared at least once a day, and hotel towels and pillows did not stand a chance.

Other money-saving schemes were more like assault with a deadly weapon. Spurred on by a desire to save money and a certain conformist tendency, many of the Raptors players were getting haircuts from the two resident team barbers, Tommy Johnston and Tim Gavello. Using only a pair of clippers, they gave players a tight fade. While I avoided our designated hair stylists, most of my teammates went under the blade and almost all exited with the same thought: in a week or two it will all blend together and look good. I would just agree with them as they laughed nervously and took a second glance in the mirror.

At Kindrick Field in Helena, a big crowd was on hand, milling around the general admission area and pacing above the Raptors dugout where the Brewers picnic section offered fans a chance to barbecue right at the game. The smell of food wafted into the Raptors dugout but Brewers fans were not about to share.

Unfortunately, my teammates decided to let the food — or something else — distract them through the first seven innings of the game, committing too many physical and mental errors to count. A comeback tied the game in the top of the ninth but was not enough as the Brewers won the game in the bottom of the inning to take the first lap of the pennant race.

To shake things up for the pennant race, Ambos and Morales juggled the roommate assignments on the road. Although I would normally pal around with Brett Smith, in Helena I made my way into town with my new roommate, Troy Doezie, another local Utah product whose wife and daughter were fixtures at Raptors home games. Bumping into Smith outside the only place in the Pioneer League to get a decent bagel — the hangout where Smith and I ate practically every breakfast and lunch each time we were in Helena — I felt as if he had caught me cheating on him. Even though I knew that Smith and I were still tight, I felt like I should tell him, "It's not what you think, we're just friends."

Although the Raptors were playing at Kindrick Field, the people of Helena were focused on the Last Chance Stampede, not baseball. The rodeo was in town. Down Last Chance Gulch a parade had the people of Montana's capital lining the curbs. Parents and children waved small American flags while dogs looked on obliviously. Women in turn-of-the-century dresses rode side-saddle and others costumed as Indians or gypsies waved to the crowd. An acid-flashback sixties float promoting flower power was decorated with the wares of a local florist, and Flintstone look-alikes rode a local construction company's dinosaur float, complete with an earthmover made up to look like a brontosaurus.

The Last Chance Stampede was personal and accessible, just like the minor leagues. As floats and riders passed the assembled crowd, I could hear participants in the parade calling out to familiar faces along the route. With the end of the parade, perhaps some of the participants and spectators would be heading out to the Brewers game and "stupid pet trick" night at Kindrick Field, where they could enjoy the same small-town accessibility and maybe a hometown win.

Neither Danny Miller, who lost for the first time, nor the consistently effective Paul O'Hearn could earn wins in our last two games in Helena. Errors doomed Miller's performance, and an inability to execute finished off another valiant effort by O'Hearn. Despite threatening in the top of the ninth, the Raptors could not execute fundamental baseball as Tommy Johnston swung through a hit-and-run ball and then failed to bring home a runner. In the bottom of the ninth, however, a perfectly executed hit-and-run completed the Brewers' three-game sweep. The difference between winning and losing was execution. One team did, one team did not. After the humiliating series we were four and a half games out of first place.

The significance of the sweep was not lost on the coaching staff, who had more than enough pressure on their hands for this road trip. Team president and part-owner Dave Baggott was along for the road trip, substituting on KLO radio for Kurt Wilson, whose father was ailing. Baggott, who was definitely a hands-on owner — often taking a break from his executive activities to tend the field, drop by the dugout, or participate in an impromptu punting contest — sometimes brought the hands-on contact too close for comfort. The road trips usually meant a break from ownership's constant habit of being underfoot, hanging out in the coaches' office, and making sure they had plenty of input about how the team was run. There was no mistaking that, even though the team president was just a radio voice for the trip, Ambos and Morales felt Baggott's eyes on them. After the third loss to Helena, the bus took players to eat dinner while Baggott, Ambos, and Morales ate near the park so they could discuss the state of the team in private.

Despite the fact that the team was in a tailspin and Baggott, Ambos, and Morales were all concerned, as our road trip extended to Butte the tone was lighthearted. In the front of the bus, discussion of baseball was at a minimum. Instead, everyone exchanged stories of favorite childhood cartoon shows. Even though the fate of the Raptors could hinge on the next few games, I fell asleep listening to Willy Ambos sing a weary version of the theme from Spiderman. "Is he strong? Listen, Bud, he's got radioactive blood. Can he swing from a thread? Take a look overhead. Lookout. Here comes the Spiderman."

"I don't need to tell you how important these next two games are," Willy Ambos said as the Raptors bus pulled up to the Butte Copper Kings Alumni Coliseum the next day. Being off the pace in the pennant race was not all that Ambos had to deal with. Losing had bred discontent and some of the Raptors players, especially those who did not see a long career in professional baseball ahead of them, were looking forward to the season's end.

"My understanding is that there are some guys who are just biding their time and waiting for the last few days to tick off on the big meter here and can't wait for the season to be over," Ambos began again, his pace quickening with emotion. "Well, if that is you, I consider that to be a tremendous yellow streak on your part, and if that is the feeling you have, please do us a favor, be a man, pack your shit and go home 'cause all I've ever asked for from day one is to go hard or go home.

"The season is winding down but I don't want the last game of the regular season to be the end of the season. I want to play that little bit further to see how far we can take this group. Any personal bruised egos, anything like that, hey, shit happens, fuckin' deal with it. It's time to step forward and do your job — now let's beat the fuck out of these losers!"

There were no hurrahs or yippees screamed from the bus, only quiet resolve. The Raptors players that Ambos's words could still reach walked off the bus with their heads down, focusing on the task at hand. The others marched into the stadium thinking that there could be only a few more talks like that left in the year.

There was a big crowd on hand to watch Billy Bird, the mascot of the Cardinals' triple-A affiliate, perform his high jinks and cheer on the hometown Copper Kings. Coming into Alumni Coliseum usually meant morose spectators and plenty of empty seats, but the visiting mascot had a good-sized crowd packing the grandstand. They had plenty to cheer about as the Copper Kings jumped out to a five-to-nothing lead in the first inning and held off the futile effort of the Raptors to win an eight-to-two decision. But suddenly, losing our fourth game in a row did not seem like such a disaster.

In Butte we abandoned the play and demeanor of a contending team and adopted the attitude of a team content to play out the season. Instead of concentrating on the score, we seemed focused on everything but baseball. As always, Jeremy Winget, who had played for Butte the previous year, had a cheering section that screamed, "We love you, Jeremy," when he came to bat. In the dugout, the league's laziest batboy slouched next to the Gatorade cooler while players had to pick up their own bats and helmets. Overly hormonal thirteen-year-old girls in the stands flirted with players on the bench.

Watching Billy Bird cavort on the field broke up the tension of losing quite nicely as he danced at third base with Shane Jones. Jones was doing his best to remain emotionally focused as his rookie season moved into its final month but was still occasionally throwing batting helmets or barking out loud bursts of profanity after unsuccessful at-bats. Seeing the intense player dancing with the mascot was encouraging. If he could only enjoy his time at the plate as much as the impromptu tango, he could focus his energies on his talents instead of his frustration with the injustices of baseball.

While the Raptors bench was in stitches enjoying the lighter side of baseball, losing just did not seem so terrible. Even when an overly aggressive umpire egged on Ambos, eventually resulting in Ambos's third ejection of the season, players could barely hide grins. On the bench we bit our lips and looked at each other, mischievously delighting in the stream of obscenities and foul protests emanating from our manager's mouth. When Ambos finally made his way up the dugout tunnel, players gleefully began to concoct scenarios to get Ambos to put on Billy Bird's costume and return to the field to get even with the umpire. Even though the bird seemed to genuinely appreciate the thought, the game continued without another appearance from Ambos.

A lifelong Phillies fan, I knew all too well what happens when the hope of the season gives way to simply playing games. When the pennant race is all but over, the play of a single player, the simple pleasures of the average game, and the fun of a day at the ballpark replace the passionate rooting for victory. I remember too many seasons watching the Phils fade from contention while the most fun of going to a game was watching the Phillie Phanatic work the crowd.

Baseball, even when played by two teams out of pennant contention, is a marvelous game. But the owners, coaching staff, and most players on the Raptors still wanted the game to be more than thrilling. They wanted it to include the ecstatic euphoria that only a pennant chase can bring, where teams are playing for their playoff lives with every single pitch. Unless something happened soon, however, the Raptors would be playing for nothing more than pride.

When Willy Ambos arose and turned to address us the next day, we prepared for the same old "this game is very important" speech, but what came was an eye opener. "I don't have to explain to you that in the first year of a franchise in an independent structure the emphasis is on winning," he said. "I also have to be honest with you. Earlier today I was almost fired. That is based on the fact that the feeling is that I've lost control of this ballclub." Ambos was measuring his words carefully as his audience was suddenly extremely attentive. With team president Baggott on the trip and seeing firsthand the Raptors carousing after the games — even after the losses — the pressure was on to whip the team back into shape. Especially after being swept out of Helena and following it up with a big loss to Butte, the Raptors were in danger of falling out of pennant contention and Ambos was in danger of losing his job.

"When I was a player I always said that if I had the opportunity to become a manager I would be a player's manager and try to make it the best learning environment possible," he said, half in apology, half in defiance. "Unfortunately, every time I have given some leniency, some freedom, to you guys, there have been some who have abused it, and now the feeling is that there's no focus, no discipline, no effort, and some of that is true. Yes, I am a first-year manager. Yes, I have made mistakes. Yes, I will continue to make mistakes. But it's never because I don't care," Ambos concluded. "I took this job because I love baseball and I want to be around baseball. I want to be around players. I want you to play hard. I want you to be a representative of Rich and myself as far as playing the game."

Stretching before games we usually formed ourselves into five lines to get loose. Trying to shake things up in Helena, we tried forming into a circle, but it was to no avail. In Butte, trainer Dan Overman suggested a new formation to break the luck. But when we were unable to agree on a new configuration, Overman threw up his arms and suggested that everybody just do their own thing. The cluster that was the Raptors stretching formation was analogous to the team itself. Players were doing their own thing. Some were just biding their time until the end of the season. Others were concentrating on padding their own statistics. Together the Raptors were a disunited team in need of a bonding experience, focus, and a victory.

A ten-to-nothing win in Butte to finish off the dismal road trip coupled with a Helena loss had us just four and a half games out of first place. Back in Ogden, where home-field advantage and home cooking could be just the recipe for a pennant run, we were excited again and ready for action.

But three days later, the words "This is the biggest fucking series of the year" written in bold capital letters on the lineup card in the Raptors clubhouse were just an unnecessary and bitter reminder of what had just happened as we filed out of our clubhouse to head back out on the road. After winning the first game, the Raptors bullpen just could not check the Brewers bats. Despite valiant efforts by the Raptors offense, led by a rejuvenated Doug O'Neill, who was suddenly scorching balls around the yard like everyone knew he could, and an inspired Jeremy Winget, who continued his assault on the Pioneer League and padding his league-leading offensive statistics, we dropped the final two games, coughing up leads and allowing late-inning Brewers home runs to doom the efforts of the torrid bats.

Losing a four-run lead in the ninth inning one night and allowing another four runs in the last two innings the next, the Raptors bullpen again proved that they were not ready for prime time. In the dugout we griped that cuts and changes should be made but also conceded that the coaching staff had the bullpen so on edge that the pressure placed on them by Ambos would be difficult for even super-reliever Lee Smith to overcome.

Despite his frustration at having been dropped to seventh in the lineup, Doug O'Neill was now slashing balls in the gap, motoring around the basepaths for triples on balls hit to left-center field, and showing why he was once touted as a prospective major-league star. Jeremy Winget was hitting with an authority unseen to that point in the season, making a good case for himself as the league's most valuable player. Unfortunately, pitching could not complement the bats, and the Raptors were once again five and a half games out of first place.

As the team filed out of the dugout after the final out of the series, Ambos just sat outside the far end of the bench pondering the significance of the loss. With an effective bullpen the Raptors could be just a game and a half out of first place, but instead we were all but eliminated from contention. As players milled around the dugout in disbelief, Ambos just stared out toward left field as if waiting for a reliever to emerge from the trees beyond the outfield wall to save the Raptors. Once in the clubhouse, however, Ambos was quite animated.

The cramped clubhouse was packed with players trying to shed the pain of the losses as they discarded their uniforms when Ambos opened the door of his office and commanded us to take a seat. We could hear the park's public address announcer in the sudden silence of the clubhouse as Ambos took center stage. The echoes of the post-game announcements were quickly drowned out by Ambos's rage.

"I've never seen anything FUCKING LIKE THIS in my whole FUCKING LIFE," he screamed. Raptors players sat in their chairs in various stages of undress listening to the words thrust at them. With his face a crimson snarl and a cigarette butt shaking in his hand he turned to the pitchers. "Does anybody got a set of fucking nuts coming out of the pen?" Finally toning down, Ambos pleaded with his team, emotion cracking his voice, "You gotta have fucking pride in what you do. And I know it's pressure. I understand that. But that's fucking baseball."

In Idaho Falls the next day, Coach Morales gathered the position players together in the visitors' locker room and focused us on not blaming the pitchers and not instinctively reacting with "here we go again" whenever the pitching staff displayed their generosity with hits and runs. After some lighthearted joshing about the recent ineptness of the pitchers, Morales talked about the reason we all were gathered in baseball uniforms, sitting in the Pioneer League, namely, to push our careers forward.

He encouraged us to be a little more selfish on the basepaths and at the plate. The season had less than thirty days remaining, which meant that the Raptors players had less than thirty days left in their baseball careers unless they could attract major-league attention. Bunt for hits, steal bases, be aggressive. It was not time to ignore sacrifice signs, but it was rapidly approaching the end of the season and time for players to make themselves more attractive to the baseball world.

Despite some here-we-go-again moments from the pitching staff, the Raptors held off the Idaho Falls Braves for a pair of close victories. Coaching first base, I could not help smiling as batters tried to bunt their way on, aggressively looked to take extra bases on hits, and took off on their own stealing second base. Where just days earlier players appeared to be playing scared, they now seemed as if they were playing possessed — by their dreams.

After the last game against the Braves, the Raptors bus stopped in Idaho Falls for a late dinner and then drove through the night to Helena. We tucked in at two-thirty in the morning and awoke late the next morning to see no sun in the sky. After fifty days of almost perfect baseball weather, broken up only by the occasional passing cloud and the odd windstorm, the Helena weather was legitimately threatening. Almost nothing could have pleased us more.

The grind of everyday baseball naturally becomes grating to the players. Physically, the nicks, bruises, and breaks made daily confrontation with the game painful. Mentally, the constant pressure to get a hit, strike out a batter, execute, and succeed was also painful. If you hit a ball four hundred feet, the next at-bat still starts with no count and could end in an embarrassing strikeout. If you dive for a ball to stop a rally, the next bloop could skid through your legs. A night off to recharge batteries, refocus minds, and recuperate bodies would have been most welcome.

But the skies in Helena would not cooperate and baseball was on for the night; after Jeremy Winget watched strike three cross the plate to end the first game, the Brewers were victorious and the Raptors were disheartened and defeated. Ambos remained in his seat watching the field for nothing in particular. Morales sarcastically exhorted his players to gather up their gear so that they might beat the Brewers to the local nightclub. After another greasy dinner at the Last Chance Casino, we retired to our rooms. A frustrated Ambos imposed a 12:30 A.M. curfew with no exceptions — no card playing and no hanging out in each other's rooms. We were under lockdown and nobody was particularly happy about it.

At the park the next day, the clash between coaches and players finally came to a head. Standing at second base during the first rounds of batting practice, I heard my name being called by shortstop Tommy Johnston, who was motioning to his head. Looking into the cage, I noticed that the batters were wearing helmets. Usually in batting practice, players went into the cage with no more protection than their game hats, but today they were fully armored.

After watching a few batters take their hacks against Ambos, I noticed that he was not throwing his usual fifty-miles-per-hour sliders —

he was throwing cheddar. Taking ground balls at second base, I watched him plunk three batters.

When it was my turn to run in and bat I got a chance to see how hard he was really throwing. Grunting between every throw, and standing only forty-five feet from the plate, Ambos was putting everything he had into his pitches, cursing and berating players between each one. When I finally got my chance to enter the cage I put on a helmet, choked up my bat, and flailed at the passing balls. Thankfully, his arm gave out during my swings and I was spared more torture. Coach Morales relieved him and finished a normal batting practice.

While Ambos iced his arm, an impromptu players meeting was called to discuss this heating up of the cold war between coach and players. Rubbing sore spots on their bodies where they had been hit during batting practice and wearing angry expressions, players gathered next to the bench along the left-field foul line that served as a bullpen. Looking at one another without saying anything, we waited in vain for a team leader to step forward and offer wisdom, indignation, or anything worth hearing. Players grumbled about the harsh treatment during batting practice, groused about going home, and shuffled their feet. Finally someone said something about playing hard, working to get a contract from a major-league organization, and trying to have fun for the rest of the year. For what it was worth, that was our meeting.

Maybe everyone was just looking out for themselves, or maybe nobody cared about our pennant race. I walked back to the dugout with the other players, unsure if the batting-practice stunt brought us together as a team or if we were beyond help.

Manipulating the pitching rotation by starting Danny Miller and placing Paul O'Hearn in the bullpen for an emergency appearance, Ambos managed one last win against Helena. Miller, giving up an uncharacteristic four runs in the first inning, yielded to Tim Salado, who saved face for the oft-maligned bullpen by putting together a strong outing, shutting out the Brewers for four straight innings. O'Hearn pitched three scoreless innings to earn a rare save and bring us back to five games out of first place.

Miller's sudden ineffectiveness could have been a casualty of nothing more than the season itself. The Raptors played in a short-season league, but for many high-school and college players, used to a few games a week, the rigor of everyday baseball was a new strain. If Miller was ever going to convince the scouts that he should move on in baseball, he would have to master the tremendous discipline to maintain high performance on the diamond day in and day out over the course of a season.

After our only other winning road trip, the coaches were too upset with us to buy beer, but after going three and one this time out, they grudgingly spotted us a few cases. A subdued celebration on the bus marked our creep to within five games of the front-running Brewers. Our work was cut out for us for the final three weeks of the season, but at least we were winning.

Unfortunately, we could not even handle our winning ways without screwing it up. Once again showing our tendency as a team to take any measure of freedom and abuse it, we enjoyed the victory beer a little too much. As the bus was peacefully driving into the night, tempers exploded. The sound of commotion burst through the bus and a heated argument roused sleeping Raptors. Drunken relief pitcher Steve Gay was apparently too loaded to make it to a bathroom and relieved himself in his pants. Unfortunately, he also relieved himself on starter Jason Evenhus, sleeping on the floor below.

Shouts soon yielded to fisticuffs. "Why you gotta be like that?" Gay kept questioning. A solid shot to the face was his only response. "Why you gotta be that way?" Smash. "Why?" Crunch. "Why?" Slap.

The fight continued in its one-sided fashion until Ambos intervened. The now-bloody Gay continued spouting off until he was hustled to the back of the bus to get cleaned up while Evenhus seethed about the origins of the fight.

The smell of urine was engulfing the bus, hastening a quick pit stop. We filed off the bus and gathered for an impromptu sermon from Ambos. We had once again let him down, shown our collective immaturity, and proved that we still could not handle ourselves as professionals. We had taken some freedom and as he appropriately put it, "pissed on it." For the rest of the season, Ambos declared, we would act like a college team — collared shirts on the road, no drinking, and more draconian curfews. It was not an uplifting way to begin the biggest homestand of the season.

The Executives

While we stewed on the bus from Helena, the Raptors ownership enjoyed the anticipation of a long homestand filled with big crowds and exciting promotions. Though our pennant hopes were waning, we still had plenty of home games to bring fans to the park and excite Ogden about the future of Raptors baseball. Waiting another year for a pennant might not even be so bad for the franchise. Rumors that spread through the clubhouse contended that ownership would be most satisfied if we were to win our division but lose the championship series. Ownership could then reap the rewards of a few extra sellouts while avoiding the expense of buying us championship rings. Whether that was true or not, it was typical of the players' perception of the Raptors owners. Naturally, we did not always see eye to eye with the owners about how the team should operate, but that was to be expected. Players needed to focus on the season and their own careers while owners needed to look at dollars and cents and toward the future. Regardless of our varying perspectives, everyone was in need of a diversion.

We needed a break from the day-to-day life of pennant racing, and our ownership needed a large crowd and a fun baseball spectacle to revitalize their bottom line. A midseason exhibition was a perfect way to restore our intensity and allow the Raptors front office to tuck away their bean counters and enjoy a raucous full house. We returned to Ogden for an exhibition that was just what we needed to remind ourselves that baseball was still a game even if the reminder was a war — a battle of the sexes. The Colorado Silver Bullets, the first all-female professional baseball team to be officially recognized by the National Association of Professional Baseball Leagues, had been barnstorming the country and were stopping at Simmons Field.

On their exhibition tour, under the tutelage of former major-league great Phil Niekro, the Silver Bullets had attracted incredible amounts of attention but few wins. When created, the women's team was to compete against teams in the independent Northern League and then travel the country playing professional and semiprofessional clubs. Unfortunately, the talent level of the Silver Bullets was not quite up to the challenge, and their games against professional opponents were either canceled or modified. Visiting the Raptors, for example, the Bullets played against a team composed of players and managers, and even owners.

The Raptors front-office staff, and partial owners of the team, were deeply involved in their team's success and had participated in everything from the painting of the Simmons Field dugouts to the selling of Raptors tickets in readying the franchise for its inaugural season. Dave Baggott, John Stein, and Holly Preston were part owners of the Raptors by day and, along with Steve Gradyan, the front-office staff of the Raptors at game time. Now, against the Silver Bullets, former minor-league players Baggott and Stein donned the home whites and took the field for the team they created. Although the return to uniform may have reminded them of a time when they had their own goals of playing in the majors, now they had new major dreams of building a new baseball entity that could foster the ambitions of young ballplayers and inspire dreams in young fans. The new owners planned to use their baseball experience to bring success to the Ogden franchise and then replicate it in bigger and better ways.

In the spring of 1993, Baggott, Stein, and Preston were all working for the front office of the Salt Lake City Trappers, an independent team in the Pioneer League. Just weeks before their season was to begin — because a triple-A team was relocating to Salt Lake City and a new stadium was to be built on the site of the Trappers' home field — the ownership of the team suspended operations and the Pioneer League invoked league rules to seize the franchise.

Under Dave, John, and Holly, the Trappers attracted a large fan following and were acclaimed for their success throughout the baseball world. Suddenly the rug had been pulled out from under them. But after moping aimlessly and mourning the setback in his career, Baggott re-energized himself with thoughts not only of working in another front office but of owning his own team. Between the spring of 1993 and the end of the year, he negotiated with the Pioneer League for the rights to the franchise seized from Salt Lake City, negotiated with the City of Ogden for a field to play on, and persuaded an investment group that included local civic leaders and Chicago Cubs third baseman Steve Buechele to join him, John, and Holly in bringing baseball to Simmons Field.

Dave Baggott did not always want to own a baseball team. Years before, Baggott was just another ballplayer looking to extend his career in the minors. A college outfielder, he was a little too short, a little too small, and a little too slow to fit the scouts' mold of what an outfielder looks like. But the gregarious kid with the blond locks and big smile found a place in Idaho Falls playing second base for a cooperative club. "For a kid who never played second base before, I had a four-month crash course and then went and played in the Pioneer League," he remembered. "I think if I would have been playing second base my whole life I could have had a good career ahead of me. There were nights I'd make a great play to my right or a great play to my left and then a slow roller would come at me and go right through my legs. But I had a great year. I had a great time. Still, nobody picked me up."

As luck would have it, those great plays always seemed to be against one particular opponent, the independent Salt Lake City Trappers. When no major-league franchise decided to sign him, the Trappers called and offered him a place on the team. Realizing that the opportunity with the Trappers was probably one last chance and one last baseball hurrah, he made the most of it. "I knew then the writing was on the wall," he confessed, "and my playing career was pretty much done. So we went out there with the emphasis on playing the game for fun and it was really a different outlook when you know it's going to be your last year. I had a ball and the best year defensively I ever had. We won the championship and I literally drove home to L.A. and opened the trunk of my car, threw all my shoes and spikes and bats and everything I had in the trunk out in front of the driveway, and called the neighborhood kids over and let them take it all away."

His playing career was finished, but the Trappers were not about to let the bright young man end his involvement with the game of baseball and the successful franchise. After a few months the president of the franchise invited Baggott to go sailing, and the former Trappers player quickly realized he was being interviewed for a job in the front office. At first Baggott wanted nothing more to do with baseball, feeling that he had fallen short of his dream and simply wanting to move on to something else. He was trying to be an industrial real estate agent, but by his own admission was not very good at it. In the end he decided to return to Salt Lake City and try to make the transition from baseball player to baseball executive.

During the 1986 season he patrolled center field for the Trappers, but as the 1987 season approached, he was working as assistant general manager. "I had like seven months, eight months working in the front office before the first game," he said, "and it didn't hit me until the first pitch was thrown on opening night and I'm standing in the press box. I said, 'Jesus Christ, I'm really done. I'm not playing this game anymore. They're out there playing and I don't have anything to do with it.'"

Although the realization that his playing days were truly over may have been a sudden shock, Baggott soon found that his new involvement with the game he loved was just as fulfilling. "It's a unique way to make a living," he said of his new profession. "A great way to put it in perspective is — I have a buddy and we were talking on the phone one day and he was telling me what a tough day he was having. He was living in Fresno and in the insurance business and he said, 'I have to hang up, I have to prepare for a big meeting. I'm presenting a proposal to a convalescent home' — and it's a lot of pressure on him. I said, 'I've got a proposal, too. I'm meeting a guy later to see if he'll sponsor the Chicken.' It's a business, but it's a unique business. In our towns that we have minor-league clubs in, we're the only ones that do what we do. So there really is no competition. It's not something you really have to go out and do a hard sell on. There's little tricks to the trade, but mostly it's selling the game itself — and the game is America's pastime, so it's not a hard sell and that's one of the things I enjoy about it."

He enjoyed it enough to stay involved, move up the career ladder of the Trappers organization, and receive recognition for his achievements in the minor-league world. He was named Pioneer League Executive of the Year and the Sporting News Short-Season Executive of the Year. After beginning his front office career as the assistant general manager, he rose to the position of general manager by the time the Trappers left the field for the final time. Now, just a little more than a year after his career again came to a crossroads with the end of the Trappers, he was not only involved with a baseball franchise again, he was president and an owner of his own team. The new focus was inspiring and exciting.

"It feels great," he said, chewing on tobacco in the trailer that served as the Raptors field office. Just as the realization that his playing days were over did not strike him until the first season began and he was in the press box, the successful birth of his own team took a while to sink in. "It didn't hit me that I succeeded with a long-term goal that fourteen months ago was just a pipe dream until I saw opening night and the players in uniform being introduced. We fucking did it, and we did it by ourselves, and we didn't do it with millions of dollars, and we got a community to believe in us as people and believe in what we were doing. They believed not only in what we were doing but what we were going to be doing for the community. That gives me a lot of satisfaction, knowing that not only is my career advancing to a new degree but also that what we do has more of an effect not only on us but on other people as well. These people in Ogden haven't had sporting entertainment for years and we're providing them the value of seeing the kids smiling, eating cotton candy, and going crazy every time we score a run. That's more of a satisfaction to me than any dollar can bring at that particular moment. The next day when you read the game reports you know from the business operation you either smile or get pissed off. But so far we're smiling."

Baggott was certainly smiling as he took the field against the Silver Bullets, and even though the women hit some of his pitches pretty hard, the stands were full of fans buying Raptors souvenirs and concession food. Everyone was having a good time and the night was attracting media attention that would increase the visibility of his franchise. It was definitely a good night to be an owner of the Raptors. Unfortunately, it was not every night that he got to parade in uniform in front of the fans, look at a packed house, revel in the good time, and put aside the burden of ownership. Owning a team was no fun when it meant trying to figure out how to pay the bills when attendance was down, it was no fun when it meant dealing with the frustrations of trying to leap political hurdles to get a stadium built, and it was especially no fun when it meant informing a player that the ownership was ending his major dreams.

"The toughest thing is when you know there's someone on the field who is going to be released after the game," he said of the darker side of the responsibility that comes with owning an independent franchise. "I didn't like it when somebody told me, 'You're not playing anymore.' Sitting there, knowing that either myself or somebody within the organization is going to tell this guy his dream is over, that is certainly one thing that we don't look forward to ever having to do. And yet the reality of it is that you have to do it because if you don't succeed with what you've got on the field, that has a direct effect on what you're doing as a franchise. Yeah, it's a game, but the business outweighs the aspect of the value of the game."

Baggott's fellow owner and Raptors vice president John Stein was the one who actually had to lower the ax to make cuts. "Having been released myself, I feel like I've been more honest than I was ever treated in being told that you're fired or that your dream is over," Stein said of his duties. "But it's something that needs to be done. It's the nature of the beast in this game, in this industry. Somebody's got to be hatchet man, and I applied for the job so I've got to handle it like every day at the office."

Stein, who threw a few scoreless innings against the Silver Bullets and then flung his body across the infield to make a diving stop of a ground ball, still had the competitive instinct on the field and wanted to make his team the best it could be. From the cutting of John Homan early in the season to the most recent release of Steve Gay and

Jason Evenhus after their drunken bus fight, Stein did the dirty work for the front office and reflected on the difficulty of the job. "The first one isn't the toughest one," he said of the cuts. "The one that got me the most this year was Steve Gay, who belligerently cost himself any further career because I can no longer recommend him as a player because of his actions on a team bus, and that hurt me. A 'local boy makes good' does not happen every day, and he was an Ogden kid who was playing for the Ogden pro team and who was having some success, and actually there was interest by some major-league scouts, and I have to tell them now that I would stay away from a guy like that because of his actions. That one hurt the most."

Being a part owner of a minor-league team was certainly not just pain for the one-time pitcher who seemed to love tooling around in his red convertible as much as he enjoyed being a part of Raptors baseball. Before games he could often be found watering the field or speaking with scouts about Raptors players, but he was never far from the action. After playing in the minors and then moving, like Baggott, through the front office and into an ownership position, Stein was extremely enthusiastic about the minor-league experience.

"Minor-league baseball is a game that, if you brought in a fan from outside the country and said to him, 'I'm going to take you to a baseball game,' and they didn't know anything about the game, after about two innings that fan has now become an expert on the game and now they are going to ask, 'Why didn't they bunt? Why did they hit-and-run?'" he said of the unique brand of entertainment. "Fans can actually go up and touch and ask for an autograph and not be charged ten dollars. Fans can see a grounder go between the legs of the shortstop and remember, 'Oh God, I did that when I was in high school.' It's more of a human game in the minors.

"The biggest difference is that wins and losses don't necessarily mean so much as entertainment does in the minor-league industry. That's why we do the catch-it-if-you-can contest, that's why we do the race around the bases. The biggest difference to me is when I used to pitch and the Chicken was in town. I hated it because it disrupted the game. I was a baseball purist. I was a player. As an operator you see what kind of dollars come through the gates and you see what poten-

Raptors vice president John Stein (left) and Raptors president Dave Baggott pose
with a model of a proposed new stadium for the Raptors. Both part-owners and former minor-league players, Baggott and Stein have high hopes for the future of Raptors baseball. Brett Mandel photograph reprinted with permission.

tially can happen monetarily by bringing in a Chicken or a Phillie Pha-
natic. I want to go in and tell the players, 'Listen, just play the game.
He's gonna mess with you — just play the game.' It's for the fans.
Minor-league baseball is for the fans."

Although there is no doubt that the minor-league baseball experience has become a huge success for the fans, it has also become a major
money maker for owners and it has a significant positive economic impact on its home communities. In their souvenir program, the Billings
Mustangs proudly proclaimed that baseball is not just the only sport
that provides a family night of relaxation, fun, and wholesome entertainment at an affordable price but that the minor-league team is a ma-

jor revenue source for the area. The program declared that the total direct economic impact of home-team supply purchases, visiting clubs' rooms and meals expenses, goods and services purchases needed to maintain the ballpark, and the significant attention focused on Billings by minor-league baseball amounted to $2,064,837 annually. An even larger economic impact could be expected from teams in the upper echelon of the minor leagues. There is nothing minor about bringing that kind of money into a local economy — in addition to entertaining the public.

The spectacle with the Raptors and the Silver Bullets was definitely for the fans, but before the crowd arrived at the park my teammates and I had been able to view the curiosity that was a women's baseball team from close up. Hours before game time, we were just wrapping up batting practice when our opponents arrived. When other teams came to town, we usually gave them scant notice except perhaps to scout tendencies during their practice. With the Silver Bullets, however, Raptors players were more interested in picking out good-looking opponents than judging their susceptibility to sliders. Pulling lawn chairs out of the dugout, we set up a front row from which to view the entertainment. There was no mistaking that my teammates were more interested in the Silver Bullets as women than as competitors.

Lisa Martinez, a twenty-nine-year-old teacher, caught the most eyes with her pink lipstick and shining face. The pitcher from the University of California who was a twenty-four-game winner with a 0.54 ERA as a softballer was turning heads not because of her fastball but because of her curves. Watching the other women run through their pregame warmups, my teammates could not resist lewdly imagining the various double-play combinations that the Silver Bullets could perform. Even though these were our opponents for the evening, it was clear that boys were still going to be boys, especially if the visiting team were not boys.

The women had managed to win five games by the time they came to Ogden, but they had lost dozens more and their record stood at five and thirty-three when they pulled into Simmons Field. Each town brought not only a baseball game but the distraction of gawking attention that made their appearance more like a sideshow. Ogden was no exception. Before the game the local media participated in a home-run derby, and during the game we were clearly playing to the crowd. Utah Jazz president Frank Layden coached third base for the home team, and a local radio station brought a cheerleading dance troupe to entertain.

The carnival-like atmosphere was just how pit boss turned Raptors marketing director Steve Gradyan liked Simmons Field. Although much of his time with the Raptors was taken up with his duties marketing and promoting the team, during games Gradyan ran the various promotions and games that entertained fans between innings. For him, half the fun of his involvement with the minor leagues was doing anything to put a smile on the faces of the men, women, and children who came out to the park.

Having honed his expertise in pleasing people as a floor supervisor at the Golden Nugget Casino in Las Vegas, Steve was an outgoing and personable addition to the Raptors front office. "It's actually somewhat similar," Gradyan said, comparing the glitz and glamour of the casinos with the atmosphere of the minor leagues. "There's a lot of action going on at all times, a lot of hectic things going on. What's so special is that the people are a lot closer. It's just apple pie and just a great place to watch relatively exciting ball and watch these kids — this one might be an all-star next year, he could be in the bigs — and that's what brings people out, and it's wholesome. They're not making $2,000,000 a year, and these guys are out there diving for balls and they're only making $650 a month, so these guys can relate to that and I think that's what draws the fans out to come see them play."

Even in a steady rain, surrounded by a circus, a professional baseball game between men and women was being played on the field. Making the night even more special for me, because of the watered-down lineup that made room for owners Baggott and Stein, Coach Morales, and Manager Ambos to come out of retirement, I received my first professional start. After shaking the jitters by ending the Silver Bullets' half of the first inning spearing a line drive, I came to bat to face their ace Lee Anne Ketcham and walked. Later in the game she tele-graphed a curve that I stroked into left field for my first professional hit.

While I was savoring my moment in the sun even though my play-ing time was in the rain, the Silver Bullets were enjoying their own op-portunity to live out their baseball dreams. Unfortunately, reviews on our mutual talent were probably the same. The women were too slow, lacked power, and needed seasoning before they could truly compete in professional baseball. If the next generation of female baseball players continues playing baseball and training with weights past Lit-tle League and into college, as my teammates on the Raptors did, maybe they will be able to participate en masse in the upper ranks of college and professional baseball.

For Raptors part owner and vice president Holly Preston, the fleeting scene of women on the ball field was just a reminder of how few women there are in the game of baseball. Preston, who was named the Pioneer League Woman Executive of the Year in 1991 and 1992, was a woman in a man's game, but the lack of compatriots of her own gen-der did not diminish her enthusiasm for baseball and the business of building a successful franchise.

"I think it's definitely a curiosity right now," she said of the visiting women's team. "They can't compete with men's teams — professional teams, anyway. It's pretty much proven. This team probably has some of the best women baseball players on it. If they formed an all-women's league, certainly there would be good competition — if there's interest, I don't know. I think it would be very difficult to gain a lot of interest. People came out in droves to see that game because there were women playing men. I don't think they'd come out the same way to see women playing women, particularly when the option to see men is still there, and that's too bad. I think women can be just as good athletes as men, but in competition they're just not as strong as men, and in a sport like this you really have to be. So I hope that a women's league can be formed that can be successful, but it would be very, very hard for them."

Her own experience has proven that a woman can not only compete in a man's game, she can excel. Preston went to school at the University of Oregon and began to study architecture but decided that was not what she wanted to do with her life. Instead she began to work with the university athletic department and decided to switch majors. She graduated with a degree in sports management. After college she interned with the Salt Lake City Trappers and was a full-time member of the front office before the season was a month old. When Dave Baggott was promoted to general manager, Holly was named assistant general manager and became one of the few female executives in all of baseball. Despite her successes with the Trappers, like the franchise itself, she was out of luck when the Pioneer League left Salt Lake City.

"We all lost our jobs — didn't know what we were going to do, it was a very hard time for everybody," she said plainly. "It was such a good thing in Salt Lake that we had going and to have it all end so abruptly and so nasty was very hard. So I started putting resumés out to all the baseball clubs, but I knew Dave had been talking to the people up here. As things progressed, I thought, 'I want to be a part of it and I'll help you,' and it got to the point where over the course of the summer I helped Dave put this thing together. I put together the investment package and helped him with things like that. He basically looked for all the investors and just because I think Dave and John and I worked so well together and had been working so long together, a percentage of the stock was held back for us because we put the deal together. Basically Dave could have held all of that for himself but instead offered a portion of it to John and I, and I accepted. It was a chance to be an owner rather than following the directions of ownership, so that's exciting. There is a little bit more stress involved, but I think down the road it will turn into a great thing. The first few years are going to be a bit of a struggle, just as most new businesses are, but being an owner is a lot of fun."

Watching her team establish itself in its first year was reason enough to look forward to a bright future. "Seeing this field being put together," she said, was the most satisfying experience in her career, "and the most exciting thing is yet to come as far as watching the new stadium go up for us here, knowing that I'm an owner and I'm going to be here for a long time, the team's going to be here for a long time. So I think some of the real exciting things are yet to come."

That excitement and enthusiasm for the future of baseball was something that not everyone shared. No sooner had the Silver Bullets left Ogden than the baseball world was thrown into turmoil. All around baseball on August II, 1994, the word was not *hit* or *ball*, *bunt* or *balk*, *home run* or *no-hitter*. The word for the day was *strike*. After their games — while the Ogden Raptors continued to pursue their dreams of making it all the way to the major leagues — the major-league players packed up their equipment and walked off the field and onto the picket line. Ogden owners were fresh from joining their players in the exhibition game and were back to the business of creating an opportunity for players while providing professional baseball to eager fans. In Helena, Butte, the other cities of the Pioneer League, and throughout the minors, players and owners earnestly pursued their dreams. But whether you understood the complex negotiations involving a salary cap, free agency, and salary arbitration, whether you sympathized with owners or players, or whether you were rooting for your team to win a frantic pennant race or wanted to see future stars in September call-ups, as a baseball fan you knew that summer without baseball was just not the same.

This eighth work stoppage since 1972 and third strike was quickly casting a pall on the baseball season and baseball in general. Like most other professional baseball players, my teammates and I suited up to play ball on Thursday, August 12, and went to perform in front of grateful fans. We beat the Medicine Hat Blue Jays, fans cheered, kids scrambled for autographs, and players went their separate ways one game closer to realizing their dreams or ending their careers. In the major leagues, Ken Griffey Jr. hit one last home run to give him forty for the year and Tony Gwynn had a few more hits to give him an average of .394. In New York the defending champion Toronto Blue Jays beat the Yankees behind Joe Carter home run like the one that won them the World Series just months before, and in Philadelphia my Phillies outlasted the rain and the Mets for a fifteen-inning win. The question on everybody's mind was not whether baseball was still thrilling, but whether it was over for the summer — and what fans would do to pass the time without baseball.

ESPN televised Michael Jordan and the Birmingham Barons on their Sunday-night telecasts, TBS aired the triple-A Richmond Braves, and football would start soon enough for most sports fans. But for the everyday fan in the minor leagues, baseball would go on as normal. Perhaps fans of major-league baseball would visit a minor-league park and be charmed by its intimate magic and spell of hopes and dreams. Maybe fans would see players who were actually in their tax brackets and owners who were actually interested in pleasing the fan and would never want to deal with millionaire players squabbling with millionaire owners again. No matter what, the Raptors players and their fellow minor leaguers were now the only professional baseball option in America.

"I was a player, now I'm an owner and an operator, and I personally side for the owners in this major-league strike," John Stein said as the season wound down. "In the majors it's money, it's endorsements, it's mediocre players making way too much money, and now it's becoming the inmates running the asylum. In America — and professional baseball can't be included in corporate America, I don't think, because it's an apple and an orange situation — the employees cannot go in and demand things, especially when there's a whole string, a whole farm system of guys sitting there saying, 'God, if they called me, would I cross the line, would I be a scab to play major-league baseball for a day for $109,000 a year? I've been chasing this dream for all my life. Would I cross the line? I can't, because someday I may be part of that union.' I just think there's a lot of things wrong with the major-league baseball system."

Fellow owner Baggott was more philosophical. "Everybody who operates a minor-league baseball team that's successful does it according to affordability. Second, behind affordability, is entertainment value," he said. "That's still at the minor-league level. I think at the major-league level that's missing a little bit. Whether or not the players are to blame or the owners are to blame, that's my personal opinion and will remain personal. Yet the ultimate loser is the fan. I think at the minor-league level everything is focused on the fans because each team operates independently as a business whether you have a major-league affiliate or not. To be successful in the business is strictly based on what you can do as an independent business to make money, and you can't make money if you don't draw any fans, and that's almost a fear factor. The bottom line is, unless you give them a product on the field they enjoy watching, and unless you can entertain them while they're there — I mean, we as operators are in a position where we have a captive audience for two and a half to three hours and we may be getting blown out seven to nothing in the first inning, so we'd better be doing something besides playing baseball to warrant these people coming back. So our goal as an operation is to do it almost where we want people to go home and not know what the score was because they had such a good time they didn't care what the score was, they forgot. And I think at the major-league level that's sometimes forgotten, and that scares me a little bit."

As the season entered its last few weeks there would at least always be a game in Ogden or wherever the Raptors played on the road, and there would be a game anywhere there was minor-league baseball. Perhaps the strike and its reverberating turmoil would affect the major dreams of the Raptors players, or maybe the only difference would be the attention focused on the minor leagues. In the weeks ahead, an Oakland Athletics beat writer, hungry for a story, would travel to Ogden to do a piece on four San Jose State alumni who played for the Raptors, and every baseball-news outlet from *This Week in Baseball* to the local evening news would focus more attention on the minor leagues in general. At the very least, more people than ever would realize that across the country, young men were still pursuing their major-league dreams far from the turmoil of the majors. Perhaps now those dreams would no longer be pursued in relative obscurity.

Sitting in the owner's seat, having been a player and an executive, Baggott viewed the strike, its causes, and the future of the game he loved. "I think talent in some areas is thin and I think that the attitudes that the young athletes have today is almost detrimental to the game," he said as an owner remembering his own time as a player. "They don't play to get paid anymore, they get paid to play and that alarms me, too. We even get that down here. Here, we're an independent club and we've had a couple kids — the first thing they say is, 'How much are you going to pay me?' If we have a kid who asks that for an independent club in the rookie league, they're not the kind of kid we want. This is just not a money league. If they play well, the money will take care of itself. Who knows, but as long as there's nine innings and twenty-seven outs in the game, I think there will always be a game."

Down to the Wire

After the frivolity of the Silver Bullets' visit, we were back to the serious work of trying to win a championship and attempting to realize the dreams of the players, coaches, and ownership of the Raptors. With just three weeks left in the season, it was clear that many changes had been made since opening night when we gathered together to listen to Ambos's speech about winning a ring and extending our careers. Many roster moves were made, and with a few final cuts and quittings we were quite a different team.

Driving Tommy Johnston back to his foster home after the previous road trip, Brett Smith and I listened to him mutter over and over that he had had enough, that he was quitting, that Smith and I could split the equipment left in his locker. Hearing Tommy talk of quitting was not new, but his tone was definitely more serious than ever. We kept telling him to come out to the park the next day and make his decision in a cool moment. But Tommy was mired with a .149 average, still nursing a sore hand from being hit by a pitch on our first road trip, and furious over the berating he had received from his coaches. For the unhappy Johnston, the target/batting practice in Helena was the last straw. When Smith and I arrived at the park the next day, Johnston was already gone. The dream of playing major-league baseball may have remained in his heart, but he had decided that it was not worth pursuing with the Raptors. Concerned about TJ but still thinking practically, we spirited Johnston's equipment out of the clubhouse — for safekeeping.

The next day we called his host family only to find that he had already headed home. Just forty-eight hours earlier, Johnston was still clinging to his dream of making it back to the Pirates organization and on to the majors in Pittsburgh. Now he was just a memory. Smith sanded TJ's name off of his bat and planned to use it in that night's game; new pitcher Don Baker was wearing Johnston's number thirty-three; and I turned double plays with Mike Carrigg in practice. Baseball and life simply went on.

It went on without catcher Brad Dandridge, who was recalled to his Northern League team like Dan Zanolla, and without the two pitchers involved in the bus brawl who were released. Days later, catcher Troy Doezie, upset about his dearth of playing time, just walked away from the game. Shuffling into the clubhouse, Baker, fellow pitcher Jay Hogue, and infielder Peter Muro joined the Raptors. Looking around the clubhouse had become a daily ritual of finding the new face and getting used to a familiar number on a new body. But the uniforms do not care who is wearing them, and with each release or resignation an opportunity ended for one player while one opened up for another.

Doug Smyly arrived early in the season to fill in for pitcher Chris McCoy, who gave up on Raptors baseball just before the season began. John Homan was replaced by Marco Contreras, Jason Pollock was replaced by Dave Bingham, and Dan Zanolla was replaced by Shane Farnsworth. Chris Amos's spot was filled by Peter Muro, and just when Jay Hogue and Don Baker came in to give the Raptors depth, the cutting of Gay and Evenhus, the resignations of Doezie and Johnston, and the recall of Dandridge left our team without much of a bench or a bullpen. The Raptors ownership was either satisfied with our diminished squad's talent or unwilling to spend for additional players — we were down to twenty-one men.

With the Medicine Hat Blue Jays in town we were five games out of first place and three men down from our opening day roster. The short roster brought opportunity for some Raptors dreamers who had been relegated to bench duty for much of the year. Brett Smith and Chris Simmons were now splitting catching duty, giving both the opportunity that they had been hustling for all season. Brett Smith had literally made an impact with his concussion-causing play at the plate against Billings and was steadily raising his offensive numbers with his increased playing time. Getting into more games even earned him a new nickname. With his prescription sunglasses shaded all around the edges like a superhero's mask, the Blue Jays took to calling him the Lone Ranger. A freak injury to his throwing hand had him sitting on the bench fidgeting with his injured hand and itching to get back into the lineup, where Chris Simmons was settling in comfortably.

To start the homestand, Simmons went three for four with two triples and a double to lead the Raptors to victory. A catcher by trade who had been filling in utility roles from coaching first base to playing second base to throwing batting practice, Simmons waited for more than forty games for his chance to play his natural position. Given the opportunity, the tenacious Simmons was doing everything he could to keep himself in the lineup so that he could try to once again beat the odds and extend his career past his season with the Raptors.

"Sometimes after the game I just sit back and go, 'Whoa,' kind of like a fairy tale, in a way," he said of his satisfaction with his efforts. "I'm doing it. I kind of want to go around to everyone else and say, 'Look at you, look what I'm doing. You guys never believed in me and here I am now.' Now that I'm at where I'm at right now, I'm greedy. I want more. You know, a lot of people can say they played professional baseball but not too many people can say, 'I was successful.' For the short part that I played I feel I am successful and I want to continue to be successful just because that's how stubborn I am. I want to go on and prove to more people."

With Simmons — who was enduring considerable ribbing for a television interview in which he said of his mother, "If it weren't for her, I wouldn't be here today" — again behind the plate and contributing to the offense with a two-for-four day, we treated our fans to a twenty-two-to-seven rout. Making the most of the blood-in-the-water frenzy that possessed the offense, Shane Jones went three for five, finally pushing his average back up above .260 even though he was far from satisfied by his season's performance. The torrid Doug O'Neill joined the hit parade with his third home run in three days — an impressive feat even if one of the blasts was against the Silver Bullets — leading the Raptors' explosion in front of a raucous crowd that cheered and cheered as we ran up the score. I even joined the fray with a couple of strikeouts. I had the opportunity to be struck out by the league's top relief man, who blew me away with a more than ninety-miles-per-hour fastball after I scattered my teammates in our dugout with a foul-line drive.

The other Blue Jays games, however, were much more dramatic and turned on our painfully short bench. When Simmons became ill during one game, Ambos was left with a bench that consisted of me — the only position player available for a roster move. When Josh Kirtlan was ejected during a ninth-inning rally, it seemed as if Ambos had encountered his nightmare scenario — insert his untested author-rookie into a pressure situation or plug a pitcher into the lineup. I would not have wanted to rest our pennant hopes on either option. The rally failed and we lost, but as fate would have it, the same nightmare scenario was played out again the following night when Brett Smith was injured in a train wreck of a collision at the plate. Smith put the opposing player out of the game with an apparent shoulder dislocation, but he was shaken up enough himself to have to be removed.

When we were down by a run in the ninth, with runners on first and third with two outs, the Blue Jays decided to intentionally walk Josh Kirtlan to face the slumping newcomer Peter Muro. With no bench moves available to bring in a better pinch hitter, Ambos had no choice but to let Muro bat and hope for the best. But with two strikes on Muro, Coach Morales sent Dave Bingham stealing home. As the crowd and players on the field became aware of the feat of baseball daring, a lusty yell echoed in Simmons Field, culminating with an outburst of joy when Bingham slid home safely to tie the game. With a delightful twist of irony that muted the effect of the bold strategizing, Muro gorked the next pitch into left field for the unlikely game winner.

For Dave Bingham, however, it was just one more remarkable comeback. Drafted by the Braves, he was cut after spending the 1992 season in Idaho Falls. After hooking on with an independent team, he moved on to the Chicago White Sox, but he was cut again. Now with the Raptors, he was chasing his dream one more time, and he was happy to steal home if that was what it was going to take to help make it to the majors.

The only black player with the Raptors as the season wound down, Bingham looked older than twenty-four as indicated on the roster sheet. I always suspected that he, like many other minor-league prospects, had lied about his age to make himself more attractive to scouts who might be timid about making a commitment to an older player. He was certainly prepared to do just about anything to get to the show, and just one look at his overstocked equipment bag was proof. He carried catcher's equipment, an infield glove, and an outfield glove so that he was ready at a moment's notice to play any position that would allow him to stay in the game. On the Raptors, he suited up behind the dish, everywhere in the outfield, and at second base over the course of the season. Over three years he spent time with four organizations — two of them independent — and he was not going to give up until someone carried him off the field. But enjoying a successful season, Bingham was optimistic. "I haven't shown them what I can do," he said, reflecting on his career. "So I'm going to keep trying 'til someone gives me the chance to play. I think if I can play, I'll be fine."

The Lethbridge Mounties then came to town for more seat-of-the-pants baseball, which thrilled our fans but led only to anxious moments on the bench as we clung to our pennant hopes — four games back with just seventeen games to play. Josh Kirtlan went three for three and Doug O'Neill blasted another home run to show the Mounties no hospitality. In Billings, the Helena Brewers were suddenly stumbling and their loss had us within three games of first place. Our pennant hopes had seemed distant just days before, but baseball was once again a game of inches — a few inches on an outside pitch, a ground ball, or a pop fly each day could mean the difference between wearing a ring forever or staring in the mirror to ask, "What if?"

With a standing-room-only crowd packing Simmons Field as a result of a free-ticket-for-a-library-card promotion, O'Neill led the Raptors to another win with an astounding triple down the left-field line to spark an eight-run first inning. Back in the heart of the lineup since his production picked up, Doug was feverishly pushing all his offensive numbers toward his preseason expectations. Although the season was not without personal disappointment, O'Neill was still capable of amazing his teammates and coaches on any given night. Tripling to left field, he left us just standing amazed in the dugout, and when Doug tore full speed after a ball hit to dead center, had the presence of mind to reach out with his free hand and remove his cap, and then reeled in the ball at the warning track, we could do nothing but shake our heads in disbelief.

Perhaps Ambos's move taking O'Neill out of the middle of the Raptor's lineup made O'Neill do some soul searching, or maybe O'Neill had finally decided to just go out and play the way everyone believed he could. With the pennant race bringing out the best in him, O'Neill finally seemed to have his concentration and his attitude in sync with his talent. Although his defense never suffered while he struggled with the bat, he was now coming to the park before practice to get a few extra swings, lashing the ball all over the park during games, and finally enjoying the game. Brightening a bit with the success, O'Neill even joined in on a laugh or two on the bench, a little more at ease as his demons of self-doubt and disappointment retreated to the stands to admire his talents.

The large crowd had overflowed from the stands and kids sat in foul territory from the right-field foul pole to the end of the Raptors dugout. After the scoring in the first inning, however, the game turned into a pitchers duel, leaving the kids little to cheer about. They quickly occupied themselves by making castles in the foul territory sand and giggling with glee as Chris Simmons, who was assigned to protect them from stray balls, ran down overthrows during infield warmups.

Walking from the dugout to coach first base before the fifth inning, I told a gaggle of sand-castle builders that I would judge their creations for a prize when the inning ended. Returning to the dugout, I was pleasantly surprised to see appropriate castles for the setting. Carved into the sand of Simmons Field were three baseball diamonds complete with bases, pitcher's mounds, and outfield walls. As the youngsters proudly displayed their creations, I sheepishly declared a tie and wormed out of my promise of a prize. None of the participants seemed too unhappy — they were sitting on the field watching a baseball game with their own private baseball-player security force protecting them from foul balls. What young fan could ask for more?

Walking into the clubhouse on Wednesday, August 17, my teammates and I were a little more anxious than usual. Besides the increasing electricity created by a pennant race that found us only two games out of first, it was also baseball-card night at Simmons Field, and we would finally receive a measure of immortality for our year with the Raptors.

For the inaugural year commemorative cards, we had posed with a fourteen-foot-tall replica of a raptor earlier in the season during our trip to the Eccles Dinosaur Park. After noting that I was the short guy in the uniform to the right of the big dinosaur, I could not suppress a smile. Even though it was a full-body shot and I was dwarfed by the ancient lizard, I was smiling, holding a bat over my shoulder — in focus and looking good. It was official, I was a baseball player with a baseball card — maybe my last, but I was certainly happy it was my first.

We spent the time after practice comparing cards, smiling vain smiles, and pretending not to be totally thrilled with the idea that we had baseball cards. The crowded clubhouse became a mad scene of players shuffling cards, carefully preserving their "mint" condition. While minor-league veterans noted their cards with cool approval, I joined the other rookies who looked again and again through the packs to make sure that my card was indeed still included. We weren't the only ones who were excited. Thousands of fans had lined up to receive free packs of cards with their admission to the park. One by one they filed in, tore open the plastic wrappers, and began to collect autographs.

The Raptors card offer had brought another big crowd out to Simmons Field, but this time the home team could not respond with a win. A disastrous outing in relief for Danny Miller allowed the Lethbridge Mounties to avoid a Raptors sweep as they scored seven times in the eighth inning. Miller just could not seem to regain the form that had made him so sharp as the season began. Suddenly struggling on the mound as a starter and also as Ambos experimented with him in relief, he seemed to have lost the bounce in his stride that he gained with his gaudy record. A little less cocky, and a little more cautious about his ability, Miller walked about the yard in a funk, trying to put his formula for success back together. It was a tough loss, but the Brewers lost again to Billings, leaving us only two games out of first place ready to head out on the road for our long trip to Canada, but without much time for a breather.

The lengthy game ended at ten-fifteen, and our bus was leaving at midnight. My roommate and I had not packed, of course, nor prepared at all for the road trip, so we had almost no time to spare. While the game progressed, I realized time was going to be short getting to the bus and tipped trainer Overman five bucks to save my usual seat — I had already tipped him so I would not have any gear to carry on the long trip and the extra cash was a wise investment if it kept me from sharing a seat from Utah to Canada. After the game, Brett Smith and I flew in and out of the clubhouse and sped back along the twenty-minute drive to our foster home. Eating, showering, and shoving every piece of clothing we owned into our travel bags and just hoping that there was underwear somewhere under the T-shirts, Smith and I piled back into his car oblivious to any Utah traffic or speed laws and made it to the bus with just moments to spare.

With sighs of relief we could finally pause to put our mad dash back from our foster home and back into the pennant race into perspective. We had won eight of our previous eleven games and picked up three games in the past week to pull within two games of first place Helena. This was just a little more impressive than the way Smith kept all four wheels of his car on the ground during our sprint from Frank and Ruby's house. Once left for dead as players and coaches talked openly about just playing selfishly instead of playing for a ring, we were again in the heat of a pennant race. Between players and coaches and their various major dreams was one of the longest road trips in professional sports and fourteen more games to close the season.

The road trip itself would extend more than eight hundred miles and fifteen hours by bus across three states and two countries from Ogden, Utah, to Medicine Hat, Alberta, Canada. It was a daunting journey, but as the card games, board games, and pillows broke out, we were in good spirits. While Brett Smith joined Doug O'Neill,

Chris Simmons, Don Baker, and Edson Hoffman in their regular card game, I teamed up with radio man Kurt Wilson against Willy and Mo for our regular game of Nameburst. Admittedly, this late in the season, Wilson and I were overmatched in the game based on identifying famous personalities from a partner's clues.

We had played the game religiously each road trip since the middle of the season for hours and hours on end. With the intuition they'd obviously developed back when they were roommates with the San Bernardino Spirit of the California League, Ambos and Morales were just too quick for us — "chubby comedian" was Fatty Arbuckle, "she doesn't float" was Natalie Wood, and "he's in the can" was Prince Albert. It was like playing against the Nameburst equivalent of the 1927 Yankees. Inevitably, Wilson and I would bicker and feud as we fell further and further behind, but at least it passed the time.

Wilson and I might have been snapping at each other, but I was certainly an improvement over the last player tapped to join the Nameburst game. Chris Simmons distinguished himself by stumping everyone with the clue "Russian ballet dancer." It was not Baryshnikov or Nureyev — Simmons was giving clues for Gorbachev. He was banned forever after giving the clue "black Motown singer" for James Taylor.

Wilson was pursuing his own dream to forge a career in broadcasting as we motored on toward Canada. He had honed his talents in the minors and developed an excellent rapport with the players and coaches that allowed him to fill the considerable amount of air time during a baseball broadcast with personal anecdotes and colorful insights. His postseason would be filled making resumé tapes and trying to push his broadcasting career out of the minors, but all that was worthless to me at that moment because Wilson could not remember the name of former vice president Dan Quayle's wife.

"I think I'm the same as every player," he said of his ambitions. "I hope to make the bigs. I think that my chances are as minuscule or even worse than the players'. There are nine players on the field, there's only one broadcaster. So if I make it to the bigs, great. If I don't, I've enjoyed what I've done and probably will continue doing it until I'm old and gray and can no longer talk."

Mercifully, the board games and card games had to shut down as we crossed the border into Canada and coaches warned us to be cool when the customs agents boarded the bus. Too much beer and too many cans of tobacco were stashed under the bus to risk any detailed inspection of our vehicle. An agent from the Canadian customs service came aboard looking no older than the youngest Raptor, and we eyed each other nervously when he asked if anyone had ever been arrested, charged with a DUI, or fingerprinted. We just spun our heads, looking for someone to be foolish enough to raise their hands, but everyone kept quiet. After we passed into Canada, the bus erupted from all directions with stories from players and coaches of their experiences with arrests, fingerprintings, and DUIs. The criminal element on the team had slipped through the loose grasp of the Canadian customs officials and was now making its way inland to pillage Medicine Hat and Lethbridge.

After fifteen hours on the road, and by the time everyone on the bus had had a chance to sample the omnipresent stack of porn magazines, our trip ended with a pleasant surprise. Walking off the bus in Medicine Hat, we were stunned to find a hotel, not a motel, for our stay. The Medicine Hat Lodge, complete with a giant water slide running through the lobby, plush beds, and spacious bathrooms, was pure luxury. "This must be the way big leaguers feel," someone remarked in the posh lobby that was overgrown with plants and resounding with the sound of fountains and children going down the slide.

Straddling the South Saskatchewan River, Medicine Hat is a small city of forty-one thousand people just west of the border separating Alberta and Saskatchewan. As Gas City, Medicine Hat prospered from the natural gas that spawned industries and local clay that built the grand buildings that ring downtown. On the banks of the river and neighboring the rink that is home to the Medicine Hat Curling Club, Athletic Park rises as a large concrete grandstand surrounding a multihued field. Red clay in the infield surrounded deep green grass and Toronto Blue Jays–blue paint coated every surface around the park. With the antiseptic concrete and metal construction of the stands and the sparse crowd, the field was a rather sterile place to play ball compared to the more homey parks we had become accustomed to visiting.

Athletic Park was made even more impersonal by the attitude it was designed to convey. When the Blue Jays visited Ogden they seemed just like another below-average minor-league team, but at home there was no mistaking that they were a farm team to the defending world champion Toronto Blue Jays. Ringing the outside of the stadium were plaques of honor listing the names of all the Medicine Hat Blue Jays alumni who had gone on to the majors, and along the outfield wall were two Labatts advertisements congratulating the Toronto World Series winners. Having watched the team from up north beat my Phillies in six excruciating games the previous year, I took all of this personally, while seeing shortstop Kevin Witt across the diamond just egged on many of my teammates. The eighteen-year-old Jacksonville, Florida, native was the Blue Jays' first-round pick, twenty-eighth overall. Even though he was not always impressing the Raptors bench, he had $470,000 in the bank as the result of his signing bonus, and everyone knew that he would get every chance to make it big because of the large investment in him. With none of the same advantages, my teammates were left to mutter bitterly that if they could only get the same attention, they would be in the show in no time.

On the cover of the *Jays Journal* at the park, the lead article touted the Medicine Hat Blue Jays who had been scouted and signed from Australia. In contrast to the leftovers and rejects brought to Ogden for a season on the Raptors, the Blue Jays organization was a finely honed system designed to fuel the engines of a successful major-league team. A worldwide scouting system brought talent to the Blue Jays, and teams from Medicine Hat, Alberta, to Syracuse, New York, funneled players up the ladder to Toronto where all the hard work and effort paid off with a world championship. In our locker room, however, a Pioneer League championship would do just fine, and we were excited to learn that we managed to pick up a half game on Helena without any effort. While we were on the bus they had lost again to Billings, and we were just a game and a half behind the swooning Brewers. But that night we were not strong, deep, or hungry enough to mount a serious challenge against the Blue Jays.

As had become a disturbing custom, Paul O'Hearn took the mound for the Raptors and, despite another strong performance, received no support from his teammates. Failing to execute properly or to score runs, we squandered a two-run complete-game masterpiece by O'Hearn. Making matters worse, Josh Kirtlan had somehow gashed his foot clowning around on the hotel water slide and was not at the top of his game when he was asked to pinch-hit. We just lacked the depth on the bench and the will to win the close ones.

A fog had fallen on the Raptors in Medicine Hat — or maybe it was just the bugs. Every night at the park brought out mosquitoes, but in Medicine Hat we were suddenly in the middle of a horror movie. Like grotesque angels, terrible moths flocked to the stadium lights and fluttered aimlessly about the field. It was as if it was snowing on the field as heavy clouds of insects swarmed down upon us. I just pursed my mouth so that I wouldn't swallow one as my teammates tried to fend off the bizarre home-field advantage.

We won only our final game in Medicine Hat, but it was enough to keep us within one game of first place, and although our bus driver took a wrong turn on the road to Lethbridge that added over an hour to our trip, we were cheerful and optimistic. Players who had groused about getting back to school or getting back to girlfriends were now talking about how many games the Raptors needed to win to sew up the race or what Helena had to do to help us out. In the front of the bus, after Ambos and Morales continued their dominance of our on-going Nameburst games, talk turned to playoff schedules, pitching rotations, and victory celebrations.

Even though the pressure was on, players were still loose and relaxed about their approach to the game. On the bench we debated whether we were trapped in the "Herbie the Love Bug" pennant race, with both teams racing backwards down the stretch and our team, at least, in danger of coming apart at the seams like the Volkswagen of Disney fame. Pregame flip contests, pepper games, and joshing around were still part of the day-to-day Raptors rituals, and even though nobody could afford to be shaken or unnerved, the occasional prank was still a perfect diversion. Putting on my batter's glove, I thought I felt a rock inside and removed it. When I found a grasshop-

The daily Raptors game of "flip" — the pregame distraction was a way to stay loose before the game, and a chance to have some fun amidst the pressure of a pennant race. Jeremy Winget, Danny Miller, Brett Smith, me, Jason Evenhus, Troy Doezie, Chris Simmons, and Josh Kirtlan join in the fun. Marty Dershowitz photograph reprinted with permission.

per instead, I almost threw it clear over the outfield wall from the dugout. After my heart rate returned to normal I was able to enjoy the laugh that my teammates had begun after I screamed. Like some of my other teammates, bugs were my weakness. Grasshoppers in handfuls of sunflower seeds were great fun in Medicine Hat, and any time Danny Miller iced down his arm he would take some of his plastic wrap off and brush it by players' ears, causing them to swat madly at nonexistent flies.

The fun certainly did not end with bugs. Jeremy Winget wore a bucket of water courtesy of Doug O'Neill and Shane Jones before the game with the Silver Bullets and then retaliated with a face full of ice cream for Jones during a television interview. Eye-black on catcher's masks or binoculars was a popular, if unimaginative, prank that never seemed to fail.

Off the field in the hotel rooms, pranks got more childish but no less frequent. A bucket of water was all you were likely to find in response to a late-night knock on your door, and I should have known better than to answer the phone after returning to my room to find teammates hanging out with my roommate — an earful of shaving cream was the only answer I received. Cups of water in the face, piles of sunflower seed shells on the caps, and gobs of chewing tobacco spat on the spikes were good for a smile any day. The laugh was just plain necessary to break the monotony of the season and remove some of the intense pressures as we raced down the stretch drive.

Established in 1885, Lethbridge was formerly known as Coalbanks from its early days as a coal-mining town in the 1800s. Alberta's third largest city and home to over sixty-three thousand people, Lethbridge is just an hour's drive from the U.S. border state of Montana. A vibrant Chinatown and scenic Japanese gardens give the city an exciting ethnic flavor and attract visitors from all parts of western Canada. Warmed by a west wind known as the Chinook, Lethbridge enjoyed above-average amounts of sunshine and warmth each year, making for many nights of perfect baseball weather at Henderson Field, which was just across the street from the Raptors' motel.

Walking into the park, nobody was expecting anything special, but what was inside was a surprise and a contrast to what we were used to — five-star accommodations. Major-league organizations invest millions of dollars in the draft picks and free agents who play in the minor leagues, but many of the facilities are subpar and some are downright dangerous. Cramped clubhouses, dank locker rooms, poorly graded fields, and inadequate treatment facilities represented conditions that could put an end to a career and ruin a million-dollar investment for an organization.

This is changing as clubs throughout the minor leagues are upgrading their facilities to meet new standards along structured timetables. In the Lethbridge locker room it was as if we were suddenly promoted to triple-A. The cavernous room was clean and bright with more than enough lockers, an office for the coaches, and an actual training room. The bathroom was modern, and the showers looked as if there was a hope of getting hot water from the faucets. Compared to the cave that was Helena's locker room, with its one working light bulb and freezing shower chamber, or Butte, where we had to trudge to a neighboring building to find locker-room facilities, Lethbridge was a dream come true.

I undressed without having to lean on or avoid other players. My gear was neatly stowed in my locker space, and with the short roster on the Raptors, I was able to recline into the vacant locker spot beside me. While it was 330 feet down the line in right in Henderson Field, it must have been 100 to the power alleys of the locker room. The dugout was equally expansive and inviting. It might have been less than quaint, but the quality accommodations were certainly appreciated.

Unfortunately, the hospitality ended with the facilities. The Mounties jumped out to a nine-to-one lead when Thurston Rockmore, a speedy outfielder, decided to begin the bottom of the sixth with a bunt attempt to pad his stats. The move enraged the Raptors and provoked pitcher Jeff Garrett to hit the next batter. The Mounties scored two more runs, but my teammates were incensed and finally ready to play ball.

Ambos gathered us in front of our dugout and told us that he was willing to concede that night, but we were going to send a strong message to the Mounties during the rest of the game that we were going to play them tough for the rest of the series. The Raptors offense began an unlikely comeback, scoring six runs in the top of the seventh and two more in the top of the eighth. Players who had been sullen and discouraged for the first six innings were suddenly on their feet at the top of the dugout — we were going to make one more improbable comeback to salvage the pennant race. But the bullpen could not hold the Mounties close enough to catch.

Although we certainly sent a message, Ambos was not satisfied. Meeting up with players later at a local bar, Ambos quietly eulogized our Raptors season. Even though he had declared that he would concede the game and use a comeback to build for the series, Ambos was now bemoaning the losing effort and declaring that the loss had doomed our pennant hopes.

The news only got worse. Helena had won and then won again the next night while we went on to lose our second straight game, pushing us once again to the brink of elimination from the pennant race. Ambos was enraged.

"We started this fuckin' trip in the pennant race and now we're fuckin' crashing and burning!" he screamed at us. "You're fuckin' professionals. Everybody wants to talk about, 'I want to go to the play-offs.' What are you willing to do to get to the fuckin' playoffs? Apparently not fuckin' much. If you think the rest of the season we're gonna sit around and ride it out and have a merry fuckin' time of it — bullshit — you still gotta win fuckin' ballgames because that's what you are paid to do and you're fuckin' professionals!"

For a quick lesson on what it means to go that extra mile, we could have just looked in the opposing dugout. Lethbridge coach Rodney McCray spent a few years in the majors with the White Sox and the Mets but was best remembered for an incident that has been replayed almost more times than Bobby Thompson's "shot heard round the world" — the time he ran through the outfield wall in Portland while running down a fly ball. The scene, which was replayed on every play-of-the-week show in the baseball world, showed McCray undeterred by the fence as he pursued the fly ball. That single-minded focus on a dream was what our team was lacking as we fell from pennant contention.

Later that evening at Rebel's, the Raptors' Lethbridge hangout, Ambos just sipped his beer and stared vacantly at the other patrons of the bar. Although our coaches saw us blatantly ducking curfew, nobody said a word. We could sulk at the motel or at the bar. At least misery had company at Rebel's. We were not mathematically eliminated, but our championship hopes had all but slipped away. All we could do was order some more drinks, enjoy the extra kick of Canadian beer, and give our pennant fever a low-key Irish wake.

Although Ambos had scolded us that we would have to go hard the rest of the year, the next day we were allowed to just show up to the park and strap it on without batting practice. With Paul O'Hearn on the mound, the strap-it-on strategy worked like a charm. We cruised to a four-to-one win, but Helena managed an improbable comeback of their own to keep us three games back.

With the win, however, we were finally in a mood to party and actually had an excuse. Second baseman Peter Muro was getting married, so our last night in Canada was a full-fledged bachelor party. We all crammed into one room to watch a stripper's performance, cheering loudly and trying to figure out how to tip with the Canadian "loonie" dollar coins. After the rowdy festivities at our motel, we once again headed to Rebel's to toast the groom to be. Even though Ambos had pushed curfew back to 1:30 A.M., we decided to ignore the rule and close down the bar.

Returning to the hotel well after two, I awoke Brett Smith, who had told me to rouse him so that we could creep over to the ballpark to steal a sign that he had been admiring all week. As we bounded across the street we were startled to hear someone yell "Hey!" behind us. It was Ambos. Apparently some of the later arrivals to the motel had awakened him, and when he realized that one of the curfew breakers was the next day's starting pitcher, he got out of bed to begin administering justice.

Smith and I were fined twenty-five dollars — at the low end of the scale — while Josh Kirtlan was fined a hefty one hundred dollars for staying out until the early morning hours. Even the groom to be was fined after he was caught out of his room with the inebriated excuse that he had "lost the room to his key." During the next day's stretches, Skip was still irate. With players murmuring beneath their breath about double standards, unrealistic expectations, and Ambos's habit of taking infractions so personally, he declared that the offending parties would also have to work — without pay — at the Raptors youth camp that weekend. After stretching, however, Ambos suddenly mellowed, joked about the incident, and even tried to coax one of the players to kiss and tell about his long evening spent in violation of curfew.

It was this tendency of the first-time manager that most irritated his players. He laid down rules, took it as a personal affront if they were broken, and then enforced them sporadically. If rules are enforced consistently and justice administered in a dispassionate manner, a manager can maintain a dependable relationship with his players. If not, mistrust and anger will naturally grow out of the confusion.

Although Ambos went crazy when that night's starting pitcher broke curfew, the previous evening Ambos had allowed the next night's starting pitcher to break curfew right in front of him. Certainly the lenient fines for Smith and myself were grossly different than the one-hundred-dollar fine handed to Kirtlan for the same offense of missing curfew. The rules Ambos so adamantly laid down after the last road trip about wearing collared shirts on the road and not drinking did not last even one day on the Canada trip. We had become accustomed to an inconsistent system of justice and, so long as nobody wanted to confront Ambos about it, we had to grumble about it when his back was turned.

For the last game of the Canadian trip our pitching and offense decided to show up on the same night, and we cruised to a win in a misty rain that never built up enough steam to stop the game. When we entered the fifth inning, we were openly praying for the weather to pick up and the game to be called, but while we could only pray for an early end, the Lethbridge crowd dispersed, leaving the wet ballpark for the comfort of home. As the game wound down, we could hear the play-by-play of Kurt Wilson from the press box echoing in the eerie silence of the park. With Wilson wrapping up the postgame show in the drizzle, we faded into the misty night to begin our journey home.

The long trip was a blur, as we slept most of the night. I won enough money playing poker to pay off my fine and even caught up on some missed sleep. Before I knew it, we were back home and ready for our final week of the season. Staggering off the bus under the weight of our baggage, we dispersed to our cars and prepared to spend a day off resting and enjoying being back in the United States. Our backs were sore, we smelled, we were tired, and we wanted to go home. We had endured more than sixteen hundred miles of road, thirty hours on the bus, nine days away, and four losses — and we were three games out of first. Passing by me as I struggled with my bags, Mike Carrigg summed it up with an earnest "That sucked."

It was finally over. Entering the road trip we were in the heat of the pennant race, but upon our return we were all but eliminated. Because Helena would prevail in a tie situation, any combination of four Brewers wins or four Raptors losses would mathematically eliminate us. We had three games at home against the Copper Kings, three games in Butte, and then a final game against Idaho Falls at Simmons Field to finish off the season. Once again the pennant race seemed out of the question and we turned our thoughts to more mundane pursuits.

At home we were lucky enough to be issued a second set of baseball cards — now we had our official pro cards and a stadium set sold only at Simmons Field. We were issued plenty of the pro cards but jealously coveted the stadium sets with their better, closeup pictures. Each player was issued two packs and no more. Disappointed but undaunted, we pocketed one set and broke open the other to trade. Players moved through the clubhouse plucking teammates' cards from the stack in exchange for one of their own. I was more than happy to participate even though my name was misspelled on my card.

Shuffling through the cards was a melancholy exercise. That morning, Paul O'Hearn left the team to be with his family for the funeral of his grandmother, bringing the total to eleven Raptors who had left the team since it was formed ten weeks before. I could relive the season through the faces of the players who were no longer with us while going through the pack for trade bait — from the first release to the first quitter all the way to Paul O'Hearn, who had gone that morning. Only thirteen of the players who sat with me in the Raptors dugout at the end of training camp were with me in the clubhouse to trade cards at the end of the season.

One casualty of every card pack was the picture of Raptors president Dave Baggott. The issuance of only two sets of cards for the players just added to the locker-room perception that the owners placed everything else before the players' happiness. We were charged full price for concession food at home, energy-draining player appearances were poorly organized, and the owners berated players about their performance. This all eroded the relationship between the team and ownership. The friction almost came to a head when Baggott rummaged through our bags in search of stolen baseballs while we practiced, but cooler heads prevailed. Upon discovering that Baggott had decided to include himself in the issue of cards, players took a special joy in depositing his card in the trash, crumpling it up, or throwing it frisbee-style across the room. The Raptors could not go on strike like the major-league players but could react in their own way to the sometimes petty ownership-player differences.

Two colossal home runs by Doug O'Neill that gave Danny Miller enough support to finally earn his league-leading ninth win certainly perked up players and ownership alike, and a Helena loss that brought us back within two games of first place made everyone forget any negativity. Like Doug, and now Danny, Jeremy Winget was also driving toward the end of the season — and hopefully a chance to extend his career — at a ferocious pace that had him contending for the Pioneer League batting crown.

The visiting Copper Kings, however, just wanted to knock us out of the running to end any pennant race drama. When they took a lead into the bottom of the ninth the following night, it appeared as if they would do just that. Even with the winning run at the plate and two outs — when I jokingly coached Pete Muro at first base to make sure he touched every base after the batter hit a game-winning home run — I was counting us out of the race. But an improbable three-run home run by Tim Gavello won the game, sending the team and the fans who stayed into wild celebration.

Finishing off the sweep of the Butte Copper Kings with a little help from back-to-back home runs by the red-hot Doug O'Neill and suddenly surging Shane Jones, we settled in our clubhouse to listen to the updates from Helena. When we learned that they had lost, we exchanged incredulous looks — we were a game out with four left to play. Tucking our gear into bags and stowing our hats in boxes for the trip to Butte for three more games with the Copper Kings, we left the clubhouse after our fifth win in a row, looking forward to making one more run at the pennant.

The next morning we embarked on our final road trip with players and coaches trying to stay as cool as possible. When our bus driver pulled off to a rest area and got off to stretch his legs, I opened a drowsy eye to the window while the truck next to us pulled out, giving me an "is that the truck moving or are we in gear without a driver" panic attack. Apparently viewing the same phenomenon, the usually cool Ambos lurched from his seat and flung himself behind the wheel, looking for the brake to avert a possible catastrophe. But it was the truck, not the bus, that was moving, and Ambos had to sheepishly walk back to his seat while we enjoyed a laugh at our skipper's expense. As we arrived in Butte, however, Ambos and his dive for the brake pedal were the only indication of anxiety in the face of the last-ditch effort to win the pennant.

"Looser bunch than this?" Ambos half-asked and half-declared as we got off the bus at Alumni Coliseum. We were joking and laughing and preparing for the final four games of the season. We knew that we just had to win our share of games and hope that Helena stumbled. It would be a tough task, but the team had been battling all year, coming back from being presumed dead too many times to count — staying loose was the only way that we could continue performing as well as we had been. During stretching and pregame warmups we laughed and hung out with the Copper Kings, with whom we had become quite familiar over the long season.

Although the season fostered friendships, it had exhausted our pitching staff. With the short roster and beleaguered throwing arms facing the top-hitting team in the league, our hurlers wilted. Even though Doug O'Neill and Shane Jones — who was having fewer helmet-throwing fits and more offensive production — again pounded home runs, it was not enough to overcome the Copper Kings and their offensive assault. We were forced to watch as our play-off chances, which had seemed so close as we replayed Kurt Wilson's call of Gavello's dramatic home run while on the bus to Butte, faded into the frigid Montana night. After the last out, we milled quietly around the dugout as Ambos and Morales signaled to Wilson for news from Helena. "They won?" called out Morales, and Wilson, who was completing his postgame show, just nodded.

On the bus the quiet was interrupted only by the sniffling of noses and the occasional whisper. Back at the motel, our bus slowed to a stop and Ambos spoke to his players. "What needs to transpire," he said solemnly, "is we need to win three and they need to lose three. We've had our backs up against the wall before. If nothing else, play for pride and win as many games as you possibly can, because as I told you before, for most of you this is it — so don't leave anything behind, don't cheat yourself, and never cheat the game of baseball. It's the best fucking thing going."

The major-league baseball strike was droning on, our season was coming to a close, and the crisp weather in Butte was hearkening the beginning of football season. With the Montana Tech football squad practicing across the parking lot from Alumni Coliseum, it was difficult not to come to the field thinking of the end of another year of baseball.

Ambos and Morales invested in turtlenecks for the final two games in Butte, and I donned a new sweatshirt. Gone were the dog days of summer and in their place were the final, cold days that would close the season. Baseball season begins in the spring when the leaves are just buds and ends as those former buds begin to tumble off the trees. It was a melancholy time, and players realized that the friendships and bonds forged over the previous weeks were going to have to be tested by the closing of the season and the separation it would bring.

On the field, a low-scoring game between the Raptors and Copper Kings built up some tension, but our hurlers were up to the task. With timely defense and a sudden invincibility from the bullpen in part-time pitcher Josh Kirtlan and our new ace reliever, Jeff Garrett, a slim lead actually stood up in the late innings. As Ambos and I recounted hockey stories on the bench while Morales fretted that our conversation would upset the baseball gods with talk of another sport, Jeremy Winget caught a line drive and doubled a man off second base to end the game.

We poured onto the field to congratulate everyone and then tried to get Wilson's attention for an updated score from Helena. When Wilson finally took off his earphones after completing his postgame show, we learned only that Helena was leading in the ninth inning. On the way to the hotel we still had not heard a final score, and a nervous silence gripped the bus. Players joked and kidded anxiously while Wilson tried in vain to raise the Brewers game on his Walkman, and we returned to our hotel rooms unsure as to whether we were still in the pennant race.

The ordeal was especially tough on the coaches, who longed to prove their worth with a title won on the field. A pennant-winning season could interest other organizations in their coaching skills, and Ambos and Morales were not shy about their desire to begin their Raptors careers with a ring winner. Morales, who, unlike Ambos, had never won a championship ring in his years of baseball, wistfully talked about how he coveted the chance to be the one "jumping up and down on the field" at the end of the season. That chance would have to wait at least one more year. Helena won and clinched the Pioneer League Southern Division with two games left to play.

The Stowaway

Although nobody made an official announcement, by the next morning everybody had heard the news that we were out of pennant contention. Everyone knew that for the final two days of the season we would be playing only for pride and for ourselves. Suddenly, talk turned to when we would be leaving Ogden and what our plans would be after the season. The previous day it had been taboo to speak of postseason plans; now players spoke softly about life after baseball. Most spoke of crossing their fingers and hoping to hear good news from other organizations or calling scouts and agents to try to get invitations to spring training or winter ball camps, but after the long season most players were interested in getting back to school or life plans and letting their baseball careers simmer for a while. I knew there would be no simmering for my career and was reluctantly facing the end of my brief involvement with the minors. After one more game in Butte and a final game in Ogden, I would be resuming a recreational baseball career, which did not have much in the way of a lucrative future but certainly had a rich past.

When my family moved to the corner of Napfle and Langdon streets in Northeast Philadelphia, the neighborhood boys came to our door and asked if the new kid could come out and play. While they were all preteens, I was only three years old. They were surprised at first, but instead of keeping me out of their pack they took me under their wing and introduced me to every variety of city sport. We played street hockey, two-touch football, half-court basketball, and any sport that approximated baseball. Without a true field in our backyard, we were forced to make due with Langdon Street, the driveway behind our houses, and anything we found nearby. I learned to play Wiffle ball, wire ball, stoop ball, half-ball, wall ball, and stickball. I spent countless hours playing lineup baseball with a neighbor — he would run through the lineup of one of the Phillies' rivals in the National League while he threw me ground balls or pop flies to imitate a real game. Somehow, the Phillies would always pull out the victory, but despite the predictable endings to the imaginary contests, it was great fun. When I was finally old enough, I was able to stop approximating and play baseball, in the Peanut League.

The years of preparation with the big kids paid off and I was able to play well on a real field. As a six-, seven-, and eight-year-old, I was always happy to play or practice and loved the success I had playing the game. At the end of my Peanut League career, when it was time to make the jump to Little League with the bigger kids, full uniforms, spikes, and stealing, my parents divorced and I basically decided to give up baseball. I suppose I was a little intimidated by the prospect of playing Little League, and with my familial structure suddenly in limbo, there just was not the urgency for me to further my involvement with the game.

I did not play organized baseball again until my junior year of high school. Even though I played two years of high-school ball, I had missed too much development and coaching during my absence from the game to excel. I started for the junior varsity but rode the pine for the varsity team and did little to move into the starting lineup when I got the chance to play. I moved on to Division III Hamilton College but was cut at the end of tryouts. The end of my scholastic playing career, however, did not diminish my enthusiasm for the game.

After college, when others were hanging up their spikes, I dusted mine off and began to play again. The camaraderie and fun of weekend ball not only satisfied my urge to play the game but rekindled my competitive desire to improve my talents. I was certainly not attracting the attention of scouts, but I was enjoying more success on the field than ever.

Unfortunately for any ambitions I might have once entertained of playing professional baseball — which, for me, probably waned at an early age, along with my ambitions to be an astronaut or a fireman — I was playing my best baseball at the same time that I was wrapping up my master's degree and making strides in my young career. That did not mean that I did not sit at my desk and wonder what would have happened if, like the other young men on the Raptors, I had dedicated much of my life to a career that could lead to the majors.

When I finally completed the arrangements necessary to become a minor leaguer and write a book about a season in the minors, I reflected that I would be living out the dream of every onetime jock and armchair manager who ever thought that the devil might offer them a deal to play ball in exchange for their souls, like Joe Boyd who became Joe Hardy in *Damn Yankees*. For one season, I could trade my wingtips for spikes, my dress socks for sanis, and my double-breasted suits for double-knit pants. For all those who ever thought, "What if?" I would have a season of dreams.

Putting on the uniform, signing autographs, and spending hours on the field during practice, it was suddenly no longer a dream but a life. Even though I took some heat at practice for somehow losing one of my stirrups in my pant leg and for the considerable supply of ice my arm required to whip it into shape, through training camp and the initial games of the season I was struck by what an incredible existence it was to be a minor-league player. There is nothing better for your ego than to be chased by ten-year-olds who want your signature, and nothing better to soothe the soul than spending sunny days on a beautiful field shagging flies, turning double plays, and taking batting practice.

I was also struck by the extremely high talent level of my teammates and our opponents. Since I grew up as a major-league baseball fan and watched countless major-league games, I was a little disappointed by the play at the first minor-league games I visited. Watching a shortstop boot a ground ball, or seeing a batter wave helplessly at a curve, it was easy to be critical. But once I practiced alongside my minor-league teammates, I could see that the young men who worked all their lives to reach this level in their careers were not far below their major-league counterparts. Where a major-league first baseman could scoop a ball out of the dirt ninety-nine times out of one hundred, a rookie-league first baseman might make the play only ninety times. If my dreams ever strayed far enough to make me believe that I could just pick up my glove, move into the minors, and successfully compete for a starting job, I was quickly assured that they would remain dreams.

After the initial excitement of waking up every day to find that I was still living a dream, playing baseball for a living soon became a job. It was thrilling to hang around and talk baseball with a former major leaguer like Rich Morales Sr. and to use the Marlboro Man in the Great Falls Dodgers Legion Park as a target in batting practice. But the exhilarating and optimistic beginning of my season in the minors soon gave way to the realization that a job in baseball had its drawbacks like any job.

We reported to work in the afternoon, put in some practice time, played a game, and then had to do it all again the next day. Most frustrating was that, especially in the small cities of the Pioneer League, when we got off of work there were few open restaurants where we could get a late dinner and even fewer entertainment options to help us blow off steam. Most nights we just ate fast food — often standing at the drive-through window after a late-ending game caused us to miss the restaurant's closing — before returning home to sleep late and pass the time until work the next day. Some days playing baseball was a great job. Other days it was just a job.

Some nights the game was so boring and the crowds so scarce that the only noise in the park was the click of the scoreboards as they noted balls and strikes. Other nights noise was a problem and the intimate settings of the Pioneer League were too close for comfort when hostile fans — sometimes our home crowd — yelled abusive comments or hurled concession food at us. It certainly beat most jobs I could think of, but every time the cannon blast that ended the national anthem in Helena made me jump out of my spikes, every time the alarm clock rang before sunrise to call us to the road, and every time I spent a getaway day lounging with a dozen other players in a tiny motel room, I was reminded that a job playing baseball was not always a day at the park.

Just as I was finding out that the dream job of playing baseball was often not much worth dreaming about, I found that my teammates were not all spending their time doing everything possible to make it to the majors. Some were happy just to be pros, others were simply focused on making it to the next level of the minor leagues. Many of my teammates were content to be able to say, "I was once a pro ballplayer," and spent their days happy to have a uniform on their backs, enjoying the attention that comes with being a ballplayer in a small town. Only the players who concentrated on their craft with every at-bat and every inning on the field seemed to have the edge that could allow them to reach their ultimate goal.

Some players not only lacked the desire and the edge necessary to continue, but as the season wore on I found myself agreeing with Ambos and Morales that they did not deserve to progress. I was astounded at some of my teammates' lack of connection with baseball's past. It was not as if they asked "Babe who?" but I gave up hoping that my teammates would understand what I meant by Murderer's Row, Tinker to Evers to Chance, or Shoeless Joe. I know that a player does not need to know who Willie Mays is to be a great center fielder, but it was clear to me that the players of the future had little concern for the past that created the game that could fulfill their major dreams.

Even more frustrating to me — as a player who was not blessed with the ability of my teammates — was the fact that many of them were just not smart ballplayers. Watching a teammate try to steal third on his own with two outs, seeing pitchers throw breaking balls to batters who did not prove they could hit fastballs, or coaching first base and having to relay signs from the third-base coach to baserunners who consistently missed them made me realize that some of my teammates were not with an affiliated team for a good reason. Baseball is the wrong sport for a player who lacks the capacity to master the cerebral aspects of the game.

Stepping off of my soapbox and basking in the simple pleasures of the minors, I could see how a player could neglect the game's past or the mental aspects of the game and decide to eschew the long odds of trying to make it to the majors just to enjoy the little show. The handsome payoff of the majors was a long way from Ogden, and there was too much to savor about minor-league baseball for even the most focused player to avoid getting caught up in at least a little of the fun.

The silly promotions like the dizzy bat race, where competitors circle a bat ten times before trying to race in a straight line, and the outlandish variety of bloopers, including a bizarre play where two Raptors runners passed each other on the basepaths — twice — brought endless amusement for the season. But it was more than just laughs; it was often a charming way of life. The wide-eyed kids hanging over the fences looking for autographs, the older fans who came to catch a game, and the storied old parks that had seen players come and go were pieces of baseball Americana that no fan could notice without pausing wistfully.

Above all, the contact and intimacy of the minors made the experience worthwhile regardless of any major dreams. My teammates and I lived with local families and became genuinely close to fans. The only time we were ever separated from the crowd was when we were in the dugout or the clubhouse. This was all driven home to me poignantly after a most unlikely occurrence during a game at Simmons Field.

I was sitting on the bench chewing sunflower seeds and talking with some other players during a game in which the plate umpire was just not cutting our team any slack. After some abuse from the bench, a pleading Willy Ambos loudly implored the umpire to "squeeze me, not my kids." Jumping out of his crouch from behind the catcher, the umpire barked at Ambos to sit back down and remain quiet.

Enthused by the volatile reaction from the umpire, the dugout around me erupted. "Tuck your ears back in your hat, rabbit," yelled one player. "Have another head of lettuce."

Taking off his mask and gesturing to the dugout, the umpire screamed, "That's it, you're out of here."

"Who? You don't even know who said it," Ambos responded.

"Him, on the end." And to the amazement of my teammates, coaches, and most of all myself, he bellowed, "Number five."

In disbelief I looked down at my jersey to see if I was wearing the wrong uniform. No, it was my number he had called, and despite the fact that all I had done was smile in appreciation at the wit displayed by my teammates, I was being ejected. For a moment, I weighed kicking dirt on the umpire's shoes, throwing a bucket of All Sport out on the field, or exploding in a rage. But looking at my laughing teammates and coaches, I could do nothing but smile. When Ambos returned from the field where he pleaded my case, he just looked at me and said, "Get out of here."

The umpires in the minors, like the players, managers, and coaches, were trying to make careers out of baseball. Throwing me out of the game was just the umpire's way of trying to reestablish control of the game so that he could continue with his work. Throughout the season we got to know the umpires of the Pioneer League. At the park we called them by name, instead of referring to them as Blue, and we spoke to them informally when we saw them around town. They traveled long hours by car to reach each new motel and hung out at the bars and movie theaters as we did to kill time. Unlike masked automatons, whether we liked them or not, they had very human faces. But this was little consolation for me as I left the dugout.

I was escorted to the clubhouse as a few fans offered me encouragement and consolation. I changed slowly into my civilian attire and prepared myself to enjoy the rest of the game as a fan. The first stop on my ballpark tour was the bullpen to relate the story of my ejection to my roommate, who was warming up relief pitchers. As I passed through the general admission section, fans who recognized me gave me an ovation for standing up to the umpires who were penalizing their team. I did not mention that I was thrown out for nothing.

Walking around the park, I was pleasantly surprised to note the familiarity that the fans had with even me, the ultimate bench player. When one father and son said hello, I stopped to talk. "When are we gonna see you out there?" the father asked. I told him that I saw some action over the weekend in Butte, but as a utility man I could only wait my turn. (It was a lame excuse, but it was better than saying that I was a writer who would see the field only if twelve guys broke their legs during fielding practice.) I was stunned when he responded that he saw in the paper that I had an at-bat but wondered when I would be in the field. The at-bat in Butte had been my only appearance in a game to that point of the season, and this fan who recognized me — not in uniform but in shorts and a T-shirt — had followed my "career" closely enough to note it. Continuing around the park, hearing kids and other fans call out my name and offer encouragement regarding my untimely and unfair exit from the game, I marveled at the intimacy of contact and connection with the fans that this level of baseball afforded.

Just as I was thrilled to be recognized by fans when I was out of uniform, I was always much happier to have someone ask me for my autograph by name instead of simply because I was wearing a uniform. Sitting on the Raptors bench, players could hear the banter from the concession stand that was just behind the dugout wall. Kids and parents kept the concessionaires busy with a steady stream of requests for hats, shirts, and all types of souvenirs. One particular souvenir, broken bats signed by players, was a big hit with the kids. While watching one inning fade into the next without much hope of getting into the game, I suddenly perked up when I heard my name. "You want a Brett Mandel bat?" I heard the concessionaire ask. It was nice to be wanted.

After a late-season home game, a young fan clutching a baseball ran me down on my way to the Raptors clubhouse. "Can you please sign this ball?" he asked. "You hit it." I looked down a bit skeptically. Unless this kid camped out down the third-base foul line during batting practice, there was not much chance that I was the player who actually hit the ball he offered. When I said I would sign but that I was not sure I was the player who supplied him with his prize, he was adamant.

"You hit it against Medicine Hat," he said, sure of himself. It was good enough for me. Not only had this young fan chased down the only foul ball I had hit at Simmons Field, he had brought the ball back to the park at another game and chased me down for an autograph to complete the memento. He wasn't asking me for my autograph just because I was suited up in uniform or because there was a crowd of people around me asking for my autograph, he wanted my autograph because my particular signature meant something to him. Although I doubted him at first, I could not have been happier to add my signature to his prize.

Even the excitement of sitting on the bench and reveling in having a front-row view for the game was reason enough to enjoy the experience. Borrowing the telephoto camera of the local paper's cameraman to scan the crowd for groupies or listening to teammates ask fans what the legal age of consent was in every new state was always great fun.

My baseball card. I'm the little guy on the right. Kids loved the cards for the dinosaur no matter which player was pictured. Reprinted with the permission of Fleer Corp. and the Ogden Raptors.

Teammates warned me that on the road I had to watch out for women with "summer" teeth — some're here, some're there.

Passing the time during the game with jokes and silliness was somewhat hazardous if Ambos caught wind of the conversation. Especially when things were not going well for us, Ambos could be ornery, frustrated, and downright cruel toward players. During one particularly awful inning, I heard Ambos react to a bad play by questioning his team with a scream: "Stupidest fucking team in baseball history?" After he paced by me on the bench I answered, "1946 St. Louis Browns?" I caught Brett Smith biting his lip, and I only smirked, too fearful of being yelled at by Ambos during the troubling inning to join Smith in the laugh.

The bench was fun even if all there was to do was yell, especially in Ogden. Because of the towering mountains that ringed the field, clear

Brett Smith and I enjoy a light moment on the bench. For me that was a steady position, but Smith played well enough to earn a starting position for the pennant race. Steven D. Conlin photograph reprinted with permission.

nights were great for hearing echoes. Perfect echoes of anything yelled from the Raptors bench would reverberate from the mountains after a short pause, which was endlessly amusing. We would "step" on each other's echoes, trying to be the last voice the mountain recognized. The winner of this echo game would be the last clear phrase shouted back at the field. Even though nothing exciting could be happening during an inning, we would be screaming our heads off, the mountain would be screaming back, and while baseball was being played on the field, the echoes game was the only game that mattered on the bench.

As the season wore on, however, not even the echoes game could quell my desire to get off the bench and onto the field, and I practiced every day relishing the opportunity to perform. I realized that my chances of playing were slim, and although the other Raptors accepted my role with the team, I sometimes felt more like a pet than a teammate. Sitting on the bench and helping out by coaching first base was a difficult way for someone with my competitive nature to spend a season. In practice I could take out some of my competitive frustrations, and before games I was thrilled to be able to compete even if it was only in a game of flip, but it was no substitute for a real chance to help the team.

Sometimes my unique perspective as an author and an outsider came in handy, and I was flattered that the coaches used me as a sounding board or asked for my input in dealing with the team. Other times players and coaches seemed a bit too anxious to help me with their own outside advice. Occasionally my teammates tried a little too hard to be quotable around me, and "Here's something for your book" was the last thing I liked to hear when I was sitting on the bench or warming up during practice. Although I would not admit it during the season, I would often later scrawl their input into my notebook after they left.

When I first arrived in Ogden I thought that it would be easy to put aside my desire to contribute and simply concentrate on enjoying the experience and writing my book. Shortly after the beginning of the summer I realized that that notion was folly. As my ability improved over the course of the season, all I wanted to do with any newfound talent was use it to help win a championship ring, but I was never able to crack the lineup, let alone be in a situation where I could assist the team. It was my silent ordeal — my roommates, of course, would report that the ordeal became not so silent back in the room — to be tantalizingly close to the game yet endure the frustration of never truly being able to be a part of the action.

Although I did not do much on the field, I was sometimes able to gain a measure of respect during practice. I have never been a power hitter, and the lack of an aluminum bat to give me some pop was no help, but as the season progressed I hit the wall a few times and threatened to surprise my doubting teammates who said that I would never hit a home run during batting practice. Brett Smith bet me a slew of dinners that I would never hit one out, and Chris Simmons said he would ante up a ten-spot if I ever left the yard.

Just when even I was beginning to doubt that I would ever do it, I hit one of Ambos's sliders out of Simmons Field. I trotted around the bases in celebration, dodged a beanball from Ambos the next time in the cage, and basked in a small triumph that made me forget about my frustrations for a moment. My teammates went wild and praised the accomplishment until game time, making me savor a couple of hours in the spotlight even more. Unimpressed, Simmons quickly offered me double or nothing on his bet.

Fun like that yielded the fondest memories of the season. Any time I could feel the simple joy of being a member of the team was a satisfaction that I will always remember. Even the adoption of the vernacular of baseball was exciting. Although I had always said "can of corn" to describe an easy fly ball, I was learning a whole new way to talk baseball. Nobody hit home runs, they went "yay-yo" or "big fly." If I was in the cage hitting well I was "throwing some head" or "mashing." And if the opposite team hit a ball hard but right at one of our players, I could taunt "gotta man there" or "that's why Doubleday put him there a hundred years ago."

I will always remember the thrill of being asked for an autograph, the excitement of getting into a game, and the fun of seeing my baseball card, but the mundane pleasures of my life in the minors will always be my best memories. Just getting into the cage for batting practice was exciting for a bench player like myself. It was my chance to show the coaches I could execute fundamental hitting and show my teammates how far or hard I could hit the ball. For most players that meant trying to hit to the opposite field, concentrating on hitting line drives, or rearing back and looking to hit home runs. With my power, I had little choice but to concentrate on line drives. Once in the cage I always took my share of good-natured ribbing about my lack of power, my talent with the pen as opposed to the bat, and my tendency to pull every ball.

When Ambos asked if I ever went the opposite way, I joked that my Peanut League team had only eight players so right field was a dead field — I was trained not to go the other way. While waiting for my next chance to swing the bat, I swapped stories with Coach Morales about mean neighbors who used to keep balls hit into their yards when the local kids would play. On Napfle Street Mr. Dragon — whose house was in right field — would come running out of his garden to confiscate any ball that dared roll too close to his yard. With my next trip into the cage, Ambos threw his trademark slider; I lunged at it to slap it between first and second. Ambos marveled at a rare opposite field stroke, and Morales called out, "Right into Mr. Dragon's yard!"

Leaving Philadelphia I was convinced that the Raptors would have little to offer me in the way of friendship, but I found myself not only enjoying their company but making close friends throughout the season. That was only in part because I was the only Raptor who could name songs and artists with the coaching staff. While the younger players struggled to identify who sang "My Generation," and "Sympathy for the Devil," I turned heads by knowing that the Strawberry Alarm Clock sang "Incense, Peppermint."

Staying up until all hours of the night playing cards, finding ways to amuse myself with the other bench players during tedious games, and really getting to know my teammates made my summer in the minors pass too quickly. I will miss laughing at the Last Chance Casino with Brett Smith and Doug O'Neill about the quality of Montana's finest Philadelphia cheesesteak and going through the same routine of silly laughs with Mike Carrigg every day warming up our arms. It was a remarkable experience.

My memories on the field, however, were a little less fulfilling, and the period during the season when I ended every sentence with "babe" was downright troubling. My big start against the Silver Bullets was great fun but was made a little miserable by the constant downpour. The next day's *Deseret News* had on the cover of its sports section a picture of me trying to turn a double play. I was glad the article did not note that I threw the ball away for an error.

Getting into a game was great excitement, but I would receive playing time so infrequently that I almost needed directions from the dugout to the plate. Any time I actually got an at-bat, the other team seemed to have their ace reliever in for an inning of work. I could look back and say that I faced the two best relievers in the Pioneer League — Medicine Hat's Mike Toney finished the seventy-two game season with a 1.05 ERA and eighteen saves while Lethbridge's Craig Farmer was not far behind with thirteen saves and forty-five strikeouts — but I would rather have been able to say that I had been hit in the neck with a pitch to force home the run that gave the Raptors the pennant.

My neck, however, was never put to good use, and as the chilled air of Butte blew us out of pennant contention, my teammates and I could think of little besides finishing the year in a way that would hasten the realization of major dreams, or at least reach a few goals. Even though we were finally out of the race, we still had reason to play hard. We had a chance to finish ten games above .500 and were in the race for team batting title. Individually, Jeremy Winget clung to the Pioneer League batting lead and threatened to lead the league in hits, doubles, on-base percentage, runs batted in, and extra-base hits. Paul O'Hearn and Danny Miller were still in the hunt to lead the league in innings pitched and strikeouts.

Every Raptor chased marks they set for themselves at the beginning of the year. Doug O'Neill had just about completed a quality season without sustaining a major injury and was regaining the belief in himself that could only make his talents more awesome. He even seemed to be enjoying himself. Shane Jones wanted to surpass his goal of ten home runs for the season, and Brett Smith wanted to improve his average and keep it above .300. Starters and bench players alike wanted to get one more chance to put on the uniform, take the field, and try to excel, but there were only two games left to try.

To finish off our final road trip, Miller picked up his tenth win, Smith went three for four, Winget went one for five, but Jones went homerless. Walking out of the stadium for the last time, everyone was doing their own mental calculus to figure out how reachable were their goals with a single game left. But it was not only in our minds that the season was racing to a close. As if we needed any more reminders that the season was ending, the Butte Copper Kings stadium was being dismantled around us. The batting cage was torn down, while the game went on, and after the final out the outfield wall was disassembled before our eyes as the field reverted to football for the fall season. By the time our bus pulled out of Butte there was almost no reminder that there had been a baseball field where we had just played. The season was ending quickly, and there was nothing we could do except try to enjoy the ride.

Before the final game in Butte I was a guest on Kurt Wilson's pre-game show, where I divulged the secret of my identity as an author and told the world — or at least the Ogden area — of my double life for the summer. It was an easy interview, partially because Wilson was an old hand at leading his guest into areas that would yield good conversation and also because I spent my time off the baseball diamond writing about everything he asked. We talked about my experience with the team, my life back in Philadelphia, and our mutual Nameburst shortcomings. Without notes, Wilson conducted his interview and signed off with a sparkle in his eyes and excitement in his voice. Even though he was actively preparing for his first game broadcasting Weber State University football, Wilson was still enjoying the waning days of the baseball season.

With Wilson dutifully telling the fans in Ogden about the game, the Raptors built up a big lead, and I had one more opportunity to get an at-bat in a Pioneer League game. I was loose as I went to the plate, probably too loose. I let a perfect pitch go by for no reason that I can recall before swinging through the second, taking the third, and waving at a curve ball that punched me out. Stalking from the plate, I was incensed. I blew one of my last best chances to get a hit with a feeble at-bat. In the dugout I threw my bat and wrestled with Ambos, who allowed me to take out my frustrations on his ample frame. I could laugh about it later, but I was just plain disgusted that I could blow the chance that thousands of others would kill for. One more game was all that stood between me and a horse collar for my career.

As the season progressed I grew more and more fixated on getting into the games and having an opportunity to get a professional hit. As the games began I was always rooting for my teammates, but I wanted a rout so that I could play. If the opposition scored a bunch of runs, I thought to myself, "As long as we're going to lose I hope they tack it on to get me into the lineup." By the end of the season my teammates would offer me consolation after a game, saying, "I thought you were going to get in." Ambos and Morales were ultraprotective against showing up the opposition and did not want me in a game unless the situation was right. Although I appreciated their gentility, I still wanted in.

Against Butte my frustrations were compounded by the fact that the Copper Kings manager was familiar with my situation and would ask me if I was going in the game when he saw a game get out of hand. I just responded that the coaching staff was saving me for the right moment. To jog their memory that I was still around when lopsided games progressed, I made a special point of loosening up in the dugout or grabbing a bat to take some practice swings in the hope that it would help me get in the game. My frustration continued despite my best efforts to prod myself into the lineup.

Before our final game of the season I traveled to a local school to talk to a class of second graders. Maybe it was because the ownership knew I could interact intelligently with children or because they did not want to tire out other players with time-consuming public appearances, but either way, I was the designated Raptor to speak to school kids. For this last visit the teacher informed me that the youngsters had just read a book about a boy who was not very good at playing baseball and asked me if I could identify with the main character of the story. Me, identify with a character who couldn't get a hit? It seemed as if the entire world was conspiring to remind me of my professional baseball futility at the plate.

After giving the usual stay-in-school pitch, we went outside so I could teach the students how to throw and hit. I may not have been able to do much with Pioneer League pitching, but that second-grade girl will think twice about throwing me a fastball — I hit her best pitch onto the roof of the school. With the extra batting practice I was all set for one more minor-league game.

Pondering the last game, I had one minor consolation and one major appreciation for my time in the Pioneer League. In my final batting practice at Simmons Field I got behind one last ball and hoisted it over the 7-Up sign on the left-field wall for another home run. While Chris Simmons tried to avoid my taunts for the rest of practice, I was just happy to have one last opportunity to feel the thrill of being part of the team.

Looking back and pondering my own experience over a lifetime of playing baseball, I walked away from my summer with an enormous appreciation for the single-minded dedication and commitment to the game that it took for my teammates to have reached the ranks of minor-league baseball. Although the highest praise and notice might be reserved for the men whose major dreams come true, anyone who has the talent and the fortune to play professional baseball has accomplished a remarkable feat. If my season in the minors showed me anything, it was that the young men who put their lives on hold to pursue the slim chance of making their baseball dreams come true are exceptional for putting up with a lifetime of toiling with bat and glove, coping with the crazy lifestyle of a minor-league player, and believing in themselves enough for them to come this far. I also learned that some minor leaguers do not make good on their bets — Chris Simmons still owes me twenty dollars.

Extra Innings: Endings and Beginnings

Seventy-seven days after our red-carpet limousine ride that kicked off opening night, we arrived at Simmons Field for the final game of the Pioneer League season. Even though we canceled batting and fielding practice, the day was still quite hectic. Players scrambled around the clubhouse to get one last souvenir for friends and relatives, one last baseball autographed for foster families, and one last tour of the battlefield. There were many good-byes to exchange, and we bid farewell to the concession-stand workers, the speed-pitch booth operator, and Elvis — Craig Holmes, our groundskeeper. Batboys cheerfully offered hope that they would see us the following year back on the Raptors, and we agreed even though it was unlikely. Elvis's son Andy sobbed.

For my last game as a professional baseball player I tried to savor every action even as the real world — and my real life — beckoned from just beyond the outfield wall. But for my teammates the possibility that this would be the final time they suited up as professionals was a sobering thought. Even the players whose year with the Raptors warranted an extension of their career had to face the possibility that forces beyond their control might end their career after the final Raptors home game. Out of pennant contention and just hours from the end of the season, the clubhouse banter was awkward. Players discussed plans for leaving Ogden, and we were all excited to have some time off. Even though talk was of getting away from baseball, the end of any discussion of postseason plans was a declaration by my teammates that after a few weeks it would be time to begin working out and preparing for the next season. Players were ready for the 1994 campaign to end but not for their careers to be over.

Some of the Raptors had already received news that boded well for their baseball future. Jeremy Winget was chosen as a first-team Pioneer League all-star at first base, and Doug O'Neill, Brad Dandridge, Dave Bingham, and Mike Carrigg all received honorable mention at their positions. It was a tribute to a season's hard work and the impressions they made on the managers they faced. Although the honor was nice, it would be truly appreciated only if it paid off in the long run. After this last game the honorees would see whether the good impression was enough to fuel their major dreams for another year — or more.

The clubhouse filled with players more than an hour before game time. Balls, baseball cards, pennants, and bats were passed from player to player in one last frenzied autograph-signing session as players stocked up on souvenirs for family and friends. In the middle of the commotion Dave Baggott and John Stein sat us down one last time and thanked us for a great season. Despite the rocky owner-player relationship that had been the norm for much of the season, the thankful speeches were heartfelt and well received. The players were grateful to have had the chance to play, owing their opportunity to the aggressive Raptors ownership; with the excellent showing on the field, the Raptors front office was similarly thankful to the players and excited for the future.

Before the game we were once again introduced and aligned along the first-base foul line for the national anthem as Mayor Glenn Mecham thanked each player personally and presented us with a small gift from the City of Ogden. "We are all very proud of your notable accomplishments this year. Best wishes for your continuing success and professional satisfaction," read the note attached to a tape of a local band wrapped in a red handkerchief.

On display for the sold-out Fan Appreciation Night crowd was a rendering of the new Raptors Stadium that was planned to be built in downtown Ogden. Computer drawings and a scale model of the future of Raptors baseball created tremendous excitement and optimism, and it would forever be the men in uniform for the 1994 season who had sown the seeds for success in future years. Long after players like Tim Gavello, Edson Hoffman, and Tim Salado would be forgotten, it would be the 1994 Ogden Raptors that had established the connection with the community and created an atmosphere in which the franchise could flourish.

Even though we had listened to it every night for the entire season, the playing of "The Star-Spangled Banner" was always a moment of significance. Before the game, the drills and routinized ballet that made up the pre-game practices served their purpose but could not affect the score. Once the anthem ended, the game was on. When "The Star-Spangled Banner" was played, players could pause to think about the game, the state of their dream, or any other notions that might cross their minds. For me the anthem served as the ticking of a clock dictating the remainder of my life in professional baseball. After the end of the tune I knew that there was one less game left in my baseball future. Now I had only one more anthem left in my career, but looking back to some of the versions I had to endure during the season, I probably was due a refund or two.

The absolute bottom of the barrel was reached at Simmons Field during our home series against Billings. With players and fans standing ready for the anthem, a lengthy pause made us realize that something was wrong with the national anthem tape. Undaunted, the public-address announcer asked the crowd to join him in singing the anthem. It sounded like a good idea, but his deep announcer voice was not prepared for the range of the anthem. Snickers and guffaws spread throughout the park as brutal tones of the tune emerged from the speakers. Then, when he could not remember the words, we reached a new low. He hummed most of the song and ended with a hurried finale. We just shook our heads at the sad effort.

The final national anthem of the year was a quality version — every word was correct and in tune. I could not complain as I walked back to the dugout knowing that I would never again hear the song with the same significance.

Another Raptor was feeling a surge of emotion as he took the field to complete some unfinished business. Paul O'Hearn returned to Ogden after his grandmother's funeral for the honor of taking the mound to close out the Raptors season. All year, O'Hearn had been putting his heart into every pitch, joining the league leaders in complete games, innings pitched, and strikeouts. Unfortunately, the team never seemed to perform behind the big righthander, and going into the final game he was saddled with a team-high four losses despite his sub-3.00 ERA. His final effort was not much different. With another large crowd on hand to cheer the home team's final appearance, the Raptors allowed the Braves to methodically run up the score without much of an offensive spark.

In the middle of the fifth inning the game was halted for the Raptors front office to hand out awards and accolades to its personnel. Chris Simmons was recognized for his hustle, Jeremy Winget for his offensive contribution, Doug O'Neill for defense, and Paul O'Hearn for pitching. Winget also won the distinctively glass-etched Most Valuable Player award, but the award I was waiting for was the fans' favorite player.

Unlike the other awards, this one was decided by the fans, with ballots that could be found at the concession stands — or in my bedroom. In the beginning of the year I stole packs of the ballots and had friends and family fill them out by the dozen during their visits. Having systematically stuffed the ballot box for weeks, I was anxious to hear the public-address announcer tell the crowd who was truly the fans' favorite player.

"In third place is Brad Dandridge," announced Dave Baggott, who was doubling as public-address announcer. I smirked, knowing that Dandridge had been gone for weeks. I must have beaten him. A little surprised, Baggott announced, "In second place is Raptors infielder Brett Mandel." Jeremy Winget, with the help of the local Winget clan, had more than twice the number of my votes. I was pleased with the result of my first-time candidacy, but chagrined that I did not stuff the ballot box for a better result — after all, second place was still first loser. As much as I would have liked to surprise the crowd by winning the favorite player award, Jeremy Winget was capping off an incredible season with a night of distinction and certainly deserved every accolade that was bestowed upon him.

After the fifth-inning awards ceremony, there was one more honor that Winget was chasing on the field — the Pioneer League batting title. Since singling in his first at-bat, he had been retired twice in a row. Going into the game he led the batting race by two points over former Raptor Brad Dandridge, who was now out of the league. When he came up again, a hit would win the batting title while anything less would lose it. In his final Raptors at-bat, Winget punched a single through the left side of the infield for the hit to win him the batting crown.

"That's it!" Winget exclaimed as he bounded back to first base. Slapping his hand from the first-base coach's box, I offered my own congratulations, having figured the significance of the hit after going through the math in my head when he came to the plate. "I don't ever want to go through that again," Winget said, happy to have won the batting title but frazzled and weary by the effort. For the last week of the season, every at-bat and every swing was do or die, but the last hit meant that his ordeal was over. The Raptors MVP and offensive star could take a deep breath knowing that his career in Ogden was over but that his tremendous season could allow him to continue his major dream, concentrate on his impending marriage, work on his tan, and get some rest before the 1995 baseball season would begin his struggle again.

Winget would make the short trip home to Murray, Utah, content with his successes in the 1994 season while I would make the trek back to Philadelphia less fulfilled. During the last game I waited in vain to get another at-bat or some significant playing time, but it was not to be. My season ended with me hitless with one RBI in five at-bats — my only certified minor-league hit was against the Colorado Silver Bullets in an exhibition game. I ended my professional baseball career coaching first base, watching Josh Kirtlan, my first-ever baseball roommate, ground out to end the game.

In his losing, emotion-tinged effort, Paul O'Hearn pitched a final complete game, setting a Pioneer League record for innings pitched in a season. Strutting off the field, O'Hearn knew that his successful year would be weighed against his age by any organization interested in his services for the next season, but that was a concern for another time.

After the game, Dan Overman asked if O'Hearn wanted any ice for his arm. "What for?" O'Hearn questioned good-naturedly, knowing that his season was over and that the next time he would need his throwing arm would not come for months — if ever.

With the last out recorded, fans poured onto the field for the post-game fireworks show and one last night of contact with their Raptors. A swarm of kids surrounded me asking for balls, bats, gloves, or anything else I would part with. During the last at-bat of the game I fielded a foul ground ball in the first-base coach's box and gleefully threw it to the crowd, taking the chance that I would not be fined for the offense. After the game I was quickly relieved of every piece of equipment I would part with.

Shane Jones sat near the bat rack oblivious to the fray. Hunched over, his head in his hands, propped up by his bat, he silently contemplated his hopes for the future and his season just ended. His final numbers — a .254 average, ten home runs, and fifty-four RBIs — were certainly respectable, but for a young man who had been passed over in the draft, Jones was left to contemplate whether the numbers were good enough to convince the legion of scouts that they were wrong to pass him by.

While I enjoyed the fleeting final moments of my minor-league life, I could only wonder if Shane pondered his — a few more home runs might have done it, maybe a couple more hits, I could have worked harder, I should have done better. From my view, Shane was one of the hardest-working Raptors, showing up early for extra work, earnestly trying during games and practices, and perhaps living and dying too much with every at-bat and chance in the field. Whether he could have performed better or had played as well as physically possible, he now confronted the eerie fact that his career was no longer in his hands. Whether he played again professionally or faced the end of his career was suddenly up to the general managers of the baseball world.

Like Jones, Danny Miller was done with the 1994 campaign and hoping that his efforts were good enough to extend his career. Having spent the night unneeded in the bullpen, he walked off the field unsure if his ten wins would be able to convince scouts that he belonged in a major-league organization.

When the lights dimmed and the fireworks began, the autograph seekers dissipated and I managed to slip quietly back into the dugout and off the field for the last time as a minor leaguer. As that chapter of my life faded with the stadium lights, I brushed past the other players in the dark, contemplating my fortune in having had the chance to call myself a professional baseball player.

Back in the clubhouse, beer was flowing freely and players were bidding a sudsy farewell to the season that was and exchanging cheerful good-byes. Taking my uniform off in a haphazard manner influenced more by the drinking than any reluctance to remove my whites for the last time, I returned my shirt, pants, belt, and stirrups to Overman, who was watching over the return of equipment like a hawk to catalog it all for next year, and popped open another beer while other players waded through the fans surrounding the stairs that led to our clubhouse trailer.

Players were making curtain calls for fans who wanted one last contact with their heroes, one last autograph, or one last Raptors souvenir. Concentrating on my drinking since there were few demands for one last Brett Mandel autograph, I was thrilled and surprised to hear a player call out my name as I was being requested at the clubhouse stairs. "It's Danny," was the simple invitation I needed to hear.

Danny was my biggest fan since the beginning of the season. He could not have been more than six years old and was a little shy at our first meeting. I asked him what he had for breakfast to open up the lines of communication as I signed an autograph for him. Charmed that a baseball player cared about his breakfast, he adopted me as his favorite player. More autographs followed, and although Danny never became much more talkative, I was always excited to see him at the yard. During Raptors baseball camp — where team members coached local kids in baseball fundamentals — he was on my intrasquad team, and before one of our last games we posed for a great picture. I don't know who was happier with the player-fan relationship, him or me, but hearing that I was being called out to address a fan one last time was a perfect way to end my career.

From the clubhouse steps I hoisted Danny up over the other fans, and although I cannot remember hearing him say anything, I was excited as ever to fire my usual rash of stupid questions at my young fan. I asked if he enjoyed his year watching the Raptors, if he was sad that the season was over, and if he was ever going to replace his omnipresent Notre Dame hat with a Raptors cap. After a big hug, I placed him back in the pack of fans and returned to the celebration.

Another fan of mine, Travis, called me out of the party to say goodbye and presented me with a shiny white baseball for one last autograph. I gripped the ball to sign it in one of the horseshoes formed by the laces when Travis's father warned me to sign big because mine was the only autograph Travis wanted on the ball. Touched and thrilled to finally get a chance to sign the ball on the managers spot, I signed my name and wrote, "To Travis, good luck," above the signature. With a final handshake and a smile, my fans were gone and I was truly finished with my life as a professional baseball player.

Although the party continued at the Dry Cow Saloon, by the time I arrived after eating dinner the magic was gone. A few players were at the bar with Willy and Mo drinking some beer and playing pool, but the night was getting late. Watching the two ex-teammates swap baseball war stories, I realized that Ambos and Morales were too tied to the game to let it slip through their grasp. Whether the Raptors performance would enable them to continue to make their livings on a baseball diamond was the decision of baseball executives across the country, but I had no doubt that they would find some way to stay close to the game they loved.

Their strong feeling for the game was evident in their approach to giving me selective playing time. Having had the good fortune to see me get into a game while visiting me in Ogden, my father approached Rich Morales to thank him for the chance to see me in action. Morales recounted that his own mother passed away before she had the chance to see him play professionally and he knew how much it would mean to my father to see me play. Hearing my father tell that story after the season, it was clear that with that kind of passion for baseball and those who play it, Morales was meant to stay close to the game.

We shared a few last beers and talked about the season that was.

Capping off the night, Doug O'Neill made a special point of telling me that I had improved as a player over the course of the season and that he genuinely appreciated the zeal with which I approached playing and practicing. Having addressed his own self-doubts, Doug had displayed all of the tools of a top prospect and was certainly on his way toward once again challenging his major dreams. Hearing the compliment from such a talented player was a thrill and a great way to end the summer as a Raptor. Brett Smith and I said some last farewells and headed down Route 15 for a final ride home.

The season was clearly over the following day when three o'clock came and went without our departure for Simmons Field. After a long summer of reporting to the yard each day, we were more than happy to ignore the coming of afternoon's call to the field, and our evening was spent on the back nine of a local golf course instead of on the baseball diamond. Instead of concession food we enjoyed a hearty home-cooked meal with Frank and Ruby — one of the few times during the whole season that we all managed to be in the same place for a meal. Brett and I thanked Frank and Ruby for their hospitality. Frank and Ruby thanked us for the experience. We signed a few baseball cards, presented them with a baseball signed by the Raptors, and swapped a few more Raptors road stories before going to a movie for the evening.

In the Raptors team picture I was posed between Doug O'Neill and John Homan — between the Raptor who first saw his major dreams end and the Raptor whose major dreams remained the most attainable. But for me, my summer with the Raptors meant my summer with Brett Smith. Throughout the season I lived vicariously through my Raptors roommate and shared his ups and downs. Like me, Smith had spent the previous year playing weekend baseball, but he chased his dreams to play professionally until he was signed by the new Ogden team.

"I had a terrible taste in my mouth about baseball," he said of his mindset after he was relegated to a recreational league when he was passed over in the draft. "I felt screwed. I was going to the park during the summer league just saying, 'I shouldn't be here, I should be some-

Tim Gavello surveys the statistics of the Toronto Blue Jays players. Looking at the organization displayed so plainly, the trip from rookie ball, through single-A, double-A, and triple-A to the majors seems tantalizingly possible. Brett Mandel photograph reprinted with permission.

where else.' I didn't like it at all." But Smith decided to give his ambitions one more chance and won a place on the Raptors.

When the season began we were together on the bench, but I watched him develop into an everyday player and a valuable member of the team. When the season ended, he was second among active Raptors in batting with a .333 average and led all Raptors catchers in throwing out runners.

"I'm glad that I can say that I played minor-league baseball," he declared near the end of the season. "I love the idea of being out there on the field every day and having thousands of people come to watch. I'm lovin' it. I'm absolutely lovin' it. I love the whole situation."

Even though I was never one to pass up a chance to tease him about his Lone Ranger glasses or the unique way he ran the bases as if he was being careful not to crush a potato chip nestled in his pants, I was more excited than anyone to see him succeed. I could not think of a better way to end my summer in the minors than by enjoying one last night out with the young man who, to me, personified what it meant to have major dreams.

A little giddy after the movie, Smith and I walked out of the theater reveling in some of the private jokes we shared over the summer knowing that we only had hours left to laugh at them. Suddenly, on a variation of a theme that had made it through the summer, Smith ended a sentence by saying, "I used to play pro ball." The whole summer we had joked about getting comps and freebies by simply dropping the line, "I play for the Raptors — yeah, pro ball." Hearing the line in past tense was just too much perspective, and he quickly resolved that he had to be picked up by an organization to play the next year if for no other reason than to put off the day when "I used to play pro ball" would be a finite statement.

For me the statement was enough. For the long summer that was the Pioneer League's short season, I lived pro ball. I rode the bus, took the field, endured the tirades, and enjoyed the life. I arrived in Ogden wondering what the talent level, the love of the game, and the pursuit of a dream would be like. Leaving, I had nothing but respect for the dedication and perseverance that the players and coaches brought to their careers, more of an appreciation for what the game means to its fans and followers, and a notion of what it is like to imagine, if only for a moment, that a lifetime of playing baseball could reward a ballplayer by making his dreams come true.

Afterword: Postseason

On January 17, 1995, four months after I returned home from Ogden, I received an envelope in the mail from the Raptors. Opening it, I was surprised to find an official Notice of Disposition — the first box of the yellow paper was checked next to the words, "You are released unconditionally." Not that I doubted the wisdom of letting go of a no-hit, no-catch impostor like myself, but it did not occur to me until I held the paper in my hands that my wild ride through minor-league baseball was truly over.

Before my release I had spoken often with other former Raptors who were settling into their postseason routines. Like me, they were occupied with new jobs and other nonbaseball activities. Once I received my official release, however, I was no longer part of their world. While many of the Raptors kept in touch, I became a spectator watching their careers from afar instead of a teammate sharing their experiences.

As spring training began, made even more melancholy by the presence of "replacement" players, it was clear that I had faded back into the real world and had no choice but to live vicariously through the news of my former teammates' progress in baseball. Looking at box scores, and even watching some of the 1994 Raptors play in 1995 preseason "replacement" games, I was able to relate to my former teammates' perspectives. I found myself no longer just rooting for my teams but rooting for my guys.

With Internet sites and baseball publications keeping me abreast of the progress of former Raptors, I watched the season with a personal connection to the players, knowing that I had crossed their paths on their baseball journey. Although I was saddened by the fact that I was no longer along for the ride, my new ability to relate to the games I saw on television or read about in the papers gave me a wonderful perspective on the game.

Why did this one succeed? I knew he would because he was so dedicated to his craft. Why did that one fail? I knew he had the talent but not the will to push his career forward. Where would a former Pioneer League opponent end his career? I could say I saw his potential despite his subpar numbers in 1994.

Returning to my Philadelphia adult baseball league, my talent had been raised a notch from my season in the minors and I was able to play with a much broader understanding of the game. Comparing notes with former Raptors teammates, many said that a similar epiphany had allowed them to advance their careers. I don't believe there are many options left for me in professional baseball, but it was nice to think that, in addition to learning a few card games, I had picked up a nuance or two about how to play the game.

Looking back, I don't know if all the players understood what I was doing on the field with them. They knew that I was writing a book and that I was dying to get into games, but I don't think they realized the incredible opportunity I had. Anyone can get close to a phenomenon and write about it, but I actually had the chance to go through the looking glass and live the experience I was chronicling.

One teammate who saw me showing up for early work and spending time working on my swing, my fielding, and my fundamentals openly wondered what it was I thought I was doing. With the obligation to make the most of the experience, and with the ultimate fantasy-camp experience at my fingertips, I was thrilled to take extra work to improve my skills and dogged in my determination to improve so I could earn playing time.

The ironic thing may be that the players who wondered what I was doing showing up early to get some extra work were the same ones who only showed up afterwards to take part in the regular practice. Most of them never considered that, like me, they were playing their last year of professional baseball. Only after the final at-bat of their careers would most of them realize that they spent their entire professional careers just one injury, one game, and one swing from that last seat at the bar reserved for the men who speak of "what could have been if." Perhaps it might have turned out differently had they joined me for early work.

After my season in the minors — even though Phillies baseball called me back to the plastic grass of Veterans Stadium — I frequently found myself venturing out of the city to visit the double-A Trenton Thunder or the single-A Wilmington Blue Rocks, where baseball attracted scores of fans who had been disaffected by the major-league strike. In those cozy confines I could watch minor players follow their major dreams as I remembered my season in Ogden and my teammates — those who moved on from the Raptors and those who baseball left behind.

Where Have You Gone?

Doug O'Neill never really took time off from baseball after Ogden. His contract was purchased by the St. Paul Saints, of the independent Northern League, and he reported to play in the Hawaii Winter League, which serves to give prospects the chance to sharpen their skills in the off-season. In the lush setting, surrounded by other legitimate major-league prospects, Doug played well and attracted plenty of notice.

Although he was still playing independent baseball with the Saints in 1995, Doug's time in the Northern League was productive. With many ex-major-league players in the league, Doug had many experienced tutors to teach him how to refine his talent.

Doug completed an impressive year — a .312 batting average with seventeen home runs and fifty-eight RBIs over eighty-four games — culminating in his being selected to the Northern League all-star team and named MVP of the Northern League championship series. When it was over, Doug finally got the break he was looking for.

Signed by a major-league organization to begin the 1996 campaign, my former Raptors teammate set off for spring training with the Florida Marlins, then to the Portland Seadogs of the double-A Eastern

League. Two years after deciding that he had to give baseball another chance, the game was once again poised to make his dreams come true.

For Tommy Johnston, dreams remained elusive. After leaving the Raptors in midseason, Johnston returned to school at Indiana University. Unable to walk away from the game, however, he signed a contract with the Mohawk Valley Landsharks of the independent Northeast League.

A step below the Northern League in talent, the Northeast League was still professional baseball and still a way to keep Tommy's baseball ambitions alive. Helping to fuel those ambitions, Tommy's numbers at the end of the year showed that he found some pop in his bat, hit .265, and belted his first two professional home runs.

Still working toward his undergraduate degree at Indiana in 1996, Johnston looked forward to another year of independent-league baseball in the Northeast League, or in one of the other independent-leagues that have sprung up across the country. After leaving the Raptors disgusted with the way he was treated, Tommy seemed rejuvenated by the 1995 season and genuinely excited about trying once again to use an independent situation to earn his way back into a major-league organization. "I'm going to keep playing in independent leagues until I decide to move on and try to get a real job," he said of his future. "I still want to play as long as I can — I'm just having fun."

Jeremy Winget, Pioneer League batting champion and 1994 Pioneer League All-Star, signed a contract with the San Diego Padres for the 1995 season. With his postseason marriage to his high-school sweetheart, Jamie, and his latest second chance in baseball, Winget went to spring training in 1995 looking to make the most of his chances.

After a strong performance in Florida, Winget's luck turned cold in the chilly Midwest. Toiling in Clinton, Iowa, with the Padres' single-A team in the Midwest League, Winget put up respectable numbers, batting .269 with five home runs and forty-four RBIs, but was not re-signed by the Padres after the season. For the first spring in six years, Jeremy was out of baseball.

"I can't complain," Winget said, looking back. "I gave it my best." In Utah, where Jeremy works as a security guard while finishing his schooling, he is happy with his minor-league memories and excited to watch brother Brad, a highly touted freshman at Brigham Young University, try to follow his own major dreams.

Danny Miller, who dreamed of becoming a San Diego Padre, had to settle for another year of independent baseball after his year in Ogden. After posting ten wins in eighteen games during the 1994 Pioneer League season, Miller played in the independent Western League, where he struggled with shoulder problems. Although his last outing on the mound ended with a three-pitch inning, Miller conceded that his time in the Western League "might be the end to a long story of baseball."

Miller, who plans to test for the California Highway Patrol and marry his fiancée, whom he met on a Western League road trip, is upbeat about his future. He admits, however, that, "it's already tough" to walk away from the game.

For Shane Jones, however, redemption was sweet. Jones returned to Ogden for the 1995 season, but with a year of professional baseball under his belt and a determination to make the leap to an affiliated club, he put together an excellent year.

Playing first base, which took some pressure off of him to perform defensively, Jones hit .323 with a league-leading sixty-nine RBIs and eight home runs. A second year at Simmons Field was just what he needed. After he was named to the Pioneer League all-star team, the Milwaukee Brewers signed Jones to a contract following the 1995 season. For the 1996 season, heading to spring training with the Brewers, Jones could be satisfied that the baseball world finally had, in effect, told him that not drafting him was a mistake.

Preparing for spring training, Jones reflected on hearing the news. "On the last day of the 1995 season I was informed that I was no longer an Ogden Raptor," he remembered "I was now property of the Milwaukee Brewers — a dream come true."

By the end of spring training, however, Jones had been cut by the

Brewers and was out of baseball. He finally had his shot, but like countless others, he came up short of making it to the majors.

After being named Pioneer League Manager of the Year for 1994 by his fellow managers, Willy Ambos returned to Ogden for a second tour of duty as the Raptors skipper. With only a handful of experienced players (Pioneer League rules prevent teams from having more than seven players with professional experience on the roster and the explosion of independent leagues across the country attracted many players who might otherwise have turned to the Raptors) Willy took one more wild ride through the Pioneer League, with which he had become so familiar. At the end of the season, however, changes confronted him.

After the 1995 season the Ogden Raptors signed an affiliation agreement with the Milwaukee Brewers. The deal meant that the 1996 Ogden Raptors roster would be filled with prospects from the Brewers system, but it also meant that the management and coaching positions would be filled by Brewers personnel.

In 1996 Willy Ambos was out of professional baseball, stoking his competitive fires by playing over-thirty ball, working for a parcel delivery service, and attempting to establish himself in a new career while continuing to look for baseball opportunities — and also working on the fundamentals with his young son, Kyle.

Rich Morales also returned to Ogden in 1995, but not before enrolling at Western Michigan University to begin work on his master's degree. Like Ambos, Morales lost his position with the Raptors after the Brewers affiliated with the club. In addition to his studies, Morales took on the position of assistant baseball coach for the university and jetted off to Brazil to teach the fundamentals of America's pastime in South America.

After a strong inaugural season in terms of performance on the field, and the development of a good relationship with the fans — a postseason fan survey conducted by the team showed that seventy-five percent of respondents had a very positive experience at a Raptors game

— 1995 was another remarkable year for the Raptors ownership. Although attendance dropped slightly from 57,707 in 1994 to 56,591 in 1995 and his team finished far out of pennant contention, Raptors president Dave Baggott was excited by the affiliation deal, which will bring new talent in 1996, and the promise of a new stadium in 1997, which will continue to build the success of the franchise. Judging those prospects by the size and enthusiasm of the newly initiated Saturday night pregame tailgate parties that brought Raptors foster families, fans, and players together, the Raptors future seems bright.

With the affiliation deal, the Brewers, not vice president John Stein, will have to deal with player-personnel issues. Stein will happily use the extra time to focus on minor-league baseball as an operation. He will also be developing his family's new personnel, John Edward Francis Stein Jr., who should be ready for the Raptors lineup in 2015.

Holly Preston and the Raptors parted ways, but she remains in the Salt Lake City area, managing a long-term airport parking facility and staying close to the region that spawned her involvement with the minor leagues.

Raptors marketing director Steve Gradyan left Ogden to return to the bright lights of Las Vegas. Although the excitement of a casino may satisfy his need to be where the action is, Gradyan says he still misses the purity of the minor-league experience and often finds himself at Las Vegas Stars games, reminiscing about his own time in the minors.

In addition to his role as the voice of the Raptors, Kurt Wilson accepted a position as director of broadcast for Ogden's Weber State University. Wilson still longs to move ahead in the broadcasting world but is content for now to make the most of his opportunities with Weber State, the Raptors, and the expanding Wilson family.

Dan Overman moved on to the Minnesota Twins organization, where he served as trainer for a single-A team before deciding it was time to step off the buses of minor-league baseball. After leaving his position with the Fort Wayne Wizards in midseason, Overman returned to Salt Lake City, where he works in a sports medicine clinic and looks forward to beginning a physician assistant vocational program.

Frank and Ruby Sanders remained avid Raptors fans and took in another couple of players during the 1995 season. Active club boosters, Frank and Ruby look forward to watching Raptors baseball in a new stadium and to the chance to see budding Milwaukee Brewers in the future.

Like me, Brett Smith received an unconditional release from the Raptors, but his quality year in Ogden was enough to interest the Bend Bandits of the new independent Western League in his talents. After hitting the first grand slam in the history of the fledgling league and being named to the all-star team, Smith's performance tailed off, but his early-season performance and ongoing effort was good enough to earn him an invitation to return for another season. Off the field, however, Smith earned his teaching certification and his new career beckoned him from the diamond. Summing up his dilemma, Smith weighed the chance to pursue his baseball dreams against his need to meet his real-world obligations with a minor-league paycheck: "I would love to play another season," he said, "but I would not be able to play for the amount that my contract says. My school loans are due. If they would be willing to increase my salary, I would be glad to play another year. Otherwise, I think I will be forced to get a real job over the summer."

Other former Raptors also took advantage of the recent propagation of independent leagues to continue their baseball careers, but now face similar questions. In addition to Brett Smith and Danny Miller in the Western League, Doug O'Neill in the Northern League, and Tommy Johnston in the Northeast League, many ex-Raptors turned to independent leagues as a convenient way to keep their dreams alive. Pitcher Doug Smyly played a season in the Mid-America League, earning recognition as a player of the week for some of his success before returning to school to earn his master's degree in economics. My steady pregame catch partner Mike Carrigg married his fiancée, Lisa, before playing in the Western League and then returning to San Jose State University to complete his degree and begin a career as a physical education instructor. Shane Farnsworth made an appearance in the Northern League but retired to law school, hoping to one day serve a role in the careers of future dreamers as a sports agent.

John Homan, cut by the Raptors after a poor start in Ogden, also found an opportunity in the independent leagues with the Regina Cyclones, of the Prairie League. His reception and release from Ogden gave him a new perspective on his ability. "My worst memory was being booed by my own hometown fans," he said. "That's why now I give it my best whenever I take the mound. So, in a way, my release made me strive to never allow someone to tell me that I'm not good enough."

Pitcher Tim Salado joined Homan in Regina, where they won a championship ring after defeating the team with the best record in independent baseball to win the Prairie League crown. After completing his studies at San Jose State University, Salado is pursuing a master's degree in sports psychology and looking forward to more independent baseball to keep his major dreams alive.

Josh Kirtlan, my first Raptors roommate, played in the Frontier League before returning home to Sacramento to begin work monitoring juvenile offenders with the County of Sacramento Probation Department. Other independent leaguers included preseason Raptors defector Chris McCoy, who played in the Northeast League, and Steve Gay, who turned to religion to focus his life and his pitching and became a Western League all-star.

Like Shane Jones, Tim Gavello and Paul O'Hearn returned to Ogden for a second year with the Raptors. Gavello, hobbled by a preseason knee injury, played in Ogden until his knee gave way as he rounded second base after hitting a double. Although postseason surgery may enable him to play again, he is completing his undergraduate degree and looking forward to becoming a teacher — facing the notion that his professional baseball career may have ended with him lying in a heap on the infield dirt clutching his damaged knee after being tagged out to end an inning.

Paul O'Hearn pitched a lackluster season in Ogden, voluntarily retired, and finished the season as the Raptors pitching coach. Returning to California, O'Hearn has hung up his glove and gone back to the working world as a business development representative for a Santa Ana bank. He stays close to the game by running a pitching school for local youths.

Some of my former teammates were talented and fortunate enough to earn contracts with major-league organizations. In addition to Jeremy Winget, who signed with the Padres for the 1995 season, catcher Brad Dandridge played single-A ball for the Dodgers in the California League. After playing winter baseball in Australia and marrying his longtime sweetheart, Dandridge moved on to double-A ball with the Dodgers and was promoted to triple-A ball during the 1996 season.

Dan Zanolla, who left the Raptors in midseason when the St. Paul Saints recalled him from Ogden, played well enough in the Northern League to win the attention of the Florida Marlins. In 1995 he played single-A ball for the Marlins in the Midwest League. Seeing little future for himself in baseball, he retired to return to finish his degree in electrical engineering at Purdue University. Catcher Troy Doezie played single-A ball for the Cardinals in the New York–Penn League, bringing his wife, Denise, and young daughter, Jaylyn, from Utah to New Jersey for the season. He is resigned to packing the family up for another few seasons if it can keep his dreams alive.

With the ridiculousness of "replacement baseball," some of the 1994 Raptors almost made it to the show — even if it was just the sideshow of the 1994–95 baseball labor wars. Pitcher Marco Contreras, who went on to play independent-league baseball in the Prairie League, was a replacement Oakland Athletic. Retiring with a Prairie League championship ring from the 1995 season, Contreras returned to Cal State–Northridge and looks forward to graduating as a kinesiology major. Pitcher Jason Evenhus was a replacement Cincinnati Red before returning to Washington State University to finish his studies, also as a kinesiology major. Pitcher Jay Hogue made an appearance for the Atlanta Braves' replacement team before returning to Texas A&M to finish his degree in speech communications. Utility fielder David Bingham was a replacement Toronto Blue Jay before returning home to finish his degree in elementary education at Lewis and Clark College. Disappointed with his experience in replacement ball and relegated to semipro ball after finding no opportunities in the minor-leagues, he is considering training his new son, Kryztopher, to be a point guard.

My former teammates pursued many baseball opportunities after our year in Ogden but only three were anywhere to be found as I scanned team rosters in 1996. Doug O'Neill, playing in the Marlins organization; Brad Dandridge, playing in the Dodgers organization; and Tommy Johnston playing independent ball in the Northeast League were the only members of the 1994 Raptors whose major-league dreams were still being fueled by time in the minors.

Other former teammates, rejected by the baseball world, anxious to get on with their postbaseball lives or just unable to endure the rigors of another baseball season, joined me in making a full-time commitment to the real world after the 1994 season. Chris Simmons did not know it then, but his last game as a Raptor was his final professional appearance. "I never thought the last night of the season would be my last time in the professional arena," he said. "I sat and watched the fireworks thinking to myself, 'I did it.' All the people that had doubted me, I wish I could line them all up and tell them to kiss my ass." Simmons remained in Utah, where he married and became a Utah state trooper. He returned to the Raptors in the 1995 season as a fan, but it seems that future Raptors should be wary if his radar gun reads much more than sixty-five while he is on duty.

Asked to return to Ogden in the middle of the 1995 season to shore up a questionable pitching staff, Jeff Garrett decided his time in baseball had passed. He returned to San Jose, where he sells automatic swimming pool covers. He is looking forward to finishing his schooling and wedding his fiancée. Chris Amos, who left the Raptors midyear after deciding that the minor-league life was not for him, worked in physical therapy before joining a car rental agency. He plans to pursue a postgraduate degree in management information.

After being cut by the Raptors, Jason Pollock moved to Idaho where he runs his own distribution company supplying convenience stores with nonfood merchandise. Still irritated with the politics of baseball but thrilled to have had a chance to realize his dreams, he relishes his freedom by setting his own hours, enjoying plenty of fishing, and pondering the notion of javelin throwing — a sport in which he had much success in the past — at the Olympic level.

Peter Muro, who dashed home from Ogden to get married before returning to the team, finally had time for a postseason honeymoon before traveling to Mexico for a tryout with the Vendados de Mazatlán of the Mexican Pacific League. After a series of disappointments in Mexico and at other camps, Muro returned home to finish his schooling and is currently testing to become a firefighter. "Not playing professional baseball has killed me," he said. "I play hard with a team in a semipro league once a week because it's better than not playing at all. I thank God for the cup of coffee he gave me in pro ball."

Edson Hoffman joined the workaday world back in Illinois and is looking to finish his schooling, but longs to get back into baseball coaching or teaching. Don Baker returned to the University of Utah to complete his studies in exercise sports science and personal training.

For the others who crossed my path or crossed my mind in Ogden, life after the 1994 season brought a mixed bag. After the Raptors' pennant hopes collapsed, the Billings Mustangs completed the 1994 season by defeating the Helena Brewers to win their third straight Pioneer League championship. The Idaho Falls Braves affiliated with the San Diego Padres, and with major-league expansion, the Butte Copper Kings and Lethbridge Mounties — renamed the Black Diamonds — affiliated with the Arizona Diamondbacks and the Tampa Devil Rays, respectively.

After canceling the 1994 World Series and playing brinkmanship with the entire 1995 season, major-league owners and players finally went back to playing baseball. Only time will tell if the game has suffered any long-term effects.

The Colorado Silver Bullets built upon their six-win season of 1994 to go eleven and thirty-three in their second year. Pitcher Lee Anne Ketchum — who yielded me my only professional base hit — even played in the Hawaii Winter League. Even as the women of summer chased their baseball ambitions, Michael Jordan gave up on his major dreams and returned to prominence in the NBA.

Of the future stars I encountered in the Pioneer League, some continued to shine but many seemed to dim a bit as they progressed up the baseball pyramid. Billings Mustang Aaron Boone was named one of the Pioneer League's top prospects by the league's managers, and by 1995 he was playing double-A ball in Chattanooga for the Cincinnati Reds' Southern League team. But Mike Toney, who blew his fastball by me at more than ninety miles per hour, may have found that not all batters are as easy to strike out as I was. He performed well with the Blue Jays' Hagerstown single-A club in the South Atlantic League, but struggled in the single-A Florida State League, posting an 8.03 ERA in twelve appearances. Blue Jays first-round draft pick Kevin Witt — whose signing bonus so irritated the Raptors players when they saw his average hover around .200 — showed promise but also indicated that he still needed some seasoning as he hit fourteen home runs but batted .232 for the single-A club in Hagerstown.

As for me, my professional baseball career will have to remain packed away with my Raptors memorabilia now that my baseball life has been pushed back to the weekends by my career. But every once in a while I dream that I am back with the Raptors, still dying to get into a game; and occasionally, when I really lay into a fastball or range to my right to field a ground ball, I wonder what might have been if I had spent more time at the cages as a peanut leaguer. In the end, all I have left are minor dreams.